# THE FUTURE OF THE MIDDLE AGES

Edited by William D. Paden

THE   FUTURE   OF

UNIVERSITY PRESS OF FLORIDA

Gainesville Tallahassee Tampa Boca Raton
Pensacola Orlando Miami Jacksonville

THE MIDDLE AGES

MEDIEVAL LITERATURE IN THE 1990S

Library of Congress Cataloging-in-Publication Data
The Future of the Middle Ages: medieval literature in the 1990s / edited
by William D. Paden.
p. cm.
Rev. papers from a colloquium sponsored jointly by Northwestern
University and the Newberry Library, Mar. 9–10, 1990, at the Newberry
Library in Chicago.
Includes bibliographical references and index.
ISBN 0-8130-1278-3 (cloth). — ISBN 0-8130-1279-1 (paper)
1. Literature, Medieval—Study and teaching—Congresses.
2. Philology—Congresses.   I. Paden, William D. (William Doremus).
1941–
PN663.F87   1994
809'.02—dc20   93-46780

The University Press of Florida is the scholarly publishing agency for
the State University System of Florida, comprised of Florida A&M
University, Florida Atlantic University, Florida International University,
Florida State University, University of Central Florida, University of
Florida, University of North Florida, University of South Florida, and
University of West Florida.

University Press of Florida
15 Northwest 15th Street
Gainesville, FL 32611

☙ CONTENTS

❦ INTRODUCTION

The practice of philology, whatever the particular domain or approach, expresses an impulse to reach toward alterity, and specifically toward the past. Such an impulse springs from a bundle of affects, both subtle and powerful, which are susceptible to influence by subtle or powerful changes in the world. Therefore, as philologists respond differently to the course of contemporary history, their impulses toward the past will differ, and they will plunge into controversy or polemic among themselves. The advancing present continually rewrites the past through a process involving discussion, diversity, and dissent.

The events of May 1968, on and around the boulevard Saint-Michel in Paris, created reverberations among a generation of French scholars and intellectuals who felt the need to make a sharp break with the past, recent or remote. More than twenty years later this conviction reached expression in philology with the publication of Bernard Cerquiglini's *Éloge de la variante: Histoire critique de la philologie* (1989), which scandalized conservative champions of historical continuity. When Cerquiglini's jacobinism echoed across the Atlantic in 1990, it aroused among contributors to a special issue of *Speculum* and their readers the same range of feelings from triumph to outrage, feelings which were complicated by an overlay ranging from sympathy to hostility toward the spirit of '68. Since this specular response occurred in the United States, where medieval European culture is more distant from political turmoil than in Europe, it was no doubt less political and more cerebral than its sources of inspiration in Paris.

Nevertheless a political overtone of distinctly American origin may have come into play, if the experience of protest against military policy in Viet Nam prepared American scholars, no longer so young but still animated by passionate memories, to embrace Parisian radicalism.

Meanwhile Europe was being rocked again by epoch-making events on the political scene: the fall of the Berlin Wall, the end of the Cold War, progress toward a single European market, and the movement, including jumps, starts, and setbacks, towards further integration. The process through which Europe is passing continues on its course, and the eventual impact of this process on the configuration of the past, though certain to come, is not yet evident. But if nineteenth-century philology served the needs of nationalism, as it did in 1870 when Gaston Paris lectured on the *Song of Roland* to a Parisian audience under German siege; if a Spanish philologist such as Menéndez Pelayo invoked a great cultural tradition as compensation for a national depression; if, by extending the same logic, we come to see that Ernst Robert Curtius invoked the influence of Romance on German culture in part because Romance culture had been glorified in defeat; then the vertigo induced by today's spinning nation-states can scarcely fail to shake philology.[1]

It would be wrong, however, to imagine philology roused from antiquarian torpor only by headlines from the world of geopolitics. As the world affects mind, so mind affects the world. Philology reacts to changes in allied disciplines which sometimes seem to accumulate by random variation, but at other times vault to a new paradigm after the exhaustion or destruction of the last. Thus resemblances to the American New Criticism, once a vibrant innovation but discarded long ago, may be adduced as a reproach to today's New Philology on the grounds of New Criticism's hostility to philology, or contrariwise as a reproach to today's Old Philology on the grounds of excessive fixation on the text.[2] And philology, too, experiences paradigm shifts generated from within its own practice, such as the Bédierist reaction against Lachmannian principles of textual edition. Such shifts may be felt as moments in a smooth overriding continuity or as jolts in a philological roller-coaster ride.

These changes in related fields and within philology, like geopolitical temblors, provoke discussion and dispute among those actively engaged. The revolutions in American literary study, as it has moved away from formalism and embraced theory, new historicism, feminism, and cultural studies, have helped form tomorrow's philologists and will therefore affect tomorrow's philology. By an inevitable *mise en abyme* these revolutions invite reassessment of medieval texts in their relation to the world and to medieval patterns of thought.[3] Current philological practices, in their relations to other disciplines and to the world, have become the subject of reassessment in the ongoing discussion among traditionalists and partisans of New Philology. The passion and intellectual force with which they speak today will propel us into tomorrow.

The essays in this volume grew out of a colloquium titled "The Future of the Middle Ages: Medieval French Literature in the 1990s." Sponsored jointly by Northwestern University and the Newberry Library, it convened at the Newberry Library in Chicago on March 9 and 10, 1990. At the conference we asked how recent changes in the world at large might affect the study of medieval literature. For a brief moment it seemed, at least to some, that we were entering a new era with high hopes for a better world. Although subsequent events have disappointed many of those hopes, deferred their realization, or developed new and unexpected problems, it remains true that the rapid evolution of recent times will inevitably influence the study of our subject. It therefore seems imperative to reassess the directions of present and future scholarship in the field.

Simultaneous with these momentous changes in the world around philology, powerful currents ran within it. Between preliminary planning and the meeting itself there intervened, in January 1990, the publication of a special issue of *Speculum*, the journal of the Medieval Academy of America, which served as a catalyst for discussion. In this issue, edited by Stephen G. Nichols and titled *The New Philology*, Nichols undertook "to explore and interrogate presuppositions underlying current philological practices." In introducing the work of his contributors Nichols asked,

> [I]f philology is so central to our discipline, why should one postulate a "new" philology, however ironically? . . . The consensus seems to be that medieval philology has been marginalized by contemporary cognitive methodologies, on the one side, while within the discipline itself, a very limited and by now grossly anachronistic conception of it remains far too current. This version, formulated under the impulse of political nationalism and scientific positivism during the second half of the nineteenth century, continues to circumscribe the "discipline" of medieval studies. (1)

The five contributors to this issue proposed various ways to break out of this circumscription and gain broader perspectives on the medieval object.

The Northwestern-Newberry colloquium embraced a range of attitudes toward the New Philology, and we have sought to cultivate that range in developing the collection for publication in the present form. Contributors differ, too, in their concern for forces of change playing upon philology from without or driving it forward from within. All the contributors assess the present condition of philology as a necessary outgrowth of the past with an eye toward the future. Nevertheless their emphases vary.

Two of these studies place present-day philology in historical context. I attempt to assess the crisis in relations between the present and the past in a cultural point of view. Taking the end of the Cold War as my point of departure, I reconsider the overarching shape of Western history, arguing that alternative ways of grasping that shape not only shed light on views of the Middle Ages which have been taken in the past by philologists both old and new, but also ensure a wealth of opportunities in the future for rethinking those views.

Hans Ulrich Gumbrecht presents a case study in the history of philology and modernism in Spain. Intellectuals of the Generation of 1898 reacted against narrow nationalism by seeking to recover contact with foreign cultures, but they also plunged into national classics in hope of regenerating Spain from within. In contrast, poets of the Generation of 1927 such as Federico García Lorca turned inward, but, like their contemporary, the scholar Ramón Menéndez Pidal, they stressed the otherness of the tradition they strove to embody. Modernist poets and philologists alike clung to the material qualities of the signifier rather than interpretation of its meaning. The Generation of 1898 anticipated the meaning-centered interest of text editors today, while that of 1927 anticipated the return to the manuscript heralded by New Philology.

At the heart of the debate lies the problem of tradition and innovation that constitutes the discipline, both intrinsically historical and ineluctably contemporary. Rupert T. Pickens and Peter F. Dembowski defend and illustrate the best of the tradition. Pickens stresses the ethical dimension, criticizing proponents of the New Philology for failure to appreciate the accomplishments of the past, and pleads for civility in philological culture, for the respect that successors have shown their predecessors in a lineage from Gaston Paris to his student Joseph Bédier, from Bédier to his American student Urban T. Holmes, Jr., and from Holmes to his students today. By maintaining the continuity of the philological endeavor from the Middle Ages to the present, Pickens argues, this tradition ultimately assures its own validity. Dembowski defines philology as the art and science of editing texts, demonstrates the subtlety and sophistication of judgment required of the editor, and emphasizes the vigor of recent and ongoing work in both practice and theory.

Stephen G. Nichols grants the central role of editing texts, but contends that it should not be the sole concern of the philological enterprise. He proposes that study of the given text as transmitted through various manuscripts should be complemented by study of the individual manuscript, the context and matrix of the texts it contains. Nichols calls this matrix "a space of radical alterity very different from the conception of textual space propounded by the critical edition," which envisions the text in a formalist and idealist way, thereby sharing postulates with the American New

Criticism. Understanding the manuscript as a cultural artifact will require newer techniques of cultural criticism. "The two goals are orthogonal in practice, but need not be antagonistic": thus Nichols attempts to mediate between traditional and innovative approaches while granting both their due.

Scanning the horizon for future directions, Joan M. Ferrante advocates greater interest in "international, interdisciplinary, and 'intersexual' studies." As a first step she proposes economical publication in computerized form of all the medieval texts that remain to be edited in French, German, and Italian. These texts must be examined not only in terms of their many languages but also for the intersecting realities—literary, cultural, historical, legal, economic, artistic—which constitute the medieval world. Ferrante calls particularly for research into the place of women in medieval literary history.

R. Howard Bloch, who also contributed to the special issue of *Speculum*, surveys trends in current scholarly practice which hold the promise of an exciting future. Like Ferrante, he believes that recent research in women's studies has opened up new approaches to gender, and that an enhanced self-consciousness of medieval studies will produce a renewed receptivity to methodologies from allied disciplines. Bloch suggests that an innovative return to Patristic studies will place the high Middle Ages in the context of late Antiquity, affording the means better to understand the entire period in its *longue durée*.

In their breadth of outlook, their variety of positions, their deep conviction and their intellectual poise, these essays invite the reader to further reflection on the future of medieval literature.

I am grateful to a number of people who collaborated on various stages of this project. Tilde Sankovitch, professor of French at Northwestern University, suggested that we approach the Newberry Library and then served as co-organizer for the colloquium. Working with us from the Newberry were Mary Beth Rose, director of the Center for Renaissance Studies, and Peggy McCracken, associate director. I wish to thank these colleagues, the contributors to the colloquium, all those who participated in the lively discussions, the anonymous readers for the University Press of Florida, and Walda Metcalf, associate director and editor-in-chief, who has seen the project to completion.

W. D. P.

Notes

Unless otherwise indicated, translations have been provided by the authors of the essays.

1. On Gaston Paris see my essay; on Menéndez Pelayo, the essay by Gumbrecht. On the criticism of Curtius by German scholars because of his "neglect of the influence exerted by . . . medieval German literature on other literatures," see Richards 14.

2. For the first argument, see the essay by Pickens; for the second, the essay by Nichols.

3. For the former, see the essay by Ferrante; for the latter, the work of Eugene Vance.

PHILOLOGY IN HISTORY

SCHOLARS AT A PERILOUS FORD

William D. Paden

ONE

We medievalists are all, both men and women, a lot like Gawain, when you come to think of it. Like him, we set out from our home base, his at the court of Arthur, ours in an academic department— though our department is unsullied, of course, by any improprieties in the conduct of our monarchs or their consorts. Like Gawain we go in search of adventure, his the search for the bleeding lance, ours for a scholarly instrument that will never run dry. Occasionally we encounter someone else like ourselves and shatter a few lances together. Gawain's adventures are chronicled in romance, ours in life's little run, the specific genre of the *curriculum vitae*. Like him we are, each of us, the greatest knight within our ken, at least until we serve as a benchmark for one greater in his or her journey toward the crowning achievement of tenure. At the present juncture in history and in the history of scholarship, we have arrived at a deep ford set between high banks. Have we the courage to make the leap?

On the other hand, though, we realize that we are light-years removed from the Middle Ages. I have sometimes fantasized about encountering Bertran de Born, the troubadour, in the flesh. If only Microsoft Word, version 47, will include an application to cut and paste oneself into a year of one's choice, say 1183, perhaps I can do it.[1] But I fear the encounter will prove difficult. Though I have scrutinized every available trace of this man's life, though I have at one point known his surviving songs pretty well by heart, I am afraid he might not know what to make of me, straight from Chicago, and I might find him disconcertingly feudal, aristocratic, intemperate, and wreathed in garlic—in a word, medieval. The acquaintance I have had with him, gratifying as it has been for me, has been inescapably mediated through the philological transaction.

That transaction is of course undertaken at our initiative, not theirs. Why do we study the Middle Ages? To say that we do so for as many reasons as there are of us would be to risk an understatement, since any of us may have many motives, including contradictory ones. Then again, however, many of us no doubt harbor reasons which may be grouped together on a level of sufficient abstraction. Joseph Owens has proposed a philosophy of medieval studies on overtly religious grounds, advocating a revival of Thomist philosophy as a vital infusion into twentieth-century Catholic thought. Others are drawn to the Middle Ages not because they have faith but because they feel the allure of an age in which faith was the grand project of institutionalized intellectual culture, even though they themselves do not believe. Thus Ingmar Bergman, the unbelieving son of a minister, naturally chose the Middle Ages as the setting for the dramatization of faith in his film *The Seventh Seal*. Others yet are attracted by surviving artifacts such as Gothic cathedrals, by the historical puzzle or the linguistic challenge, or by aesthetic qualities such as the high imagination of romance or the artful grit of the *fabliaux* or Villon.

When we choose to concentrate our scholarly attention on the Middle Ages, we presumably feel that it somehow offers a combination of distance and closeness that is right for us. It is far enough away to pose the challenge of strangeness—cultural, historical, linguistic, literary; it is farther than more recent periods that may be approached too easily for our taste; but it is close enough for us to feel capable of projecting humanity into it, unlike remoter times such as classical antiquity, ancient Egypt, or the culture of the Hittites. The decision to study the European Middle Ages ineluctably implies an orientation toward Europe, a congeniality with its products, an investment in its culture.

WILLIAM D. PADEN

For whatever reasons we choose to study the Middle Ages, our choice is bipolar, an act of communication, dateline today, between ourselves and that other, earlier time. As we change, so must the communication. If we persist in calling this time a Middle Age or several Middle Ages, we must say what it is or was in the middle of, unless we are willing to let the very name of our study lapse into antiquarianism, like the name of the Pont Neuf, new in the sixteenth century, its name preserved for us in language like a fly in amber. Just as Christo wrapped the Pont Neuf, we must attempt to package our subject anew, no matter how fragile the wrapping, before we expose it once more to the passage of time.

5

TWO

Many observers agree that we have arrived at a turning point, at a moment of acceleration of history. Such an acceleration seems rich in the implication of change from what we have recently been toward what we shall soon become. We are told that we have witnessed the end of English (Eagleton), or the end of books (Coover), or the end of art (Danto), or the end of history (Fukuyama), or the end of nature (McKibben); we have evidently seen the end of understatement, and perhaps a return to the apocalyptic mentality with its thrilling menace of imminent closure (Kermode). For John Lukacs the twentieth century ended in 1989 and the Modern Age, following the Ancient and the Medieval, has subsided into a transition toward something new and as yet unnamed. A visionary cultural critic such as O. B. Hardison, Jr., emerging from his early career as a specialist in medieval and Renaissance literature, proclaimed that, like Ganymede, "who was captured by Jove and brought to heaven to be his cupbearer," we shall shortly doff our carbon constitution in favor of silicone, and then disappear through the skylight of our humanity (289).[2]

It is easy to say that speculations such as these will surely be upset by the course of future events. *Le monde* quotes an interview with François Mitterrand from the *Wall Street Journal* in which the President of the Republic is reported to have said, "L'histoire peut aller aujourd'hui dans un sens ou un autre, et nous ne pouvons pas savoir dans lequel" (Amalric; "Today history may go one way or another, and we cannot know which")—and we cannot even feel certain whether these words are Mitterrand's own, cited directly by a French reporter who may have witnessed the interview, or are cited in French as quoted by the *Wall Street Journal* (improbably), or have been translated into English by the *Journal* and back into French by *Le monde,* or got there by some other circuitous route. But new beginnings are merely the converse of old endings, so if we wish to gauge our relation to the past we must make some effort to determine where we are. Nor is it enough to demarcate our relation to the past by erecting a string of posts between ourselves and it, using such lumber as the poststructural or, nearly everybody's favorite these days, postmodern. Rather we should look over the fence in an effort to see the lay of the land we are walking on, no matter how difficult it is—to give some sort of positive identification to the relation between where we are and where we have been. If we are at the end of something, can we speculate on the new shape of history? What implications can we draw, if any, for the study of medieval literature?

THREE

An initial observation about world politics, one that would have seemed implausible until very recently, is that the Cold War has ended. The present significant moment therefore connects with another: the end of World War II. This time-span includes the entire scholarly maturity of almost all of us today. Though the brief moment since the Cold War ended has already revived some older conflicts and ushered in some new ones, they are definitely post–Cold War conflicts. We find ourselves in a time we cannot name.

It seems likely that this development will make it more difficult to practice Marxist literary study, that it will distract attention from an approach such as that of the late Erich Köhler, who analyzed troubadour lyric and Old French romance in fundamentally Marxist terms.[3] A broader implication may be that literary scholarship during the period of the Cold War will seem in retrospect to take on a coherence which passed unsuspected during that period itself.

WILLIAM D. PADEN

In rereading discussion of a specific lyric genre, that of the *pastourelle*, I have been struck by such coherence among time periods conceived on a comparable scale. After the end of the Middle Ages, gentlemen scholars and enthusiastic amateurs toyed with the pastourelle until 1868, when with unexpected suddenness it came to be treated as an object of serious inquiry, subject to evidence, by a young German scholar named Julius Brakelmann, holder of the recently invented doctoral degree. Brakelmann's methodological advance outpaced his literary-historical convictions, with the result that he manipulated historical evidence to support his preconceived conclusion that the pastourelle must have originated in northern France, and not among the troubadours; but the evidence he introduced withstood his prejudices so well that later scholars were able to dismiss his argument with a flick of a footnote. After Brakelmann was killed at the age of twenty-six in the Franco-Prussian War, other scholars debated on the historical grounds he had defined until the turn of the century, when they seemed to run out of words. After the War to End All Wars, discussion revived with a new appreciation for the sophistication of medieval culture. Scholars turned from the issue of historical origins and began to assess the literary tone of the genre; the simplicity perceived earlier in the medieval text yielded to an awareness of internal tensions, to the discovery of satire directed against one of the protagonists, either the peasant Robin or perhaps even the knightly narrator. The new respect for the subject revived the discussion of influences from classical or medieval Latin; the international diffusion of the genre came to be seen not as servile imitation but as spontaneous reinvention; even the music of the pastourelles was investigated with interest. Since World War II, the characteristic innovation in pastourelle research has been, perhaps, the effort to seek a larger context in which to set the genre so that we may understand it in a consciously chosen perspective. Approaches have been developed as diverse as the folkloric, the sociological, the mythic, the comparative, the structuralist, and the feminist.[4] Each of these lines of inquiry has roots in the work of earlier periods, of course; moreover, the characteristic pursuits of earlier periods have continued to be cultivated through research in textual analysis, literary history and formalist reading. Scholars in this period have gone so far as to show signs of respect for their predecessors, as their predecessors rarely did for those who preceded them. The eclecticism and diversity of pastourelle scholarship during the Cold War reflect the same qualities we see in the architecture of those years, an architecture which has come to be called postmodern.

The word "postmodern" may well, I believe, be applied to the period of the Cold War. Postmodernism is not usually thought of as beginning so early, since the idea gained renown with the publication of Lyotard's *La condition postmoderne* in 1979, its translation in 1984, and the discussion that spread everywhere during the rest of the decade.[5] But the *Oxford English Dictionary* has found the primary architectural reference of the word as early as 1949, when John Hudnut spoke of the owner of a "post-modern house," declaring that "he shall be a modern owner, a post-modern owner, if such a thing is conceivable. Free from all sentimentality or fantasy or caprice" (2d ed., 1989, s.v. *post-modern*). Hudnut clearly felt he was dealing with a neologism, and just as clearly the sense of the word has evolved since that time to permit, or even to require, qualities of fantasy and caprice in postmodern architecture such as Philip Johnson's 1978 AT&T building (p. 194). Following Hudnut, the *OED* finds Arnold Toynbee, in 1956, writing of "our post-Modern age of Western history." Nicolas Pevsner wrote in 1966 of "the existence of a new style, successor to my International Modern of the nineteen-thirties, a post-modern style, I would be tempted to call it, but the legitimate style of the nineteen-fifties and nineteen-sixties." When Lyotard reported on the postmodern condition in 1979, he created a deliberate Anglicism.[6]

Postmodernism has blossomed once again in the special number of *Speculum* edited by Stephen Nichols and published in January 1990 with the title *The New Philology*. Of the five scholars who address the issue, four proclaim their own perspective as that of postmodernism, though they fail to make clear what they mean by the term except that they intend to mark themselves off from their predecessors of "the 'old' philological persuasion," as

Nichols calls it (3).[7] Howard Bloch, the only one of the five who identifies himself unambiguously as modern ("our own modernism," 39), dates the development of the New Philology "in the decades between World War II and the present" (46). The collection closes with Lee Patterson's plea for renewal of the profession of medieval studies, and Patterson closes (108) with reference to an address on "American Mediaevalists and Today" delivered by E. N. Johnson in 1953, in which Johnson spoke of the social value of medieval studies confronting the dangers of the time, "the McCarthyite witch-hunt and the recent development of the hydrogen bomb." Patterson asserts that "it is sadly true that neither of the problems that moved Johnson to speak has been much alleviated, although now we seem more likely to suffocate ourselves than blow ourselves up, and repression comes in less flamboyant, more insidious forms." He concludes in concert with Johnson that medievalists must justify their interests by contributing to the solution of problems of the day, "[and we] shall not get it done by merely attending as usual to our own comfortable, irrelevant, esoteric, and academic busy work while the world goes to its ruin and we together with it" (Johnson 854).

Patterson joins the chorus of apocalyptic prophets. I take his heartfelt unanimity with Johnson as confirmation that postmodernism is approaching its half-century mark. I am astonished that he believes the danger of McCarthyism has not been alleviated (despite the repressive aspirations of a Jesse Helms), and that the danger of nuclear holocaust has remained unchanged since the 1950s. I think it symptomatic that Patterson wavers from "postmodern" to "modern," implying that his perspective is already long in the tooth.[8] Now that what Ronald Reagan called the "Evil Empire" has become our client; now that Mikhail Gorbachev has been awarded the Nobel Prize for Peace so shortly before his slide into obscurity; now that the Russian government is selling the United States highly enriched uranium from its dismantled warheads for use as fuel in nuclear power plants; now that meaningful disarmament seems a foregone conclusion; now that the Cold War is well and truly over, surely times have changed. The confrontation between Communism and liberal democracy, which Francis

Fukuyama regards in a Hegelian perspective as the culmination of ideological conflict, has collapsed under the depressing weight of life in Marxist states.

Not unrelated to the end of the Cold War and the emergence of American culture has been the expansion of the English language as a language of the globe, spoken today by more people for whom it is a second language than for whom it is their first, indeed by about a quarter of the people on the face of the earth.[9] Hubert Curien, Minister of Research and Technology in the government of François Mitterrand, has observed to *Le monde* that the Francophone world now produces about 8 percent of all scientific discourse, but that among the scientists who produce the other 92 percent, not one is ignorant of English (Dufour and Nouchi). When the biologist James Watson was pursuing postdoctoral studies in Denmark and Italy, it apparently never occurred to him that it might be useful to understand Danish or Italian (18, 22)—and it probably would not have been. We may infer that an essential element in the education of a scientist today is mastery of English, at least scientific English, known as B.E. ("Broken English") in the laboratory of CERN in Switzerland—formerly the Conseil Européen pour la Recherche Nucléaire, now renamed the European Organization for Nuclear Research, with the same acronym. One reason, then, why American universities receive so many foreign students in scientific fields must be the need to learn English, just as, in the thirteenth century, the majority of students at the University of Paris went there in order to learn to speak and read Latin and left when they had done so (Lerner 212)—once they had satisfied their language requirement, as it were. In Italian *licei classici*, students in increasing numbers now opt for English rather than Latin, which is being displaced on its native soil. The implications for the Italian perception of the past, and for our own, are earth-shaking.[10] As for French, after centuries when English borrowed words across the Channel it now makes frequent loans, to the discomfiture of linguistic conservatives like Étiemble. As the European Community moves toward a single market, more than one observer has wondered if the organization will some day choose an official language, and if so, what language it will be.[11] Already some consider English "well on its way to becoming the unofficial international language of the world community" (Katzner 43)—the Latin of the third millennium.

The emergence of English as a global language cannot fail to af- fect all those involved in the study and teaching of foreign languages in the United States. In specifically medieval terms, it extends the movement of *translatio studii*.[12] Readers of Chrétien's *Cligés* have in the past, I suspect, felt largely in agreement with the narrator not only that the seat of universal learning has shifted from Greece to Rome to France and remained in France, but also with his fervent hope that it will stay there:

> Dex doint qu'ele i soit maintenue
> Et que li leus li abelisse
> Tant que ja mes de France n'isse
> L'enors qui s'i est arestee. (ed. Micha, vv. 34–37)

> God grant that [learning] be maintained there,
> And that this place be so pleasing to it
> That the honor which has come to rest there
> Never depart from France.[13]

Chrétien's narrator has been felt to be saying something self-evident, true, agreed upon by the reader. When Gertrude Stein received Hemingway, Joyce, and Picasso in the rue de Fleurus, her company of cultural émigrés would probably have agreed; so would the historian Amy Kelly have agreed, as she composed her dithyrambic praise of the capital as the intellectual center of the twelfth century.[14]

I doubt, however, that readers will feel the same tomorrow. More recently we have seen Marguerite Yourcenar, a denizen of an island off the coast of Maine, become the first female member of the Académie française; Boston University has appointed Elie Wiesel, a memorialist of the Holocaust who writes in French, as professor of humanities; New Orleans has provided the myth of the American South for Louis Malle, a French *cinéaste* turned American movie-maker; after a series of forays at Yale, Jacques

Derrida has ventured as far as the West Coast to establish a beach-head at the University of California–Irvine; and Michel Serres, a tenured professor at Stanford, has joined Yourcenar in immortality. The *translatio* has flowed to the west.

Nevertheless the topos retains its interest for the French. It is a significant choice that the Opéra de la Bastille (p. 195) scheduled as its first production, on March 17, 1990, Berlioz's *Les Troyens*, with its book adapted from the *Aeneid* (Henahan). Cassandre and Didon were sung by the Black American sopranos Grace Bumbry and Shirley Verrett; Pier Luigi Pizzi was the stage director, and Myung Whun Chung conducted the Paris Opera Orchestra (after the departure of Daniel Barenboim to Chicago). The opera house, you recall, was designed by Carlos Ott, the Canadian architect with the Catalan name born in Uruguay and now headquartered in Paris. The spectacle implied a sweeping historical continuum by depicting the transfer of culture from Troy to Rome, by playing out that transfer on the symbolic site of the fall of the *ancien régime* and the triumph of the Revolution, and by inaugurating a new impulse in diffusion of nineteenth-century French culture to all the corners of the waiting world.

If the *ouverture* of which François Mitterrand is fond of speaking is in truth an opening onto internationalism, onto a global culture, the implications seem more auspicious than if it is an opening onto a "Dynasty" made in Hollywood.[15] But insofar as the preponderance of cultural prestige has passed to the English language, and perhaps to American culture, the narrator in *Cligés* will seem old-fashioned, provincial, a prisoner of the past. When Gene Kelly won the heart of Leslie Caron in *An American in Paris* (1951), he anticipated the shift in the world art market from Paris to New York and staked a claim for the translation of study across the Atlantic.

FOUR

Then again, perhaps our time of transition connects not with the end of the Cold War but with another, remoter significant moment. Perhaps the phase we see ending arches over a longer stretch of history, a larger period containing Postmodernism as its conclusion. Perhaps we are witness to the end of a period that began around the beginning of the nineteenth century with the advent of Romanticism, a period that was marked in politics by the Napoleonic drama. In 1927 Clive Bell traced "the whole glorious history of modern art" from Géricault, Delacroix, and Constable (*OED*, 2d ed., 1989, s.v. *modern*). It is arguable that the flow of Western tradition made its sharpest turn up to now around 1800. Although our enjoyment of opera, for one thing, suggests that the continuity from Romantic tradition is far from ending, some of us have played Saint John on Patmos, proclaiming that repetition and eclecticism mark our time as a "twilight of modernism."[16]

In this focus we may see ourselves as latecomers in the age of Freud, and I suggest that this perspective is appropriate to an understanding of the stance of critics who take a psychoanalytic approach. In *The New Philology* Stephen Nichols invokes Lacan explicitly when he suggests that analysis of text and miniature in illuminated manuscripts offers "a dual route of penetration to the underside of consciousness" (8), presumably a collective unconscious in which both poet and painter are involved. The reference to Lacan or Freud or both remains implicit in the contribution by Howard Bloch. Bloch undertakes a discussion of the *Lais* of Marie de France in these terms: "My purpose is, in fact, to link (*lassar*) the notion of the *lai* as written residue to the question of the law and, finally, to show the extent to which the poetess and a certain medieval (and also peculiarly modern) notion of poetry are implicated in what seems in the *Lais* to be an obsession with linguistic transgression" (48). The continuity between medieval and modern, as Bloch calls it, is mediated by a technique appropriate for the disclosure of an obsession. Elsewhere in the article Bloch writes as an analyst of dream, when he describes the fairy lady in *Lanval* as "a dream of possession" (50), or as an analyst of fantasy, when he calls her "the literary incarnation of a fantasized solution to the material problems of the class of unmarried, unendowed, and wandering 'jeunes' " (50). Bloch undertakes to perform a psychoanalysis of these young medieval knights as a group, or of Marie de France as she internalized and expressed their mentality, or, to put it more simply, a psychoanalysis of the text.

His method follows from that purpose. The sentence I have quoted makes overt word-associations between *lai*, "the genre Marie writes," and *lassar*, "to link" (in Occitan, not French), and implicitly synthesizes what Bloch has just written about *legs*, "residue" (as in the *Legs* of Villon), and *loi*, "law." These are what Bloch calls "homophonies," and he is permissive, if not latitudinarian, in the words he accepts as sounding the same: *lai, laie, lede, lié, las, leu, la, laisse, laz, loi.* These words all have initial *l* in common, but little else: the initial *l* may be followed by as many as six different vowels or diphthongs; the vowel or diphthong may or may not be followed by another consonant; and there may or may not be a second syllable.[17] A few pages later Bloch declares, "Given the fact that Old French poetry, even though written, was intended for the ear (either to be recited or read aloud), there can be no difference between the words *traire* and *trahir*" (55).[18] Such an assertion offers the delight of baiting the Old Philologists, of course, but aside from that playful function it implies what Bloch is in fact doing: positing word-associations which may be thought to reveal an unconscious in the text. Such word-associations have no need of strict philological identity.[19] At the end of his analysis, Bloch claims to have accounted for "the fundamental masochism which lies at the core of Western eroticism" (58). He has done a psychoanalysis not just of a few *lais*, not just of one poet, not just of medieval poetry or culture, but of Western eroticism—including us. Surely if Bloch can accomplish all that by twisting the neck of a monosyllable, the price to pay is a small one.

Then again, wordplay is not limited to psychoanalysis. If Isidore of Seville could derive the word *lucus*, "grove," from *lucere*, "to shine," because groves are dark with shadows (Curtius, *European* 497), perhaps he implied a certain playfulness in the Creator of language, who instituted such a resemblance. Although Bloch's homophonies are startling if we think of them in linguistic terms, it is true that Isidore might have read Marie de France the same way, just as Freud or Lacan might have. As Bloch points out (46), Old Philologists who have multiplied their conjectures over a textual crux have read with no less fertile fantasy, even though they believed they did so in search of an objective truth. Other philologists who have cultivated word associations in a Freudian vein include Roger Dragonetti, Jean-Charles Huchet, and Laura Kendrick.[20] The skeptic might be willing to grant that such readings employ a technique which is useful in relation to other projects, but object that its practitioners have not justified their grounds for extending it to medieval literature. That is, granted that similar techniques are an established instrument in psychiatry,[21] on what grounds may one extend them to philology? Are the Freudian critics so persuaded of the truth according to the Viennese doctor that they seriously consider it an obligatory presupposition for any understanding of medieval poetry?[22] Or do they adopt it more playfully, as one perspective with interesting applications? If their attitude is the latter, are their results properly considered as instances of critical play? If their criticism is intrinsically playful, does it differ in this respect from the present paper? Does the *episteme* of our age compel us, or at least invite us, to playful knowledge? Such a proposition has been put forward in all seriousness by students of modern culture including Hardison, who wrote: "It is fair to say that the dominant movement of twentieth-century theoretical science, especially mathematics, physics, and cosmology, has been away from certainties and toward masks and games" (49).[23]

Bloch posits a descent of philology from Vico's *New Science* and the Romantics—despite what he calls the "interval" marked from 1869 to 1949, when the field was institutionalized under the aegis of positivism—down to the "New Medievalism," launched by Robert Guiette with his *Poésie formelle en France au moyen âge* (1949) and carried forward by Paul Zumthor's *Langue et techniques poétiques à l'époque romane* (1963). In this model of fat and lean years, the objectivity proclaimed by positivism implies a subjectivity in the Romantics—and in the New Medievalism. Whether or not such an element may be detected in Guiette or Zumthor,[24] it does characterize this essay of Bloch's. On the micro level it corresponds to his psychoanalytic approach; on the macro level, to his nostalgia for the Romantic *mysterium* and his intimations of a religious impetus, as when he writes that today's reader "cannot fail to recognize the pertinence of medieval literature to any attempt to situate the literary sign with respect to Being" (39). Bloch's Romantic roots underlie his identification of himself as a modern rather than a postmodern.

FIVE

Flipping channels from one master narrative to another, I would now like to sketch the outline of a yet longer view. Perhaps today's transition connects even farther back, all the way to the Renaissance of the thirteenth through sixteenth centuries, and what we see ending is a great project set in motion by events in Italy six centuries ago. We might call this period the Long Renaissance, or the Greater Renaissance as we speak of a city including its extensions, or more simply the Great Renaissance by analogy to the Grand Louvre which is one of its temples.[25] In terms of the history of climate, the Great Renaissance corresponds to what has been called a "little ice age" between two eras of relative warmth—the high Middle Ages and the twentieth century (Brochier).

I think such a view has much to recommend it. Perhaps we teeter on the brink of something different from these past centuries with their consistent privileging of classical culture, from Petrarch through the founders of Northwestern University, who staffed the institution in the 1850s with four professors: one in Greek, one in Latin, one in mathematics, and one in chemistry.[26] Renaissance humanism was alive and well in the 1890s, when Joseph Bédier and Alfred Jeanroy published theses on Old French lyric poetry which were written in Latin. It was flourishing still in 1925, when a student at Yale was required to study Greek or Latin in order to receive the prestigious Bachelor of Arts degree (should I say *Baccalaureus Artium?*); without Greek or Latin he could only settle for the Bachelor of Philosophy, as my father did. Perhaps humanism ended in France in the events of May 1968, although it lingers in its particular French form in the shelving of books for ready reference, or *usuels*, down the center aisle of the department of printed books at the Bibliothèque nationale, where the most accessible subjects are French literature of the seventeenth through nineteenth centuries, with a sparse representation of the twentieth century, sparser still of the sixteenth, a handful of medieval works—and the complete Guillaume Budé collections in Greek and Latin. We sometimes fail to realize how natural it was for Ezra Pound to read the classical poets.

The consistency of those centuries is marked by their use in painting of classical perspective, which was defined by Alberti in 1435, and which began to come apart in the work of the Impressionists, as their interest shifted from the object and the perceiver to the medium of perception; it was deconstructed by Erwin Panofsky, and it has quite disappeared from the work of a Jackson Pollock or a Frank Stella.[27] In philosophy the Great Renaissance ran from Montaigne to Wittgenstein, but now "the political supremacy of Europe has ended, and the hegemony of European ideas is ending too" (Toulmin 3). In psychology it ran from Burton's *Anatomy of Melancholy* to Freud, but now we have cognitive science; in economics, from Malthus to Marx, but now we have McDonald's in Moscow, located directly across Pushkin Square from a heroic statue of the poet. To Pushkin the golden arches must look strange among the onion domes.

The same periodization extends into the sciences. The characteristic Renaissance preoccupation with the passage of time reached biology at last when Darwinian evolution supplanted the taxonomy of Linnaeus, but Darwin was supplanted in turn when Watson and Crick founded the new science of molecular biology, joining genetics and biochemistry, by their demonstration that the structure of DNA takes the form of a double helix. In physics Newton quantified the force of gravitation in terms of movement of bodies in space and time, but Einstein integrated gravity into the special theory of relativity as an effect of the curvature of four-dimensional space-time (Hawking 4, 184). Renaissance technology was marked by two inventions: one by the devil, gunpowder, which culminated in the invention of dynamite and the endowment of the Nobel Prizes, only to be overshadowed by nuclear fission (Di Salvatore); the other by God, the printing press, which may now be yielding to the computer.

The geographical discoveries of the first Renaissance culminated in the era of colonialism, but with the last wave of independence in the 1950s we have entered a post-colonial age. In politics the Great Renaissance was the age of the nation-state, the concept imported to Russia by Ivan the Terrible and continued, as Eisenstein implied in his film on Ivan, into the age of Stalin. Today Stalinism is dead and we have launched into something new. The European Community is struggling toward a voluntary social integration on a scale without precedent.[28] "The international system is at a crossroads on the concept of what is a nation state," according to Madeleine K. Albright, the United States representative to the United Nations, and observers wonder whether the two hundred–odd countries now in the world may grow to fifty more in the next fifty years, or may become five thousand (Binder and Crossette).

Our culture has moved beyond the Renaissance definition of itself as the continuation of glorious antiquity, after the dark medieval parenthesis. Both inside and outside the academy, this master narrative with its strong chronological valorization and its strictly European horizon has simply lost any impact on much contemporary thought. Such an observation would by now be self-evident in any circles but those of specialists in classical antiquity, the Middle Ages, and the Renaissance. The disdain for medieval poetry expressed so abundantly by a Renaissance scholar such as Brunetière,[29] or even by a medievalist such as Jeanroy,[30] reflected their position in the development of literary study out of Classics. Pioneering medievalists transferred classical techniques of reading and editing from ancient literature onto medieval, but sustained the Humanist condemnation of all things medieval and so condemned themselves to a form of self-hatred which today seems irrational. Their normative outlook, their vision of medieval simplicity (as exemplified by Gaston Paris), the whole framework within which the founders of modern philology perceived medieval literature, has changed radically. This is the underlying reason why scholars writing on the pastourelle seemed to gain such respect for their subject in the period between the wars, and

WILLIAM D. PADEN

why the condescension toward medieval poetry which older medievalists still express from time to time seems so gratuitous to younger ones. Scales have dropped from our eyes. No longer bound to define ourselves as better than the Middle Ages, we have become able to see them with a new disinterest, a new objectivity, a new receptiveness.

Hence the call for recontextualizing medieval literature, for seeing it in its own terms rather than those of the Humanists. Eugene Vance proposes a reading of Chrétien de Troyes grounded in the trivium, as James F. Burke does for the *Cantar de mio Cid*. A yet closer sense of immediate physical context envisions the text in its manuscript form. Cerquiglini argues that the concept of the text which has informed traditional philology is specific to nineteenth-century modernity, part of the eventual working out of the implications of print, but that the time has come to vault over such an anachronism back to an embrace of textual variance, or, as Zumthor called it, *mouvance*.[31] Cerquiglini has been influential in Stephen Nichols's call for a return to the manuscripts of Old French literature and a rejection of the unique authoritative text implied in the practice of critics such as Leo Spitzer not so long ago. That unique authoritative text owed more to Gutenberg than to any medieval poet, and when we have conceived such a text, we have read as members of print culture. Similarly, Suzanne Fleischman urges us to attend to discourse phenomena in syntax beyond the sentence, beyond the authoritative period and capital letter of the printed book which succeeded the more fluid punctuation, often rhythmic rather than syntactic, of Old French manuscripts (cf. Cerquiglini, *Éloge* 47–48). John Dagenais goes further, arguing that we must replace our outdated critical paradigm centered on text and author with a new one centered on manuscript and reader, if we hope to understand the life of medieval literature in its difference from classical textuality. The uniformity and quantity in communication which are characteristics of print distinguish the Great Renaissance from its medieval predecessors and arguably from us its successors, with our dwindling print runs of increasingly specialized books and journals. Once we all link up our computers on MedNet we shall be able to dispense with camera-ready copy and publish through a modem; just think of the *mouvance* then.[32]

These sweeping changes cannot fail to affect our reading. An example is the *Song of Roland.* In 1870 Gaston Paris lectured on the epic at the Collège de France in the midst of the German siege of Paris (see p. 180). In that lecture Roland symbolized the besieged French nation, and the *Song* was, like Eisenstein's film of the life of Ivan the Terrible, a hymn to the state.[33] When we theorize the *chansons de geste* in terms of social collectivity in contrast with romance as an expression of the individual, we come very close to implying a concept of the nation. But if the nation (at least in Europe) is changing with the emergence of the European Community, then insofar as our personal identity is informed by our sense of belonging to a nation, our reading must change as well, or perhaps has already changed. Perhaps new readers will find it increasingly difficult to sympathize with a patriotic experience such as that of Gaston Paris. Perhaps they will find it easier to find irony in the *Song of Roland* or to respond to the Latin version of the legend, long scorned by admirers of the Oxford version, partly because the Latin narrator penetrates the inner experience of Ganelon and portrays Roland as afraid—which has scandalized some older readers, but may pique the interest of younger ones.[34]

SIX

There are other schemes. Although Hardison focuses his attention on tracing the Pythagorean and Democritean traditions from Greece to the present, he suggests in passing that a transition analogous to the one we are experiencing has not occurred since the advent of Christianity with Saint Augustine. Perhaps this implies a master narrative of Antiquity, Christianity, and the Twentieth Century. Aside from the disproportion among these parts, however, for the student of the Middle Ages such a scheme seems to miss the point, since by melding the medieval and Renaissance periods (either great or small), it effaces the possibility of identifying the Middle Ages in contrast with what followed.[35] Another way of thinking, predicated on the end of the Great Renaissance, groups the Middle Ages and the Renaissance together with Antiquity, all under the rubric of Early Studies, as in "early music." This terminology, however, loses contact with any recognizable character in those times except their earliness, their distance from noon or evening, whenever it is we live now. Yet another outlook disputes beginning modernity with Romanticism, and prefers to push it back to the pre-Romanticism of Rousseau, the politics of revolution, and the culture of Enlightenment. For Priscilla Parkhurst Ferguson, "So much has happened in Europe in so short a time that future historians may well decree that the twentieth century ended in 1989. Not since the end of the eighteenth century have so many elements of closure seemed to cohere: end of an age, end of the old order, and, of course, end of the century. Not since 1790 has a final decade promised so much change."[36]

What seems clear to me is that the age of the single hegemonic master narrative told by the Renaissance is past, and that we have instead an abundance of alternative stories, so many that we may switch from one to another like a cinematographer switching lenses, experimenting with different ways to see our object and ourselves. There is utility in many different narratives, because ours is a kaleidoscopic age. We have varying affinities with our past. We may choose to promote affinity with this or that moment or span in the past. We may witness a clamor of rivalry among those who promote various versions of the past. Such clamor makes ours an interesting time, and in particular, I suggest, an interesting time to be a medievalist.

SEVEN

If it is true that we have reached the end of the Great Renaissance, the implications for the study of the Middle Ages are double-edged. On the one hand, if today's culture no longer defines itself at the expense of the Middle Ages, that far distant time may simply lose whatever negative interest it once had as the epitome of all that was unenlightened. Thus some departments of literary study have cut the early period out of their curriculum. At Northwestern a new graduate program in German defines its interest as beginning around 1750; I am told that at Johns Hopkins the English department has become indifferent to literature written before the sixteenth century, thus eliminating not only *Beowulf* but Chaucer. On the other hand, however, if we have at long last outgrown the need to define ourselves at the expense of the Middle Ages, we may become able to consider that time with a more open mind. In the years to come we shall see whether study of the Middle Ages thrives better in an atmosphere of threatened indifference than it did in one of lively scorn.

Because I think it is such an interesting time, I demur from the cries of alarm which have been put up by some of our colleagues. Stephen Nichols, introducing the papers in *The New Philology*, ends on the dismal note of a "sense of absorption and isolation of medieval studies," of a "medieval ghetto" (10). Nichols refers in turn to the paper by Lee Patterson, who opens with this volley against complacency:

> In the current academic milieu, at least in the Anglo-American world, medieval studies is a marginalized institution. Most literary scholars and critics consider medieval texts to be utterly extraneous to their own interests, as at best irrelevant, at worst inconsequential; and they perceive the field itself as a site of pedantry and antiquarianism, a place to escape from the demands of modern intellectual life. (87)

Patterson's alarm for medieval studies, I believe, is created in large measure by his perception of a hegemonic Renaissance. He writes that the ultimate cause of the marginalization of medieval studies

> must be sought in the pervasive and apparently ineradicable *grand récit* that organizes Western cultural history, the gigantic master narrative by which modernity identifies itself with the Renaissance and rejects the Middle Ages as by definition premodern. According to this universal scheme, the Renaissance is the point at which the modern world begins. . . . The ubiquity of this master narrative needs no emphasis. It is almost impossible to conceptualize Western history without it. (92)

To the contrary, I find numerous ways to depart from the scheme that causes Patterson such distress. Whether we are involved in the end of postmodernism, or of modernism, or of the Great Renaissance, or of some other way of conceiving our heritage, the implications for rethinking the Middle Ages are manifold and challenging.

In his gloomy assessment of our professional condition, Patterson overlooks some major factors. In spring 1962, 150 medievalists gathered in Kalamazoo, Michigan—not then a household word, as veterans attest—for a congress of medieval studies, the first to be held there. In May 1992 the twenty-seventh International Congress of Medieval Studies brought together more than 2,600 registered participants. Meanwhile the Modern Language Association has continued its hospitality for medieval interests, as has the Kentucky Foreign Language Conference, and there is a steady stream of meetings on specific medieval topics. Publication on medieval subjects, like publication in other areas, continues to grow beyond all anticipation. We have witnessed the launching of the Middle Ages Series at the University of Pennsylvania Press, the Garland Library of Medieval Literature, French Forum Monographs, the Grant and Cutler bibliographies, the Medieval Institute Publications at Kalamazoo, and the Regents Studies in Medieval Culture at the University of Nebraska Press, to name some of the most conspicuous new series in the field.

I have amused myself by looking up the dates when about 50 journals that I try to keep up with were founded. Only one began publication before 1870: *Archiv für das Studium der neueren Sprachen und Literaturen*, founded in 1846. In that title "neueren" meant newer than the classical languages out of which medieval philology had sprung. Between the Franco-Prussian War and World War I, a rash of journals that still interest me saw the light. The earliest ones had names involving the root of the word "Romance" in implicit contrast with "classical," titles such as *Revue des langues romanes, Romania, Zeitschrift für romanische Philologie, Romanic Review*.[37] The word "modern" enjoyed a vogue, especially in English, with the *Publications of the Modern Language Association, Modern Language Notes, Modern Philology*, and *Modern Language Review*. Between the wars the rate of founding continued to rise with a turn toward more titles in the medieval manner, especially in Latin, titles like *Speculum, Medium Aevum, Mediaeval Studies, Medievalia et Humanistica, Traditio.* Since World War II even more journals have started up, although some decline in frequency is perhaps detectable since 1965. None of the journals on my list which have been launched since the war use the word "new" in their titles, an omission which implies that the contrast with "old," meaning "classical," is quite dead. (The omission is therefore symptomatic of the end of the Great Renaissance.) Only one uses "modern," *Forum for Modern Language Studies;* some continue to use "Romance," such as *Romance Philology, Romance Notes, Romance Quarterly* (originally *Kentucky Romance Quarterly*). Characteristic are the "medieval" titles which continue to appear, either in Latin (*Viator, Encomia, Exemplaria*) or more commonly in vernacular languages (*Studi mediolatini e volgari, Cahiers de civilisation médiévale, Olifant, Tenso*).[38] Furthermore, as more and more journals have entered the field, the proportion which use English as their primary language has increased. Of the ten on my list which have been founded since 1970, nine use English as their primary language.[39] Old French studies are not only burgeoning, they are following the *translatio studii* by riding the Gulf Stream of global English. The field of medieval studies we wander through is no wasteland—it is more like an enchanted forest.

However, by citing all this frenetic activity I am not really answering Patterson and Nichols directly, since they are concerned not with the state of medieval studies as a thing in itself, but rather in relation to other fields perceived as more central. I think they are talking about academic politics as displayed in departmental meetings, committees, appointments, enrollments in graduate courses, and the choices graduate students make for their specialties, particularly for their dissertations. I have a friend in history who once confessed to me the disappointment he feels because so many of his undergraduate students do not go on to become historians. Like him we in literature must bear our cross, the certain knowledge that many of our students will not specialize in the medieval period. But would we really wish to have it otherwise?

WILLIAM D. PADEN

We may ascertain something about the prosperity of medieval French studies in relation to other periods by consulting the annual survey of "Dissertations in Progress" published by the *French Review* since 1963 (see McCann). As of 1991, the total number of dissertations listed in nearly three decades was more than 5,500. Half of them were in nineteenth- or twentieth-century studies. The other 50 percent were divided more or less equally among five remaining groups: Medieval, Sixteenth Century, Seventeenth Century, Eighteenth Century, and a group of less populous areas including General Literature, Francophone Literature, Linguistics, and Pedagogy. Dissertations on medieval subjects accounted for 11 percent of the total, one percentage point less than the eighteenth century but one more than the seventeenth and three more than the sixteenth. If we look more narrowly at production of dissertations since 1980, we find that medieval subjects accounted for 10 percent of the total, ranging from year to year as low as 5 percent or as high as 19 percent. Other periods of study have had their ups and downs as well.

I find in these reports on dissertations in progress no reason for alarm over the state of Old French studies, much less any reason to fear that we occupy a ghetto in the shining city of our more modern colleagues. Our great strength is the intrinsic interest of our subject, but we also have the strategic advantage, within the departmental arena, of the longest available perspective on ourselves. Because the medieval perspective contains the other modern areas and because the medieval background informs subsequent history and literature, we must understand those intervening times in order to think our way back from the present into the medieval past. More significantly yet, the past we have chosen to study implies by its name a transition between Antiquity and the Renaissance. If, as I claim, we have emerged from the Renaissance, then we have a new, wider perspective on these three periods. No other period in the French department can claim to imply past and future as the Middle Ages do. They are the buckle in our sword-belt, the boss on our shield. If we grasp the full significance of our period, it is the keystone of the Western tradition.

There is a commonplace called *laudatio temporis acti*, praise of time past, or of the good old days. As a normative vector it may be considered the direct opposite of the *translatio studii*. Although the topos has an impeccable medieval pedigree, we may not wish to adopt it. We risk doing an injustice to our colleagues and to ourselves if we mutter monkishly with the narrator of the *Life of Saint Alexis*, "Good was the world in the time of the ancients, for faith there was, and justice and love—and medieval studies." I have no doubt that over the lengthening century since the Ph.D. degree came into being, the initial preeminence of medieval studies has declined. I think it had to, since the institutional study of modern literatures was born in the shadow of the Classics, and only that discipline, the legacy of Renaissance humanism, could confer upon it the necessary letters of nobility (Douglas). Study of modern literature had to reach maturity by outgrowing philology. By doing so, modern study developed an organon of methods which stands to benefit medieval literature by enabling us to read it as though it were alive, even as we respect its alterity. Under the renewed affinity of our culture for medieval culture, with ever-evolving approaches to modern literature at our disposal, we have an opportunity without precedent to reread medieval literature now.

NOTES

1. "Close to naked singularities it may be possible to travel into the past," according to Hawking (89). A singularity is "a point in space-time at which the space-time curvature becomes infinite"; a singularity would be called naked if it were not clothed in a surrounding black hole (Hawking 88–89, 185–86). It remains to derive the implications for the study of courtly love and the fabliau.

2. Man disappears in another way for Michel Foucault, who sees the death of God as inevitably entailing the death of Man (*Les mots et les choses*).

3. For reservations regarding Köhler's approach, see Kay 112–31. At the 1990 Convention of the Modern Language Association of America, the Division on Literary Criticism organized a timely meeting with the title "After Glasnost: Whither Marxist Criticism?"

WILLIAM D. PADEN

4. See the study by Gravdal and my response, "Rape in the Pastourelle."

5. At the time of this writing (1992) the Northwestern University Library catalog carries 195 items under the subject heading "Postmodernism," of which 190 were published since 1984.

6. "I have decided to use the word *postmodern*. . . . The word is in current use on the American continent among sociologists and critics; it designates the state of our culture following the transformations which, since the end of the nineteenth century, have altered the game rules for science, literature, and the arts" (Lyotard xxiii).

7. For the term "postmodern" see *The New Philology* articles of Nichols (7); Fleischman (19, 37); Spiegel (59); Patterson (87).

8. Patterson frequently uses "postmodern" in reference to his own situation, but judges that "Hamlet . . . expresses our modernity" ("On the Margin" 97).

9. McCrum, Cran, and MacNeil (19–20) estimate the number of people who use English as at least 750 million, perhaps closer to one billion, out of a world population around 3.5 billion. Lukacs distinguishes between American English, "the language . . . of all airports and airlines," which is the "computerized, scientific, business language employed from nine to five, in Tokyo and Singapore as well as in London and New York," and the language of leisure "that the Japanese or English businessman speaks after five, when he is at home at the kitchen table"; he believes that "it is the latter that counts," because "leisure . . . is the basis of culture, not the other way around" (221–23).

10. Even in the Vatican, Latin is yielding power to the vernaculars of the Polish Pope and the Italian bureaucracy (Woodward). A flyer announcing the Eighth International Congress of the Academia Latinitati Fovendae at Louvain and Antwerp, 1993, written in Latin and English, includes these statements: "Since WW II the situation of Latin all over the Western world has been changed radically. In secondary schools it has lost its preeminence almost everywhere on the programme and even where it survives, teaching has been reduced drastically and pupils leave school with a rather limited knowledge of the language. . . . In fact, nowhere in the world, not even in Rome, is academic teaching done in Latin today, which means that among latinists and theologians, not to mention other scholars, the practice of spoken Latin has almost entirely disappeared."

11. The declaration of French as the language of France, in June 1992, represents a defensive gesture against the encroachments of English (Riding).

12. On the theme of *translatio studii* see Gilson 182–86. For Bernard Cerquiglini (57), the very name "Chrétien de Troyes" suggests a translation from ancient Troy to Troyes in Champagne, from pagan antiquity to medieval Christianity. This ingenious reading is a good one by the criteria we apply to poetry, but implausible as history—it is far more ingenious, for example, than Chrétien's straightforward assertion of the *translatio*.

13. My translation. At the conclusion of his chapter on "L'humanisme médiéval" (196), Gilson quotes these lines with passionate sympathy. Freeman has offered a reading of *Cligés* informed by the *translatio studii* topos.

14. Amy Kelly, *Eleanor of Aquitaine and the Four Kings*, chapter 4: "O Paris!"

15. On the other hand, we must applaud the awareness of English literary tradition and critical contributions shown by Cerquiglini in *Éloge de la variante*, an awareness which we have not always seen in Gallic scholarship.

16. Nelson 555–56; more recently, Lukacs 284–85.

17. For more detailed discussion, see Pickens in this volume (his third section, "*Éloge de la variance* and the 'New' Philology").

18. Medieval *traire* and *trahir* were pronounced quite distinctly, as are the corresponding forms in Modern French.

19. "When we hear of people rejecting Lacanian formulae such as 'the unconscious is structured like a language,' or 'the unconscious is a discourse' in the name of a purist adherence to the principles of linguistic science, we can consider them as dismissing, with too hasty a stroke of the pen, the richness of such analogical recourses" (Lemaire 100–101, quoted by Meltzer 161).

20. See my critical review of Kendrick's book *The Game of Love*. For a lively defense of this school of thought, see Delany.

21. On puns in Freud and Lacan see the contributions by Fineman and Meltzer to the volume edited by Culler; on word association in Jung, see Meier 66–69; in clinical psychology, Berg and Pennington 137.

22. For reservations concerning the application of Freudian techniques to Renaissance literature, see Greenblatt. One serious critic of psychotherapy in many forms is Masson.

23. "A scientific theory is just a mathematical model we make to describe our observations: it exists only in our minds. So it is meaningless to ask: Which is real, 'real' or 'imaginary' time? It is simply a matter of which is the more useful description" (Hawking 139). My colleague John Ketterson, Professor and Chair of Physics and Astronomy at Northwest-

ern University, has stated that in physics, mathematical model-building is recognized as a valid form of science even if it has no connection with reality.

24. The objectivity of Guiette's formalist criticism contrasts with his production as a poet; Zumthor departs from his usual objectivity in the subjective introduction to *Speaking of the Middle Ages*.

25. A different proposal for the term "Great Renaissance" has been made by Le Goff.

26. Williamson and Wild 17–18. The Classics department has since grown, but no longer comprises half the faculty.

27. Recent discussions include those of Snyder and Pinkus.

28. We are told, perhaps not surprisingly, that the Pope favors a medieval Europe (Svidercoschi).

29. "Si l'on commence par poser résolument en principe, ou en fait, que notre littérature du moyen âge, nos *Chansons de geste* elles-mêmes, nos *Fabliaux* (ou *Fableaux*), nos *Mystères* aussi n'ont aucune valeur littéraire, alors, mais seulement alors, il devient aisé de s'entendre" ("If we begin by resolutely positing, in principle or in fact, that our literature of the Middle Ages, our *chansons de geste* themselves, our *fabliaux* [or *fableaux*], our *mystères* too, have no literary value at all, then and only then does it become easy to understand each other"); Brunetière (189), quoted by Bloch ("New" 43).

30. At the age of 75, after a lifetime spent in study of the troubadours, Alfred Jeanroy sprinkled his analysis of "La chanson: Sa forme et son contenu" with scornful derogations and concluded with this one: "Le caractère conventionnel des images est, en somme, le pire défaut du style des troubadours. Je n'ai pas dissimulé qu'il n'était pas le seul" (*Poésie* 2:134; "The conventional character of their images is, finally, the worst fault of troubadour style. I have not concealed the fact that it was not the only one.") Following Gumbrecht's analysis in this volume, one might ask if Jeanroy expressed a national inferiority complex in relation to German scholars in the wake of the Franco-Prussian War. See also my forthcoming assessment of Jeanroy's work.

31. Cerquiglini, "Modernité textuaire," in *Éloge de la variante* 15–29; compare Zumthor, *Essai* 64–82. As Cerquiglini says himself (111), his book constitutes an "hypothèse forte"; his assertion, for example, that "l'auteur n'est pas une idée médiévale" (25), calls for discussion in view of studies such as that of Minnis.

32. Cerquiglini (112–15) proposes as a solution to the quandary of the textual critic today that texts should be published on floppy disks, which

would allow entry of each version or manuscript in a distinct document, so that one could consult various versions simultaneously in separate windows. It is not clear that such innovative publication would differ essentially from publication of multiple versions in a traditional bound book, such as Pickens's edition of the songs of Jaufré Rudel; in fact it might be an inferior solution, since a book such as Pickens's allows the reader to consult as many versions of the text as the editor proposes, whereas the computer screen is limited in its capacity to show many windows at once (the one at which I am writing cannot show meaningful passages on more than four). For discussion of the more sophisticated concept of hypertext as it could be applied to Shakespeare's *Tempest*, see Hardison 262–65; for more on hypertext see Coover. "MedNet" in the sentence above represents a playful fiction, but has already been realized in the electronic bulletin board called Medtext-L, sponsored by James W. Marchand of the University of Illinois. Already it is possible to transmit a formatted document (such as an article or book) through e-mail.

33. Paris ends his peroration on a note of patriotic fervor : ". . . et souhaitons par-dessus toutes choses, comme Roland, qu'on ne puisse jamais dire de nous que, par notre faute, la France a perdu de sa valeur!" ("Chanson" 118; ". . . and let us hope above all else, like Roland, that no one will ever be able to say that our shortcomings have cost France any of its greatness!").

34. For an ironic reading, see my "Tenebrism in the *Song of Roland*"; for a new edition of "De Tradicione Guenonis," see Paden and Stäblein.

35. Alexandre Leupin sees the Middle Ages as continuous with modernity (that is, the present time), discounts the significance of the Renaissance, and distinguishes culture as Christian versus pagan: "Ce n'est pas une fiction du tout innocente, la fiction de la tradition occidentale: nous en connaissons tous les effets dévastateurs. Elle repose évidemment sur l'idée d'une continuité entre les Grecs et nous, qui saute le Moyen Âge. C'est un des phantasmes les plus ravageurs de l'histoire. Mais je ne peux souscrire à [la] formulation de la Renaissance comme lieu coupant le Moyen Âge. J'affirmerais que le Moyen Âge est essentiellement moderne étant donné que la coupure se situe non pas entre moderne et ancien, mais d'après Kojève, entre chrétien et païen. Dans ce sens, je ne pense pas que le Moyen Âge, historiquement parlant, soit notre Autre" (Haidu, Leupin, and Vance 28; "It is not an innocent fiction at all, this fiction of the Western tradition; we know all its devastating effects. It is founded, of course, on the idea of a continuity between the Greeks and us that leaps over the Middle Ages. It is one of the most ravaging fantasies of history.

But I cannot subscribe to the formulation of the Renaissance as a space cutting off the Middle Ages. I would affirm that the Middle Ages are essentially modern, in view of the fact that the cut-off does not separate modern and ancient, but according to Kojève, separates Christian and pagan. In this sense I do not believe that the Middle Ages, historically speaking, are our Other").

36. Ferguson, xv; likewise both Habermas and Lukacs. Foucault defended situating the beginning of modernity in the early nineteenth century; Weightman stoutly defends our continuity with Enlightenment thought. I am indebted to Peter Dembowski for the reference to Weightman.

37. On the concept of "Romania," see Curtius, *European Literature and the Latin Middle Ages*, 30–35.

38. Recent contributions to the history of scholarly journals in medieval studies have been made by Duby, Joris, Dufournet, and Bourel de la Roncière on *Le moyen âge*; by Hempel, with a gallery of portraits of some sixty publications; and by Owens on *Mediaeval Studies*. Specialized journals founded recently in France such as *Perspectives médiévales* (Paris, Société de langue et de littérature médiévales d'oc et d'oïl, 1975–) and *Médiévales* (Vincennes, Université de Paris VIII, 1982–) are received by few American libraries, perhaps because of the spiralling costs of subscriptions in general.

39. The only exception is *Medioevo romanzo*, which also publishes articles in English.

A PHILOLOGICAL INVENTION OF MODERNISM

MENÉNDEZ PIDAL, GARCÍA LORCA, AND THE HARLEM RENAISSANCE

Hans Ulrich Gumbrecht

The inception of this essay was a presentation that I gave at the 1991 MLA Convention in the context of a workshop on "Philology and the Foundations of Modernism" organized by R. Howard Bloch. It was part of a larger network of panels and meetings focusing on "Essentialism and Fundamentalism in Philological Perspective." For two reasons it seems indispensable to mention the original framework of my argument. First, because I am using, as my main orientation, a double pair of concepts—"philology/modernism" and "essentialism/fundamentalism"—which had been elaborated by Stephen Nichols in a remarkable (and remarkably complex) outline for that MLA debate. While I greatly profited from the implicit provocations of this conceptual configuration, I will simply treat it as a given, as a starting point for my article—and hence not discuss its theoretical and historical pertinence. Secondly, I want to emphasize that the materials that I am going to present regarding the history of philology and modernism in Spain between 1898 and 1927 will be used in the sense of a case-study; that is, they are meant to illustrate a hypothesis about different (and perhaps culturally specific) attitudes in dealing with texts. Such a perspective subordinates the specificity of modernism and philology in Spain to the relative abstractness of my argument and justifies, I hope, the fact that on the historical level I am largely (although not exclusively) recurring to previously published results of research.

ONE

My first reaction to Nichols's outline of the topic "Essentialism and Fundamentalism" was to associate the pole of "essentialism" with what I had myself been trying to describe as the "hermeneutic space" in a number of recent essays concerning the emergence of the concept of "literature" and the historical foundations of the philological disciplines.[1] Within the hermeneutic space, as within philological essentialism, texts matter because they are supposed to carry "meanings," both in the sense of a more or less complex semantic structure that they "contain" and in the sense of their ability to "refer" to phenomena in the extra-textual world. It is normally taken for granted that such meanings are anchored in the intention of an author-subject and that, therefore, the author's intention can be used as a criterion to validate the meaning identifications or interpretations of professional and nonprofessional readers. At the same time, however, the hermeneutic/essentialist approach acknowledges the possibility that individual texts (or at least specific types of texts)[2] can be credited with a multiplicity of meanings or readings. Whenever this assumption is made, the variety of the meanings is seen as emerging out of differences between an original situation of text production and those subsequent situations in which texts are received. According to Hans-Georg Gadamer (290 ff.), the practice of relating individual texts to varying situations can be called "application." Often the distance to be bridged by application—chronological distance, cultural difference, situational diversity or psychic deviance—requires a high degree of sophistication and has hence justified the claim that hermeneutics/interpretation is an art. But while hermeneutics brings interpretation as a technique of meaning production to unheard-of levels of perfection, it generates a largely unresolvable problem. By opening a horizon of different meanings for each text, interpretation raises—and leaves unanswered—the question upon which criteria the identity of these texts can be grounded. The "materiality" of the signifiers, which constitutes a level of self-identity through different situations of application, cannot be invoked to solve this problem, because it cannot be reconciled with the principle of multiple meanings.[3] Therefore the hermeneutic/essentialistic gaze often presents itself as bypassing, or as simply penetrating, the textual "surface" constituted by the signifiers and as primarily (if not exclusively) focusing on the "depth" and complexity of the signified. Through this topology hermeneutics devalues the surface of the text and the materiality of the signifiers.

In opposition to essentialism, philological fundamentalism falls outside the hermeneutic space. What hermeneutics tries to bypass as the textual surface and sees, at best, as a starting point for the constitution of meaning cannot be clearly separated from the level of meaning in the context of fundamentalism.[4] Therefore fundamentalism is much more concerned with the preservation of the original wording than with interpretation. From its particular perspective, any modification at the level of the signifiers has inevitable consequences for the level of the meaning, and therefore such changes are considered illegitimate within most forms of fundamentalism. Instead of loosely relating meaning to an author's intention, as essentialism does, fundamentalism tends to protect both the signifiers and the signified through taboos, which are often religiously motivated (Assmann and Assmann 63 ff.). Accordingly, translations between different languages are regarded as highly problematic, and even as finally impossible, as long as the requirement of maintaining meaning identity is strictly observed. Whatever is seen as an "application" in the hermeneutic space must be prohibited as a dilution (if not as a dissolution) of the original meaning within fundamentalism, and hence appears as a symptom of moral, cultural and philological decay.

If essentialism overlaps with hermeneutics, it is certainly possible to discover a certain convergence between fundamentalism and the "new philological movement" in medieval studies (see Nichols, "Introduction"). The most salient fundamentalist aspect of New Philology lies, of course, in the meticulous attention paid to identifying the original textual status as materialized in the

HANS ULRICH GUMBRECHT

manuscripts. What, in addition, sets New Philology apart from hermeneutics and from the hermeneutically based technique of "critical" text editing is its radical unwillingness to sacrifice any details identified on the level of the textual "surface" to hypotheses about the meanings or intentions of supposed authors. While it would certainly be an exaggeration to say that the dimension of textual meaning disappears within New Philology, there is no doubt that the primary attention of its practitioners is directed to the materiality of the signifiers. Rather than attempting to bridge any hermeneutic gap, they stress historical otherness.

Here, however, the possibility of establishing a coherent typological contrast between essentialism/hermeneutics and New Philology/fundamentalism seems to end. For if New Philology and fundamentalism agree in not conceding the existence of a gap between the level of the signifiers and the level of the signified, the new philologists' interest in the wording of each individual manuscript leads to production of inventories of textual variants that are not meant to be reduced to a single meaning. In contrast, it is the desire of identifying such single meanings that motivates the textual conservativism of the fundamentalists and on which their unconditional moral claims are normally grounded. At this point in my reflections about the topic of the above-mentioned MLA discussion, I was also wondering whether colleagues such as Bloch and Nichols might want to see their positions associated with a connotation of the ideological and intellectual narrowness that the word "fundamentalism" bears in everyday language. Finally, it seemed inconsistent to extend the adjective "popular," with which Nichols had characterized fundamentalism, to the new philological movement; not only because it is a purely academic movement, but also because, so far, it certainly has fewer followers among literary critics than the hermeneutic forms of interpreting and editing.

Thus what had initially appeared to be a relatively easy task, namely the discussion of two contemporary practices of text editing from the perspective of the notions "essentialism" and "fundamentalism" (and their potential relation to literary modernism), turned out to be a most complex and confusing enterprise. My hope that a rethinking of the interplay between philology and modernism in Spain between 1898 and 1927 might shed a clarifying light on this complicated scenario is based on a threefold observation.

First, unlike most of the other national academic traditions in Europe (especially in Germany and Italy), Spanish "national philology" has never developed a dominant tradition of hermeneutically based ("critical") text editing in the Lachmann style.[5] While this situation was normally experienced (and deplored) as a shortcoming, it can now be argued that the philological style inaugurated by Ramón Menéndez Pidal anticipated certain aspects of New Philology through the specific attention it paid to variants and textual detail.

Second, until very recently the social status of Spanish national culture could be characterized through a specific condition of immediate presence.[6] There seemed to be no need for the hermeneutic sophistication of historical bridging and of application. This presence offers itself as a relevant perspective for the understanding of the particularities in the history of text editing in Spain.

Finally, the fact seems to be relevant that, during the twentieth century, the work of academic philology became more popular outside the university in Spain than in any other European context. Such popularity was a precondition for the strong impact that a non-hermeneutic philological style had on the emergence of modernist poetry.

TWO

It is not easy to explain historically the impression of immediacy that used to surround the Spanish classics and their texts like a shining halo. As its precondition, I would invoke a specific flexibility—a capacity of oscillation—through which the historical environment of the century between 1550 and 1650 had inscribed itself into the Spanish classical texts. This environment was constituted by the effort to reimpose a theologically grounded cosmological order upon an astonishingly "modern" intellectual and behavioral style which entailed a high degree of subjectivity. Lazarillo de Tormes's double life of boundless personal greed and an equally boundless opportunistic adaptation to officialized social norms, Teresa de Avila's struggle between an extremely intimate form of religious experience and a continuous effort to observe the demands of the ecclesiastic hierarchy, and the multiple perspectives in which Cervantes presents his hero Don Quijote are but some of the most widely known textual examples for a general condition that made the culture of the *siglo de oro* invite different styles of reception in the changing historical situations of their posterity. If such a condition made the texts relatively resistant to the effects of historical distance, this potential was constantly activated, after 1700, through the habit of invoking Spain's great cultural tradition as a compensation in varying contexts of political dependency and national depression. More important than the invention of new readings and interpretations was the insistence on the sheer presence of the classical corpus and the claim that it was still "alive" for each subsequent generation.[7] I will try to demonstrate that this condition is crucial in order to understand the specific functions that philology adopted in Spain during the late nineteenth century and its impact on the emergence of poetic modernism.

Before doing so, however, it is necessary to problematize a prevailing historiographical tradition that distinguishes the history of philology from the history of literature. On the one side, this tradition claims a continuity between the founding figures of Spanish philology, Marcelino Menéndez Pelayo and Ramón Menéndez Pidal, and on the other it connects literary modernism exclusively to the models of French Symbolism and of the Nicaraguan poet Rubén Darío. I will argue in contrast that two considerably different attitudes towards textuality separate Menéndez Pelayo and Menéndez Pidal, whereas the latter's philological practice shares a number of key concerns with the poetics of Spanish modernism.

Although historiography often presents Marcelino Menéndez Pelayo (see p. 182), who was appointed professor of Spanish literature at the University of Madrid in 1879, in a role comparable to that of the Grimm brothers in Germany or of Gaston Paris in

France, he was neither the first Spanish representative in the academic discipline of literary studies nor the first to inaugurate a research practice of specific methodological rigor.[8] Instead, his quantitatively monumental work and his considerable influence within the most conservative political circles of the late nineteenth century mark the culminating moment in the pattern, just described, of pointing to the texts of the Golden Age as a compensation for national inferiority complexes. It was Menéndez Pelayo's ambition to make evident (from our perspective, to construct) an uninterrupted and unaltered continuity of "Christian Humanism" stretching from the triumphant national moment of early modern imperialism to his own present. The medieval centuries on the Iberian peninsula, which we are beginning to discover as a period of complex multiculturalism,[9] were excluded from such canon-building and dismissed as a period of contamination. Thus, Menéndez Pelayo's approach to texts was that of a rudimentary essentialism: he was uninterested in strictly philological issues (hence the notoriously low quality of the editions and series that were published under his name), and his interpretations were exclusively informed by the harsh binarism of orthodoxy versus heterodoxy. With such extreme clarity orienting his view of the cultural tradition, Menéndez Pelayo's scholarly work increasingly materialized in bibliographical repertoires, some of whose exclusions (the most famous being the work of Luis de Góngora) were to motivate considerable resistance among the following generations of Spanish intellectuals.

Despite the widespread convention of presenting him as Menéndez Pelayo's successor, the philologist Ramón Menéndez Pidal was always eager to insist, however politely, on their intellectual distance (Gumbrecht, "Lebende" 84 ff.). Much more important than the one year of courses that he took from Menéndez Pelayo at the University of Madrid in the 1880s were the mediated influence of German philological rigor with which he had became familiar through his work under Maurice Morel-Fatio at the University of Bordeaux, and the intense interest that some of his relatives had taken in Castilian folklore. Thus, Menéndez Pidal defined his professional goal as a program of maintaining and contributing to the life of the national cultural tradition, and he believed that stressing the otherness, the archaic character of this tradition was the most efficient way of underscoring its aesthetic appeal: "Cuánto más el ideario y los sentimientos choquen con los modernos, más deben atraer el artista capaz de revelarnos la novedad del arcaísmo, haciendo revivir esa raza de hombres desaparecidos" (*Epopeya* 244).[10] It was not only the paradoxical principle of archaism as a precondition for contemporaneity that set him apart from Menéndez Pelayo's reliance on a flat (and unhistoric) spiritual continuity, but also his conviction that such archaism became most evident and palpable on the level of textual materiality. Therefore Menéndez Pidal's philological style was characterized through palaeographic editions that included the broadest possible range of variants, instead of sacrificing them, in the style of "critical editions," to hypotheses about the intentions of possible authors. He took the multiplicity of the variants as a direct symptom for the life—sometimes for the almost physical vitality—of the tradition:

> La poesía vive, rebrota en cada nuevo acto de recitación, está en perpétuo devenir, siempre diversa, aunque siempre pretendiendo ser fiel al modelo fijado por el común consenso del recuerdo tradicional. Por eso es preciso poner ante los ojos tal número de versiones que dejen percibir en cada frase, en cada verso, reflejos rielantes y hagan ver el texto del poemita como corriente de un rio rizada de cambiantes centelleos. La publicación del Romancero que ahora comenzamos quiere presentar así el romance tradicional en toda su vitalidad.[11]

The most important observation, however, from the perspective of our typological interest, lies in the fact that interpretation and an interest in the meaning of the texts from the national tradition were certainly *not* the motivating forces behind Menéndez Pidal's philological work. This omission sets him further apart from essentialism. It was his ambition to become a living part of that tradition which he helped to keep alive, and he took the capacity to memorize and to recite the words that constituted its texts as the ultimate criterion for his success. Keeping the tradition alive became equivalent with integrating the philologist's body into the life of the national culture: "Yo me encuentro así que soy el español de todos los tiempos que haya oído y leído más romances. Las versiones que agradan a mi imaginación tan llena de recuerdos tradicionales, las que me gusta repetir, las que doy aquí al público, creo que son una partecilla de la tradición" (*Flor* 41).[12] This attitude explains why, from his very first publications on, Menéndez Pidal was eager to practice what we can today call a technique of "thick description." He would never separate the presentation of his research results from lengthy narratives concerning the biographical and situational circumstances under which these discoveries had been made. His pioneer edition of the *Cantar de mio Cid*, published in 1908, included photographs of the historical sites associated with his manuscript findings and with what he believed to be the historical truth of the medieval text. In May 1900 he had even organized his honeymoon as a field-research excursion through Castile (*El romancero* 100 ff.).

THREE

Whereas Marcelino Menéndez Pelayo's entire lifework, until his death in 1912, remained dedicated to the conservative legacy of Spain as the Catholic nation that heroically resisted the temptations and transformations of modernity, Menéndez Pidal, more through the style of his research than through high-sounding ideological declarations, became part of the mildly revolutionary intellectual generation that emerged as a reaction to the loss of Cuba and the Philippines, Spain's last transatlantic colonies, in the year 1898. Its discourse was based on the concept of *regeneracionismo*, of revitalizing Spain as a cultural nation, and thus provided the most appropriate environment for Menéndez Pidal's philological program of keeping a cultural tradition alive. The insistence, among the authors of 1898, on the premise that this tradition had been overshadowed and repressed by a reactionary form of nationalism and was hence a historical layer to be rediscovered (for which Miguel de Unamuno cast the catch-word "*intrahistoria*") made research activities look like the most adequate materialization of such a project; the implication that *intra-*

historia could only be found in popular culture led to a strong interest in folklore, which Menéndez Pidal shared with the Generation of 1898; and, finally, the representatives of this generation converged with Menéndez Pidal in their ultimate goal of becoming themselves part of the revitalized national tradition. Perhaps this was the most "Romantic" moment in the history of Spanish culture, but it completely lacked that component of Romanticism which doomed the full reappropriation of the national past as impossible—and for which Schiller had invented the notion of "sentimentalisch."

In their attitude towards foreign cultures, the Spanish intellectuals of 1898 were unambiguously ambivalent. On the one hand, they were convinced that the *regeneración* of their nation could—and had to—come from inside; on the other hand, the binary logic of their resistance against a narrow nationalism as it had been incarnated by Menéndez Pelayo, and in which they saw the main reason for Spain's decay, confronted them with the obligation of a cultural opening. Therefore the intellectual climate around 1900 was characterized both by enthusiastic initiatives of rereading the national classics and by an often painful willingness to reestablish contact with cultures beyond the Spanish borders.[13] It is my impression that, following the discourse model of "external influence," literary historians have widely privileged the latter side of this double movement. Even the fascination with Latin American poets that characterized the lyrical *modernismo* of the 1890s and the early twentieth century in Spain was grounded on the hope of regaining a cultural legacy that had undergone the double estrangement of a transcontinental migration and of a direct confrontation with Central European modernity.[14] The self-reflexive turn, however, took over again with a younger group of poets, called the Generation of 1927, whose works have been regarded as Spain's greatest contribution to twentieth-century literature. In February 1922, when he was only twenty-four years old, Federico García Lorca, the most famous representative of this group, gave a lecture on the Andalusian gypsy tradition of "El cante jondo," which marks the beginning of his work towards his masterpiece the *Romancero gitano*, published in multiple versions from 1928 on. In the final paragraph of the lecture on the *cante jondo*, Lorca's words come as close as possible to the concepts that Menéndez Pidal, who was then preparing an early version of the *Romancero* edition, used to describe his philological project. It was their shared goal to keep threatened traditions of national culture alive, and it was their shared strategy to achieve this goal by bringing the otherness of the tradition into contact with the culture of their own present and its future:

> A todos los que a través de su vida se han emocionado con *la co-pla lejana que viene por el camino,* a todos los que la paloma blanca del amor haya picado en su corazón maduro, a todos los amantes de la *tradición engarzada con el porvenir,* al que estudia en el libro como al que ara la tierra, les suplico respetuosamente *que no dejen morir las apreciables joyas vivas de la raza,* el inmenso tesoro milenario que cubre la superficie espiritual de Andalucía y que mediten bajo la noche de Granada la transcendencia patriótica que unos artistas españoles presentamos.[15]

At this point, it should no longer be surprising that what fascinated Lorca was much less the often trivial and barely understandable content of these poems, than the music that they helped to incorporate and, especially, the sound quality of those words that articulated pain without conveying any specific meaning. Exactly the same interests led to the programmatic rediscovery of Luis de Góngora's poetry at his 300th anniversary in 1927, the year that gave Lorca's poetic generation its name. In this context, however, the intellectual closeness, if not the cultural identity, between Spanish modernist poetry and the new form of national philology became explicit (see Gumbrecht, "Warum gerade Góngora?"). An important reason for the enthusiasm for Góngora felt by Lorca and his friends was the exclusion of Góngora's works from Menéndez Pelayo's Christian Humanist canon; his negative claim that Góngora's poems were void of meaning motivated the philological project of the young poet Dámaso Alonso to translate them into easily understandable contemporary prose.[16] Lorca himself undertook the task of demonstrating that the sensuality of Góngora's much admired metaphors was grounded in the national popular tradition. The circumstance that such a proof is impossible to make from a historical and philological standpoint only emphasizes Lorca's dependency on the ideology of 1898 and on the program of Ramón Menéndez Pidal. By invoking his name and ironically contrasting it with Menéndez Pelayo's at the beginning of his lecture "La imagen poética de don Luis de Góngora," delivered in Granada in 1927, Federico García Lorca tried to dignify his interest in baroque poetry and thereby inscribe himself within the contemporary intellectual field:

> El insigne Menéndez Pidal dice que el humanismo "abrió" los ojos de los doctos a la comprensión más acabada del espíritu humano en todas sus manifestaciones, y lo popular mereció una atención digna e inteligente, como hasta entonces no había logrado. Prueba de esto es el cultivo de la vihuela y de los cantos del pueblo por grandes músicos. . . . No quiero nombrar a Menéndez y Pelayo, que no entendió a Góngora, porque, en cambio, entendió portentosamente a todos los demás. (64 f.)[17]

Due to their shared emergence out of a movement of national regeneration, the perspective of poetic modernism in Spain, with its concentration on sound, rhythm, music and very often (especially in Lorca's case) also on the written or printed page, had come extremely close to the intellectual style of the national philology. But while the modernists' eagerness to find associations between their own works and popular traditions seems to be a constitutive element of their poetics, its *national* cultural perspective was probably just accidental. During the year 1929–30, which Lorca spent in New York as a student at Columbia University (see p. 184), probably seeking distance after the end of his relationship with the sculptor Emilio Aladrén Perojo, there was nothing that fascinated him more than the culture of the Harlem Renaissance. As with the interest he had previously taken in the *cante jondo*, it was again the sound of an unfamiliar language and the rhythm of strange bodies that attracted his attention:

> Y me lanzo a la calle y me encuentro con los negros. En Nueva York se dan cita las razas de toda la tierra, pero chinos, armenios,

rusos, alemanes siguen siendo extranjeros. Todo menos los negros. Es indudable que ellos ejercen enorme influencia en Norteamérica y, pese a quien pese, son lo más espiritual y lo más delicado de aquel mundo. Porque creen, porque esperan, porque cantan y porque tienen una exquisita pereza religiosa que los salva de todos sus peligrosos afanes actuales.

Si se recorre el Bronx o Brooklyn, donde están los americanos rubios, se siente como algo sordo, como de gentes que aman los muros porque detienen la mirada; un reloj en cada casa y un Dios a quien sólo se atisba la planta de los pies. En cambio, en el negro hay como un constante cambio de sonrisas, un temblor profundo de tierra que oxida las columnas de níquel y algún niñito herido te ofrece su tarta de manzanas si lo miras con insistencia.

Yo bajaba muchas veces desde la Universidad donde vivía y donde era no el terrible mister Lorca de mis professores sino el insólito *sleepy boy* de las camereras, para verlos bailar y saber qué pensaban, porque es la danza la única forma de su dolor y la expresión aguda de su sentimiento. . . .

Yo ví en un cabaret—Small's Paradise—, cuya masa de público danzante era negra, mojada y grumosa como una caja de huevas de caviar, una bailarina desnuda que se agitaba convulsamente bajo una invisible lluvia de fuego. Pero [cuando] todo el mundo gritaba como creyéndola poseída por el ritmo, pude sorprender un momento en sus ojos la reserva, la lejanía, la certeza de su ausencia ante el público de extranjeros y americanos que la admiraba. Como ella era todo Harlem. (Maurer 113 f.)[18]

Not unlike Menéndez Pidal's work, which was motivated by the goal of becoming himself a living part of that tradition which he tried to revive, Lorca's poetry, and especially the series *Poeta en Nueva York*, of which he began to publish isolated pieces from 1931 on, seems to dwell on the desire to be surrounded by those past and foreign worlds whose sounds, rhythms and forms inspired his language—and perhaps by the desire to die with them (Maurer 133). Therefore Lorca wanted his readers to believe that he had established a relation of closeness and immediate understanding towards these cultures, a relation that was not based on the meaning of words: "pude sorprender un momento en sus ojos la reserva, la lejanía, la certeza de su ausencia ante el público de extranjeros y americanos que la admiraba." When he travelled from New York to Havana, he was obsessed, for the same reason, by the intuition that the black rhythms of Cuba were those of the Andalusian gypsies: "Y salen los negros con sus ritmos que yo descubro típicos del gran pueblo andaluz, negritos sin drama que ponen los ojos en blanco y dicen: 'Nosotros somos latinos' " (Maurer 125).[19]

FOUR

It would be all too pretentious to claim that any "conclusions" regarding the future of medieval studies can be drawn from this outline of a case-study on the philological invention of modernism in Spain. If anything, the undeniable parallels that we discovered between Menéndez Pidal's academic practice, Lorca's poetics, and our contemporary New Philology permit a more appropriate assessment of the latter in terms of the concepts of "essentialism" and "fundamentalism."

What brings these three positions close to fundamentalism and sets them clearly apart from hermeneutics/essentialism is the attention that they all pay to the material qualities of signifiers. For them the textual surface does not disappear with the deciphering of the signified. One could therefore hardly imagine a García Lorca interpreting *cante jondo* stanzas or a Menéndez Pidal working on an English version of his editions of the *romance*. Textual interpretation was, at best, a secondary concern within their poetic and philological practice. Whereas hermeneutics tries to bridge the gap between the texts' past and the interpreters' present by a content-centered act of application that fuses the horizon of the past with that of the present (see Gadamer 289 f., 356 f., 476), it seems to have been the ultimate goal of Menéndez Pidal and García Lorca to let their own linguistic production be inspired by a confrontation with the otherness of linguistic materials from different cultural worlds. Thus "becoming part of the tradition" implies two radically different operations on the two sides of our typology: for hermeneutics, it is the reconstruction of meaning-structures constituted in the past and their adaptation to present situations; for philology and modernism in Spain after 1900, it meant keeping alive a continuity of textual production.

If the most obvious result of our case-study is the line of distinction that it enables us to draw between the New Philology and its forerunners on the one side and hermeneutics/essentialism on the other, this typological possibility should not make us overlook at least two features that set apart the genealogical line of New Philology from the current use of the concept "fundamentalism." Fundamentalism is eager to eliminate textual variants in order to preserve the purity of a single, canonized, authentic version of the text; and it does so because what ultimately matters for fundamentalism is a single, canonized, authentic meaning. Given the emphasis New Philology places on the preservation of a multiplicity of variants—an emphasis that it shares with the historical paradigms we have been analyzing and through which it can be distinguished from fundamentalism—one could expect it to become less concerned with the act of interpretation. Yet New Philology has so far not made any programmatic statements about a possible change in the role of interpretation within its practice. It is, therefore, an important open question to ask whether "understanding," in the hermeneutic sense of the word, can still be the main target for a historical discipline that is in the process of shifting its main attention from the "depth of the signified" to the "surface of the signifiers." Perhaps the new philological movement is, after all, but a small symptom of a larger transformation in the social functions of historical culture and in the desires through which it is motivated. We have become reluctant to say that we hope "to learn from history," and we still feel embarrassed to admit that what drives us is the *illusion of becoming part* of those worlds that constituted past cultures.

NOTES

1. Gumbrecht, "The Body Versus the Printing Press: Media in the Early Modern Period, Mentalities in the Reign of Castile and Another History of Literary Forms"; "L'auteur comme masque: Contribution à

HANS ULRICH GUMBRECHT

l'archéologie de l'imprimé"; "Beginn von 'Literatur': Abschied vom Kör-per?"; "(N)On (Literary) Interpretation"; "Bulky Baggage from the Past: The Study of Literature in Germany"; "A la sombra del reino hermeneutico."

2. Structuralism in literary studies used to present a "polysemantic status" as an exclusive defining element for literary texts.

3. See my forthcoming *Materialities of Communication*, which contains some of the most relevant theoretical contributions from two previous volumes in German which I edited with K. Ludwig Pfeiffer: *Materialität der Kommunikation* and *Paradoxien, Dissonanzen, Zusammenbrüche: Situationen offener Epistemologie*.

4. I have recently tried to describe this reevaluation of the "surface" constituted by the signifiers as a point of convergence between different contemporary theoretical positions ("Das Nicht-Hermeneutische: Die Theorie weiss von der Unmöglichkeit des Verstehens").

5. See my articles "Lebende Vergangenheit: Zur Typologie der 'Arbeit am Text' in der spanischen Kultur" and "'Las versiones que agradan a mi imaginación,' oder: Von Menéndez Pidal zur postmodernen Editionspraxis."

6. For a more detailed analysis of this phenomenon, see my "Klassik in Spanien."

7. I have discussed and documented this specific cultural function of the "classical texts" within Spanish culture in *Eine Geschichte der spanischen Literatur* 474 ff.

8. See Gumbrecht and Juan José Sánchez, "Menéndez Pelayo—¿per omnia saecula saeculorum?"

9. Brilliantly evoked in María Rosa Menocal's forthcoming book on 1492 as a foundational moment for Romance philology.

10. "The more ideas and sentiments conflict with modern ones, the more they must attract the artist capable of revealing to us the modernness of archaism, bringing back to life that race of vanished men." (Trans. W. D. P.)

11. Seminario Menéndez Pidal, ed., *Romancero tradicional* 5 f. "Poetry lives, puts out new shoots in each new act of recitation, is in a state of perpetual becoming, always new, even though always pretending to be faithful to the model of traditional memory fixed by common consensus. For this reason it is necessary to put before our eyes such a number of versions that they will allow us to perceive glistening reflections in each phrase, in each verse, and make us see the text of the little poem as the current of a river flecked with dancing sparks. The publication of the *Ro-*

mancero that we now undertake attempts to present the traditional romance in this way in all its vitality." (Trans. W. D. P.)

12. "Thus I find myself the Spaniard who has heard and read the most romances of all time. The versions which please my imagination, so full of traditional associations, those that I like to repeat, those that I present here to the public, I consider as one small part of the tradition." (Trans. W. D. P.)

13. I have tried to reconstruct the cultural atmosphere of this historical moment in my article "Inszeniertes Leben: Alltag und Kunst in der spanischen Provinz um die Jahrhundertwende." Its most representative historical document is the journal *Alma española*, which was reedited in 1978 by Ediciones Turner (Madrid).

14. I owe this insight to conversations with Florian Nelle (Freie Universitaet Berlin), who is working on a dissertation under the title "Paris—Hauptstadt der lateinamerikanischen Intellektuellen im 19. Jahrhundert."

15. García Lorca, "El cante jondo" 56; my italics. "To all those who throughout their lives have been moved by 'the faraway stanza that comes down the road,' to all those whom the white dove of love has pecked in their mature heart, to all lovers of the 'tradition linked to the future,' to him who studies in a book as to him who ploughs the land, I respectfully beg them 'not to let die the precious living jewels of the race,' the immense timeless treasure that covers the spiritual surface of Andalucía, and to meditate, under the night of Granada, the patriotic transcendence that we, a few Spanish artists, offer to them." (Trans. W. D. P.)

16. This translation of Góngora does not contradict the hypothesis that textual meaning had only secondary status within the poetics of Lorca's generation, because this status was exclusively motivated by the intention to prove Menéndez Pelayo's opinion wrong. Dámaso Alonso later assumed the chair of Spanish literature at the University of Madrid and became President of the Royal Academy of Spanish Language. His biography was thus an inversion of Nichols's concept of the "philological invention of poetic Modernism."

17. "The excellent Menéndez Pidal says that Humanism 'opened' the eyes of the learned to a more perfect understanding of the human spirit in all its manifestations, and that the popular deserved a worthy and intelligent attention, such as it had not received until then. Proof of this is the cultivation of the *vihuela* and of songs of the people by great musicians. . . . I do not wish to name Menéndez y Pelayo, who did not under-

stand Góngora, because on the other hand he understood all the others prodigiously." (Trans. W. D. P.)

18. Quoted from a lecture which Lorca gave in Madrid (March 1932). "And I hurl myself into the street and meet the blacks. In New York the races of all the earth agree to meet, but Chinese, Armenians, Russians, Germans remain foreigners. All but the blacks. It is indubitable that they have an enormous influence in North America, and, whatever anyone may think, they are the most spiritual and the most refined of that world. Because they believe, because they hope, because they sing, and because they have an exquisite religious laziness that saves them from all their real, threatening anxieties.

"If you go through the Bronx or Brooklyn, where the white Americans are, you feel something held back by people who love walls because they keep out your glance; a clock in every house and a God who is scrutinized no further up than the soles of his feet. On the other hand, in the black ghetto there is a constant exchange of smiles, a deep trembling of the earth that oxidizes the columns of nickel, and a little child, hurt, offers you his piece of apple pie if you look at him insistently.

"I would often go down from the University where I lived and where I was not the terrible Mister Lorca of my professors but the unexpected *sleepy boy* of the housemaids, to see them dance and know what they were thinking, because dancing is the only form of their pain and the sharp expression of their feelings. . . .

"I saw in a nightclub, Small's Paradise, where the mass of the dancing public was black, damp and viscous as a jar of caviar, a naked dancing woman who was shaking convulsively under an invisible rain of fire. But while everyone shouted as though they thought she was possessed by the rhythm, I managed to glimpse for an instant in her eyes the reserve, the distance, the certainty of her absence before the public of foreigners and Americans who were admiring her. All of Harlem was like her." (Trans. W. D. P.)

19. "And the blacks come out with their rhythms which I realize are typical of the great Andalusian people, black children without pretension who roll their eyes and say, 'We are Latin.' " (Trans. W. D. P.)

HE FUTURE OF OLD FRENCH STUDIES IN AMERICA

THE "OLD" PHILOLOGY AND THE CRISIS OF THE "NEW"

Rupert T. Pickens

*Il en est de l'art d'éditer les anciens textes
comme de tous les autres arts: il a évolué au
gré de modes qui meurent et renaissent.*
—Joseph Bédier

SPECULUM PHILOLOGIAE: VETUS PHILOLOGIA ET NOVA

According to Romance scholars writing in a recent number of
Speculum, philological scholarship is in a state of crisis. [1] In his
introductory essay Stephen G. Nichols states that, on the whole,
his contributors agree that "medieval philology has been marginalized by contemporary cognitive methodologies, on the one side,
while within the discipline itself, a very limited and by now
grossly anachronistic conception of it remains far too current" (1).
Nichols continues by defining the current practice as having been
"formulated under the impulse of political nationalism and scientific positivism during the second half of the nineteenth century" (1); it is the purpose of the volume to scrutinize this
practice. Much discussion naturally centers on editorial policies
because textual criticism lies at the heart of philological endeavor.

I shall argue, to the contrary, on the basis of a close examination
of pertinent scholarly work (both studies supporting the view of
philology-in-crisis and those affirming its opposite), that the
Speculum volume has missed the mark in declaring the irrele-
vance of traditional philological activity. Caught up in a rhetoric

of polemics and revolution, the Romance contributors fail to comprehend how, in Europe and North America, philological methods and practice lay claim to their own modernity within the historical continuum in which, to be sure, "scientific positivism" has its place; yet, as seen in a more complete history of philological practice than is offered by any exponent of what the *Speculum* volume calls the "New Philology," positivism is surpassed, transcended, in a continuing process of transformation and renewal. Because they have fallen heir to the anti-philological bias of American New Criticism, moreover, the "New Philologists" do not understand that their work is also engaged in such a process and must inevitably be judged by its standards. In this light, it is not traditional philological activity (the "Old" Philology) that has reached the point of crisis, but the "New" Philology its detractors have proclaimed.

Suzanne Fleischman takes up the alarm sounded by Nichols. She writes: "Philology . . . has come to be equated in the minds of many with a desiccated and dogmatic textual praxis which, through the minutious methodologies of paleography, historical grammar, and the textual criticism of 'Monsieur Procuste, Philologue,' has reduced medieval literary 'monuments' to the status of 'documents.' "[2] A " 'crisis of philology' . . . is still very much at hand," Fleischman continues. In "the intellectual climate of postmodernism," we must "reexamine the premises and presuppositions of our traditional methodologies and disciplinary practices and . . . renovate or replace them if need be with alternatives which can make the old texts speak to us in ways more consonant with our modern, now postmodern, episteme." We are "at a crucial moment of charting new directions that will justify . . . continuing to 'do philology' at all" ("Philology" 19).

While R. Howard Bloch seems uncomfortable with exaggerated proclamations of absolute newness, he too recognizes the existence of fresh practices, the "new 'New Philology,' " with roots in the 1950s ("New" 38). For Bloch this most recent "New Philology" stands in harmony with Romantic principles, and in contrast with positivistic values as embodied in the editorial and interpretive work of Karl Lachmann and Gaston Paris. But positivism still has the power to jeopardize modern scholarly enterprises (39–41); a 1988 contribution is characterized as "absurd and rigidly superannuated," and it "demonstrates the impotence of the positivist philological method to establish a meaning" (47 n33).[3] Like Fleischman's, Bloch's article is intended to illustrate a palliative method of reading.

Nichols and Bloch frame discussions in terms of the history of philological scholarship. Bloch in particular exposes some of the more absurd extremes of positivistic thought (42–46), but he contributes little to our understanding of philological practices after the *bédiériste* reactions against Gaston Paris's Lachmannianism in the 1930s. In mentioning contributions of Wellek, Spitzer, Auerbach, and Curtius, Nichols advances the history by a decade or so (2–4). But none of the Romance specialists suggests that, until now, anything of lasting significance has occurred since the 1950s. We are led to understand that philological practice became fossilized in the wake of the European masters' influence in the United States; indeed, since philology allegedly finds its exemplary figure in Gaston Paris himself, it must have reverted generally to a pre-Bédier state of primal ignorance.

One work all three Romance specialists cite approvingly is Bernard Cerquiglini's recent *Éloge de la variante*. Cerquiglini's view of the history of modern philological practice resembles theirs in scope and emphasis, and their references to his book acknowledge his as a kindred mind. In fact, the influence of *Éloge* on the Romance contributions is so pervasive that it appears to serve as a source text for the "New" Philology.

Cerquiglini's pamphlet is less a work of scholarship than a piece of radical polemics. It may therefore seem inappropriate to judge it as though it had been meant to convey truth about a program of research seriously undertaken. Yet sophisticated readers like Nichols, Fleischman, and Bloch have failed to recognize the full extent of its playfulness; in ascribing to it a seriousness of purpose and a scholarly weight it does not and cannot bear, they have also been blind to the profound misinformation that defines it as a work of political persuasion and not of fact. Since the contributors to the *Speculum* volume legitimate *Éloge de la variante* as a

THE FUTURE OF OLD FRENCH STUDIES IN AMERICA

product of learned research, it is worth examining Cerquiglini's work in some detail before returning to the exemplary *mises en pratique* of the "New" Philology it subtends.

"MONSIEUR PROCUSTE, PHILOLOGUE"

In a chapter bearing this title (*Éloge* 31–54), Cerquiglini discusses the essential mobility of the medieval vernacular text in terms of the *variance* of its written expression in particular manuscripts. The Procrustes image introduces a major theme—and the primary butt—of Cerquiglini's polemic: the positivistically inclined philologist who forces the medieval text to conform with ill-founded preconceived formal and linguistic patterns. Karl Lachmann and, more especially, Gaston Paris are cast in the role of Procrustes (see p. 187), the mythical Greek robber who forced his victims to lie on a bed which they were stretched out or cut down to equal in length. First Joseph Bédier and then, implicitly, Cerquiglini himself play the avenging Theseus.[4] Bédier wrote "un long article qui . . . *enterrait* Gaston Paris" (95, my emphasis),[5] while Cerquiglini offers an off-the-cuff psychoanalysis reflecting on Oedipal dimensions imputed to Gaston Paris's relations first with his real father, the "Romantic" medieval scholar Paulin Paris, and then with other alleged father-figures, his teachers in Germany (78–81). Rejecting the editorial methodology of his father, Gaston Paris embraced the principles of Lachmannian textual criticism. Bédier "buried" Gaston Paris, but we are led to suppose that the Lachmannian's spirit lives on, animating latter-day Procrustean philologists. Only later does Cerquiglini observe that, in France and English-speaking countries especially, Gaston Paris's influence in matters of textual criticism is today virtually nil by comparison with that of the liberator Bédier (95).[6]

Imprecision, hyperbole, and polemic mar Cerquiglini's discussion of Chrétien de Troyes's *Conte del graal* and the scribe Guiot. Cerquiglini has discovered, in the single-manuscript editions by William Roach (manuscript *T*) and Félix Lecoy (manuscript *A*, Guiot's copy), that "Il y a bien deux *Perceval*, au moins" (64; "There are certainly two *Percevals*, at least"). But there are in fact many others, as the apparatus in Alfons Hilka's critical edition clearly shows.[7] Cerquiglini admits that the *Perceval* might well provide a "contre-exemple" to his observation that by its very nature medieval writing produced *variance*. The reason for his hesitation is that the *Perceval* "fut très célèbre, et son influence est lointaine ainsi que durable; on peut penser qu'on le copia avec grand soin" (64; ". . . was very famous, and its influence was widespread as well as long-lasting; one might think that it was copied with great care"), that is, with a degree of attention approaching the care devoted to transmitting a sacred text, where conscious scribal "interventions" would have been minimal. William Roach had already stated in his edition of the *Continuations* of Chrétien's *Perceval* that the first Grail romance was transmitted with relative fidelity, thanks to Chrétien's prestige (1:xxxiv). The fact remains, however, that the *Perceval* does indeed exhibit a significant degree of textual movement.[8]

Of all medieval *Perceval* texts, the one found in the manuscript signed by the scribe Guiot, who worked in Provins, apparently late in the first quarter of the thirteenth century, has received the most scholarly attention, despite the success of Roach's widely respected edition of *T*.[9] Generally speaking, in fact, Guiot's copies of all of Chrétien's romances are considered to be the most reliable (Micha, *Tradition* 290–93). Thus Cerquiglini's remark that Guiot is the philologists' darling (65) is, in a sense, justified; furthermore, in a possible argument that would assert the equal validity of *all* extant versions,[10] his polemical tone might not seem altogether inappropriate.

Cerquiglini apparently directs his sarcasm against philologists who, in his view, have wrongfully ascribed primacy to Guiot's copy.[11] But as he develops his case, the blame cast upon modern philologists must be shared as well by Guiot, the medieval copyist: "enfant chéri des philologues (car il fut, au vrai, le premier d'entre eux)" (65; "the philologists' fair-haired boy [for he was, in fact, the first among them]"). The "philologist" Guiot also submitted his text to the tortures of the procrustean bed: "Si l'on considère ce manuscrit, on constate qu'il est plus court de deux cent soixante-quatorze vers que le manuscrit T et présente au moins cinq cents variantes notables avec lui" (65; "If you study this manuscript, you will note that it is shorter than manuscript *T* by 274 verses and that it manifests more than 500 significant variants with *T*"). The latter figure is substantiated by reference to Micha.

Cerquiglini's hyperbole obscures the fact that Guiot was by no means the first vernacular copyist to put his text to the rack and the block. On the contrary, twelfth-century manuscripts bearing the *Chanson de Roland* and the *Vie de saint Alexis* offer earlier examples, as Cerquiglini well knows (85–86); and, more to the point, inscriptions of "*mouvance* topoi" from as early as the *Cumpot* of Philippe de Thaün (1113) suggest the pervasiveness of the practice.[12] The impressive statistical data might therefore serve to strengthen his argument. But they are inexact for several reasons. (1) Micha compares the significant variants in Guiot's copy not with manuscript *T,* but with the established text of Hilka's critical edition. (2) The line numbers in Roach's edition of *T* do not provide an accurate count of *T*'s length, but refer to corresponding lines in Hilka's edition; in fact, *T* is 36 lines shorter than Hilka's established text; Hilka's text is some 200 lines longer than that of his base manuscript, *A*. (3) The difference in length between *A* and *T* is on the order of 240 lines, not 274.

In applying the term "philologue" to Guiot, Cerquiglini sets in motion a process that will eventually undermine his primary thesis. He will conclude that the history lying behind specific textual manifestations is irrelevant—that, for example, each variant *Perceval* has merit in its own right (68–69 and 110–12).[13] But the very procedures by which a particular scribe accomplished his recreative acts are necessarily regarded as having resulted in the mutilation of an exemplary model, a model which has receded beyond our power to recapture it. Cerquiglini berates Guiot, as a predecessor of Gaston Paris, for producing a variant text that, in another perspective, he can only praise. In the end, the only one to suffer by such a paradoxical demonstration is Cerquiglini himself. As the point of focus moves from the modern philologist to the medieval scribe-philologist, the glare of the polemicist's ironizing light reflects back on himself.

RUPERT T. PICKENS

Cerquiglini's intent seems to be to valorize Guiot's version as well as that of *T* and whatever others may exist.[14] But he cannot resist the temptation to turn his summary appraisal of Guiot's personal style against the Procrustes-like philologist:

> La critique, *on s'en doute* [my emphasis], a vu dans l'aisance, la légèreté, l'originalité du manuscrit A (copie de Guiot) la preuve qu'il était un bon témoin de l'aisance, de la légèreté et de l'originalité qui furent, par définition, celles du grand romancier Chrétien de Troyes. A cela nous pouvons répondre, avec un même degré de présupposés (et, à la limite, un moindre anachronisme), que le grand romancier médiéval est celui qui joue subtilement des canons, des règles et des *topoi* dont il a hérité. Le débat, on le voit, est irrémédiablement vain. Car la question est ailleurs. (68)

> [Criticism, *as one might expect* ⟨my emphasis—R. T. P.⟩, has seen in the easiness, the airiness, and the originality of manuscript *A* (Guiot's copy) proof that it is a good witness to the easiness, the airiness, and the originality that, by definition, were the great romancer Chrétien de Troyes's. To that we can answer, with a like degree of presupposition (and, at the outside, less anachronism), that it is the great medieval romancer who plays with the canons, rules, and *topoi* he has inherited. Debate, it is clear to see, is irremediably in vain. For the question lies elsewhere.]

So Cerquiglini dismisses the problem of textual authority. But the innuendo of his *on s'en doute* introduces an argument that has, to my knowledge, no basis in reality. Of all the reasons offered by scholars for regarding the *Perceval* text produced by Guiot as the most suitable manuscript to serve as a base for a modern edition, impressionistic stylistic comparisons between Chrétien and Guiot have never been tendered as persuasive or conclusive in themselves. On the contrary, attention has focused on such questions as the relatively early date of Guiot's copy, the Champenois cast of its language, the quality of his sources, the fact that his codex transmits all five of Chrétien's major romances, its close textual relationships with other very early manuscripts bearing the complete corpus or the *Perceval* alone—thus, in sum, the apparent likelihood of its temporal and geographical closeness to Chrétien de Troyes and to the text as it was released for publication.[15] The question of Guiot's reliability is by no means closed, nor is the matter of textual authenticity or authority in general.

Cerquiglini's treatment of Chrétien's *Perceval* shows specific ways in which his polemical style overrides the concerns of scholarship. But a far deeper fault causes the book's central arguments to collapse upon themselves. For the fact is that nearly everything of any importance in this book has been said before—and repeatedly in many cases—by philologists and by theorists of literature and textual criticism. The list is long and telling.

The problem of textual change has, of course, been at the center of medieval literary studies since the origins of modern scholarship in the field during the eighteenth century, as attested, for example, by the transcriptions of troubadour texts made by Canon Gioacchino Plà and by and for Lacurne de Sainte-Palaye[16]—not in the post-1830 period, as could be inferred from Cerquiglini's discussion (73–74). Quite correctly, however, Cerquiglini remarks that the history of textual criticism has been the history of changing attitudes towards the phenomenon he calls *variance* and resultant editorial methodologies. He traces that history through the Romantic, positivistic, and Bédierist phases (73–101). But he drops his historical survey after a summary discussion of inadequacies of Faral's 1938 edition of Villehardouin's *La conquête de Constantinople*. It is as though no significant changes had occurred between the 1930s and Cerquiglini's proclamation of *variance* some fifty years later. The reason Cerquiglini gives for not continuing the historical account subverts his own attacks on Procrustean philology: "Les idées de Joseph Bédier connurent en France et dans les pays anglo-saxons un succès complet, et en partie regrettable; une fois admises, pratiquées, elles ne suscitèrent plus aucun débat, marquant depuis plus d'un demi-siècle une sorte de fin de l'Histoire philologique, l'activité éditrice régulière, mais fort paisible, la réflexion assoupie se soutenant d'une Vérité révélée" (95; "Joseph Bédier's ideas enjoyed complete success in France and the Anglo-Saxon countries, which is somewhat regrettable; once admitted and put into practice, they no longer stirred debate, marking, more than a half-century ago, a kind of end to philological History: honest but peaceful editorial activity, with a dulled capacity for reflection sustained by a revealed Truth"). In fact debate did not cease, and many important and relevant events did take place in scholarship that Cerquiglini either ignores or summarily dismisses.

One is the first important theoretical formulation of the problem of textual *variance* in a modernist/postmodernist perspective: Paul Zumthor's discussion of *mouvance* in his 1972 *Essai de poétique médiévale*, which focuses on the essential instability of the medieval vernacular text. Zumthor argues that the various written manifestations of a vernacular work are traces of "un texte en train de se faire" (73; see 65–75 and 507).[17] Cerquiglini's developments on the subject are essentially little more than elaborations on that kernel; for example, "L'œuvre scribale est un commentaire, une paraphrase, le surplus de sens, et de langue, apporté à *une lettre essentiellement inaccomplie"* (58–59, my emphasis; "A scribe's work is a commentary, a paraphrase, a 'surplus of meaning,' of language, given to *an essentially unfinished text"*).[18]

It is Zumthor's argument in *Essai* that began in the mid-1970s to focus attention on *mouvance/variance* as a positive, not a destructive, force in medieval textual transmission, with the inevitable result that experimentation with an editorial practice reflecting that value was soon undertaken. In respect to the Romance lyric, discussion centering on the trouvères had begun as early as 1962 (Lucas, "L'édition des textes lyriques"), but the first widely recognized edition attempting to incorporate a procedure to account for recreative textual change appeared in 1978 and was devoted to a troubadour.[19] Cerquiglini does not acknowledge such positive approaches to *mouvance/variance,* and he dismisses other well-known multi-text editions with condescension.[20] The editions Cerquiglini cites and many others like them, some in circulation for nearly fifty years,[21] succeed all the same in bringing the *variance* of the medieval scriptorium into the study of the modern scholar. Yet these are, in Cerquiglini's estimation, "tentatives sympathiques, fort utiles, qui traduisent un besoin, mais laissent insatisfait" (112; "pleasant efforts, quite useful, that express a need, but leave you unfulfilled"). The reason, as will be seen, turns on technological rather than scholarly questions. Meanwhile Cerquiglini consistently ignores or devalues the work of his predecessors.

He also dismisses the significance of another important body of relevant work. The polemical intent of his history of modern textual criticism aside, its content closely parallels the similar, more expertly argued presentation in a book published in 1979 that has already become a classic of American scholarship: Alfred Foulet and Mary Blakely Speer, *On Editing Old French Texts*.[22] But Foulet and Speer include the necessary discussion of post-Bédierist theoretical developments ("Towards a New Consensus?" 28–39) that is sorely lacking in Cerquiglini. It is curious, in view of the way Cerquiglini's own history of scholarship develops (not to mention his overriding preoccupation with editorial principles), that he dismisses Foulet and Speer's contribution with a curt "Les discussions méthodologiques en ce domaine sont, *on s'en doute*, riches d'intérêt" (69, my emphasis; "Methodological discussions in this field are, *as one might surmise*, rich in interest"). Both Foulet and Speer have continued to publish on the subject after their initial collaboration: Foulet, before his death, primarily on issues pertaining to Chrétien's *Lancelot*,[23] culminating in the publication of the text with his coeditor, Karl D. Uitti, in 1989; and Speer, on matters of further theoretical interest, including assessments of *mouvance/variance*–centered editorial policy dating from 1980,[24] and most recently in her own 1989 multi-text edition of *Le roman des sept sages de Rome*. This body of work, complemented by articles in a 1987 issue of *L'esprit créateur* edited by Uitti on *The Poetics of Textual Criticism*, reflects the work of what might well be called the "Princeton School," all the more so since the post-Bédierist "new consensus" referred to by Foulet and Speer guided the work of Princeton University's *Roman d'Alexandre* project.[25]

The work of the Princeton School and related projects are by no means the only important scholarship relevant to his arguments that Cerquiglini has ignored. Notable by their absence are references to the theory and practice of textual criticism in Germany since Lachmann or in Holland, Belgium, Switzerland, and Great Britain, as well as in North America (but Italian "neo-Lachmannianism" is cited—and denounced [notes 46–47]). Such omissions are symptomatic of the provincialism characteristic of some scholarly practice in France. Ironically, they are indicative of the very "enclavement" that Seuil's "Des Travaux" series, which Cerquiglini's book inaugurates, is designed to alleviate by publishing "Des traductions d'ouvrages étrangers dont nous avons besoin pour *désenclaver la recherche en France*" (*Éloge* 7, my emphasis; "translations of foreign works which we need in order to *open research in France up to the outside*"). Seuil/"Des Travaux" would do well to contract with Mary B. Speer for a French translation and update of *On Editing*. It should also be clear by now that the *enclavement* imprisoning Cerquiglini's thought is historical as well as cultural, for in essence he condemns Gaston Paris and the producers of multi-text editions before the invention of wordprocessing, not to mention Guiot-as-philologist, for being the products of their own times. As Peter Dembowski states succinctly ("Intertextualité" 17), particular fashions in textual criticism fully participate in the prevailing intellectual climate of their times.

ÉLOGE DE LA VARIANCE AND THE "NEW" PHILOLOGY

Proclamations and exemplifications of the "New" Philology by Romance scholars reflect the polemical tone and intent as well as the cultural and historical *enclavement* of Cerquiglini's book. Unlike authors in the *Speculum* volume representing other disciplines, the Romance specialists offer a grossly misleading depiction of current philological practice. Fleischman uses Cerquiglini's "Procrustean dinosaur" as a theme to inform her article, and Bloch, like Cerquiglini, delights in the quaintness of scholars writing in another age, while he fails to account for trends in recent philological scholarship. They are caught—like Cerquiglini himself—in the paradox of beatifying Joseph Bédier for having led a triumph over the Procrustean Lachmannian, Gaston Paris, while pretending that the practices they condemn still constitute the norm some fifty years later.

In cultural context, Cerquiglini's polemics and political agenda may be partially understood in light of the gap in editorial practice dividing France from the rest of Europe, perhaps in light of a certain rivalry among institutions of higher learning located in and around Paris. Cerquiglini's excesses are so blatant, however, that he seems motivated, too, by a desire to *faire scandale,* to *épater les bourgeois,* in order to command the attention of the broader reading public.

For an American writer, the motivation to adopt such a strategy is less clear. Controversy for its own sake, perhaps. A wish to be on the cutting edge of trends taken to be fashionable in France is suggested by Fleischman's identification of herself with a "Paris School" of Romance philology. When she says "I and Romance philologists working in Paris" ("Philology" 22), she specifies Cerquiglini, Christiane Marchello-Nizia, and Michèle Perret; she most assuredly does not mean Philippe Ménard ("Philology" 28 n31), Jean Dufournet, Emanuèle Baumgartner, or François Suard. Fleischman is also drawn into Cerquiglini's *enclavement.* Her scholarship is generally presented as partaking of only the very most recent developments, for she cites very few sources published before 1975. For example, only the "latest" Zumthor deserves full references: *Introduction à la poésie orale,* 1983 (20, n3); "The Text and the Voice," 1984 (22 n11); *La poésie et la voix dans la civilisation médiévale,* 1984 (24 n17)—but not Zumthor's 1972 description of *mouvance* in the written tradition; meanwhile, Zumthor's discussion of *monument* and *document* from thirty years ago merits only a cryptic allusion ("This useful heuristic distinction was introduced by Paul Zumthor," 19 n2), without mention of the seminal 1962 *Langue et techniques poétiques à l'époque romane.* Fleischman further imitates Cerquiglini and his scholarly provincialism in her nearly absolute neglect of American philologists: except for herself, she cites only Noel Corbett (once, with approval [34 and n52]) and William W. Kibler (once, unfavorably [28 n31]).

Also like the author of *Éloge*, despite an avowed concern for language, manuscript, and literary interpretation, the recent exponents of the "New" Philology have approached these subjects with varying degrees of expertise and competence. Fleischman professes interest in manuscript text, yet relevant examples do not come from her own readings; she fails therefore to establish her own credentials as a philologist capable of reading and understanding the medieval language in the medium in which it is preserved. At one point (20 n4), she refers to a list of samples from two *Lanval* manuscripts that is found in an article by members of the Paris School who, for their part, rely on transcriptions by Rychner; the sampling purportedly offers proof that one scribe normally wrote enclitics before vowels and the other proclitics (*nel aime* versus *ne laime*).[26] Fleischman fails to notice that the Paris philologists do not observe the scribes' inconsistencies and omit word divisions that contradict their thesis.[27]

Fleischman's article is weakened by its naïve incorporation of *Éloge de la variante* and by its reliance on manuscript readings from Rychner via "L'objet 'ancien français.'" It therefore fails in its attempt to celebrate "newness" in philological practice. The substance of her contribution can nevertheless be read as a legitimate linguistic investigation of Old French, that is (despite her own polemics), as a philological enterprise in the traditional sense. Her methods are not immune from question,[28] but they could well be justified within purely philological frames of reference (Fourquet, "Linguistique et philologie"); her practice does not necessarily reflect the anti-philological bias she proclaims.

In contrast, Bloch's defiant disregard of the phonological facts of Old French is a scandal. In discussing Old French *lai*, "song," as it pertains to Marie de France, Bloch evokes a wide variety of word associations. He mentions as "variants" *lai, lay, laye, laie, laiz, laes,* asserting that all "can be used as an adjective to connote the secular realm and as a substantive to designate a lay person" ("New" 47). In other words, *lais/lai,* "song" (with and without flexional *s*), along with different orthographic variants like *lay,* is homophonous with *lais/lai,* "layperson," which is true. Introduction of feminine forms for "lay"/"layperson" confuses the matter, however, because the bisyllabic form cannot be homophonous or interchangeable with *lai*, "song" or "layperson," except in the oblique case before a vowel.

Ever more serious problems arise as Bloch expands his list of "variants": "*Lai* and its homophones *laid*, *lait* . . ." (47). *Laid*, "ugly," and *lait*, "ugly" and "milk," are indeed perfect homophones, along with *lait*, "injury," but they are not homophonous with *lai*, "song," which lacks the final dental stop; consequently, depending upon the dialect and the period, the vowels would also differ: if, as happened early in Anglo-Norman, the diphthong /ai/ is considered to have been leveled to /e/, then in final position, as in *lai*, "song," it is close; but preconsonantal, as in *lait*, "ugly," "milk," or "injury," it is open (Pope §529).

The confusion and errors redouble as Bloch's associations continue: "The adjectival homophones *lé, ley, lay, let, lait, leit, laé, lede* specify that which is wide or large. . . . *Lié, liet, leé, le* [for *lé*?] summon the idea of lightness, happiness, joy . . . , while *las, lax, lais* connote sadness, misery, misfortune" (47). The problems introduced here are of several orders. (1) The leveling of the diphthongs /ai/ and /ei/ to /e/, implied in the assertion that *lai* is homophonous with *ley* and *lé*, "wide," is a matter, first, of dialect distinction and, second, of dating. (2) *Lié*, "happy," is not homophonous with *lai*; the significance of the loss of the palatal element apparent in the spelling *le* (for *lé*), which makes "happy" theoretically homophonous with *lai*, likewise depends upon which dialects and which periods are being referred to (see Pope §1155). (3) Adding derivatives of Latin *lassus* further muddies the waters. On the one hand, *las*, "tired," could have been only imperfectly homophonous with *lais*, "song," before the diphthong in the latter leveled to /e/, or else late in twelfth-century England /ai/ could have simplified, sporadically, to /a/ (Pope §1155)—yet the former event alone is assumed to have taken place in order to justify the previous associations. On the other hand, *lax/lais*, "tired," are spellings representing palatalization of /a/ primarily in Eastern dialects (Pope §E xv) that have no bearing on reading Marie de France except in terms of specific local receptions. (4) The form *laé* (for *leé*) is bisyllabic, with stress on the second syllable, and is therefore not homophonous with *lai*. (5) The archaic feminine lede (where *d* represents an interdental), "wide," is also bisyllabic, as is non-homophonous feminine *lede*, "ugly" (with a dental).

Other difficulties arise as the arguments continue, and Bloch's associations bear fruit of dubious quality as his discussion turns to Marie's poetics.[29] Discussion of the topic culminates with *lai/ loi*: "Finally, the word *lai* is used in its Old French forms *loi, lei, ley* to designate custom, usage, justice, or the law" (48), that is to say, a word, variously spelled, that is homophonous with *lai*, "song," means "law," etc. (it is curious that Bloch omits "religion"). Here two observations are in order. First, there can be little doubt that in large areas of western France and in Anglo-Norman territory the words *lai*, "song," and *lei/ley*, "law," were homophonous by the time of Marie de France (Pope §§226, 230, 523, 1157– 58). Second, elsewhere, and especially in Francian territory, the word for "law" had undergone another development altogether, as is indicated by the spelling *loi*. This other process produced the highly differentiated diphthong /oi/ which then shifted to /we/ (open) (Pope §§518–20). Thus, two distinct dialect forms of the same word existed at the same time. The association Bloch would make between *lai*, "song," and *lei*, "law," is not universally possible in Old French; homophony occurs only in England and in the westernmost dialect areas on the Continent. In Francian and the other continental dialects, no poetic identification of *lai*, "song," and *loi*, "law," was at all functional.[30]

The philologist might raise here the question of authorship of the *Lais*. Was the Marie to whom these stories are attributed the same Marie "de France," that is, from the Francian dialect area, who translated fables from English into French?[31] Did she say something like /le/ (close) for "law," or did she say something like /loi/ or even /lwe/ (open)? Other readers of the *Lais* might follow Cerquiglini (cf. *Éloge* 108–11) by responding that the attribution of authorship is irrelevant, that only the manuscript manifestations matter. The point would be well taken, for we know very little about the Marie who signed the *Guigemar* prologue or any other late twelfth-century writer by that name, and most attempts to identify her depend upon arguments largely external to any of the literary texts at hand.[32] No one denies that different manuscripts have different significations thanks to the forces of *mouvance/variance*. But in the case of Marie's *Lais*, the "New" Philology has thus far failed to demonstrate that it is equipped to deal with the fundamental diachronic and synchronic problems of dialect variations. In reference to Bloch's readings, the association of "song" and "law" is appropriate only when his text is Anglo-Norman; the identification is impossible when he is reading manuscripts copied on the Continent, where "song" and "law" are not homophonous, but constitute a minimal pair. Meanwhile, other associations are possible in other dialect areas, but are without validity in the western regions.

Bloch's efforts to marshall such information as a means of providing critical perspectives on Marie's *Lais* are bound to fail when his dazzling array of lexical items is subjected to informed philological scrutiny. The exuberance that inspires the *lai* associations betrays him utterly when he turns to an analogous treatment of Old French *traire*. Bloch is right to explore the broad semantic field of this verb: "shoot," "treat," "draw out," "draw," "translate," etc. (55). But with alacrity he jumps to another observation:

> As translation, *traire* implies the transformation of the same into the other; and if it means "to shoot," "to distance," or "to introduce difference" [i.e., extending the process of translation/*translatio*], it is because such terms of alienation are the homophone of "to deceive." Indeed, given the fact that Old French poetry, even though written, was intended for the ear (either to be recited or read aloud), there can be no difference between the words *traire* and *trahir*. "To draw or shoot" and "to betray" stand as proof of the treacherousness of a homophonic lack of difference in the sound of a word that can also mean "to differ." (55)

But there are indeed differences—fundamental differences— between *traire* and *traïr* in Old French, as in modern French, that deny the possibility of homophony. Attempts to make them homophones—for example, "To write or treat (*traire*) is to betray (*traire*) [sic]" (56)—are doomed to defeat.

Bloch's article, intended to defend and illustrate a "New" Philology, instead bespeaks the excesses of a groundless pseudo-philology. As the Romance articles in the *Speculum* volume demonstrate so profusely, in fact, the "New" movement in scholarship the authors set out to celebrate is a house built on sand that is bound to collapse. Can anything be salvaged from the wreckage?

THE POSTMODERN MACHINE: EDITING ON-SCREEN

As philology is concerned with matters of text, the question of textual edition is central in all discussion pertaining to the present controversy. We recall Cerquiglini's dismissal of multi-text editions, which apparently represent no advance over editorial scholarship as it was practiced in the 1930s: "Tentatives sympathiques, fort utiles, qui traduisent un besoin, mais laissent insatisfait" (*Éloge* 112). He continues:

> Tentées par la copie diplomatique, ces éditions se prennent au fantasme du fac-similé, de la fourniture probe et maximale de données intactes, dont le lecteur fera son bien; n'ayant d'autre option que la générosité loyale, elles oublient que toute édition est une théorie: il faut donner à voir, mais surtout à comprendre. Ensuite, on ne quitte pas avec elles l'espace à deux dimensions de la page imprimée: l'écriture médiévale est mise en regard, et non pas en mouvement. La solution est ailleurs. (112)[33]

> [Tempted by diplomatic copying, these editions cling to the fantasy of the facsimile—the proper supplying, to the greatest extent possible, of intact data—which the reader will take possession of; having no option but their forthright generosity, they forget that every edition is a theory: you must give something to be seen, but above all to be understood. Moreover, with them you don't get away from the two-dimensional space of the printed page: the medieval writing is put into view, but not into motion. The solution is somewhere else.]

Cerquiglini dismisses the book with ironic finality in order to propose computer technology as alone capable of suggesting medieval textual *variance:*

> L'écran qu'élaborent et raffinent toujours plus les techniciens est à la fois dialogique (il offre une interaction constante du consul-

tant et de la machine) et multidimensionnel (il permet la consultation conjointe, par fenêtrage, de données appartenant à des ensembles disjoints). Utilisant ces deux propriétés, on peut concevoir un type d'édition d'une oeuvre médiévale, issue de cette réunion d'ensembles disjoints qu'est le codex, qui ne serait plus soumise à la structure bidimensionnelle et close de la page imprimée: une disquette accueille des masses textuels variées, que le lecteur consulte en les faisant apparaître diversement sur un écran d'ordinateur. (113)

[The screen, which technologists are forever improving and refining, is at the same time dialogic (it offers constant interaction between user and machine) and multidimensional (it allows the user to bring together, through use of windows, data from unrelated sources). Making use of these two features, one can imagine a way of editing a medieval work, itself born of that collection of disparate units which is the codex, that would no longer be bound by the two-dimensional structure of the printed page: a diskette accepts varied masses of text which the reader looks at by bringing them up in different ways on the computer screen.]

So Cerquiglini launches his polemical *Éloge* in order to declare a technological revolution comparable to the invention of movable type in Germany (115). At the dawn of the new age, we are on the verge of sweeping aside the book as we know it, including all editions, even the most forthright in accounting for *variance*. Students and scholars alike are to be riveted to the cathode ray tube, never again to turn a page. But even the prophet must admit that the appropriate ideal technology, in the form of compatible software, does not yet exist; indeed, he is forced into a kind of "nostalgia of the future," when ever greater technical elaborations and refinements will have produced the desired programs.

It is singularly ironic, then, that such a traditional philologist as Karl D. Uitti, in the study which Bloch calls "absurd and rigidly superannuated" ("New" 47, n33), should have so thoroughly anticipated Cerquiglini in this respect. Uitti envisions a time when "computer-assisted technology and the development of suitably sophisticated programming [will] make it possible to render easily and pertinently accessible to interested readers . . . 'textual multiplicity' . . . within given traditions (as well as certain corresponding specificities)—that is, . . . [when] the books and the libraries to which we are accustomed themselves become useless and outdated" ("On Editing" 291). Uitti directs a team of researchers at Princeton University that has been at work for the past few years on the texts of Chrétien de Troyes's *Lancelot*; they are in the painstaking process of developing necessarily complex techniques for inscribing manuscript text in all its intricate subtleties.[34]

The promise the computer holds for revolutionizing scholarship and for the transmission and storage of knowledge has not faded—unlike the once-heralded potential of microfilm and microfiche. The computer is now useful for producing conventional printed editions of medieval text via simple word processing. But Uitti's statement strongly affirms, as Cerquiglini's discussion feebly implies, what anyone knows who has seriously thought about using the computer to reproduce or to transmit manuscript text in any meaningful new way: that in practical terms we do not yet possess, nor will we soon have, the technology to produce a computer-based multi-text edition that would be readily comprehensible to any readers other than the ones who had processed it.

In order to grasp the size of the problems involved, one need consider only such basic questions as the following: (1) How should we access medieval manuscripts—by using photocopies or going directly to libraries? (2) How should we transfer information from the manuscript to the computer—by scanning a manuscript or a photocopy? by keyboarding directly from a manuscript or indirectly from a photocopy or handwritten transcription? (3) How should we reproduce abbreviations? (4) How should we account for the peculiarities of individual hands and establish limits of tolerance for variations in script? (5) How should we show changes in hands? (6) To what extent would it be legitimate to edit as we transfer information? (7) Should we strive to reproduce on the screen, directly or schematically, all characteristics of the original manuscript texts, or should an editor mediate to make the texts somehow more accessible to a broad audience including non-philologists?[35]

In other words, should we use the computer to its fullest potential by maximizing specialization in ways that might be uncongenial to humanists, or, at the other extreme, should we adapt the conventions of the more familiar printed book to the machine? Until these and countless other difficulties are resolved and the appropriate software developed, the modern book which Cerquiglini so disdainfully denounces—might one say, as a Procrustean falsification of medieval textuality?—remains the only means by which textual critics can bring medieval texts to the attention of their readers.

PHILOLOGIA ET MODERNITAS

The *Speculum* volume and Cerquiglini's *Éloge* both incorporate a postmodern and quasi-politicized equation of newness and revolution. In order to proclaim and to practice the "New" Philology, in that view, it is necessary to exorcise the past, to wrench our freedom from what has gone on before. But the philologist whose professional values include respect for modern scholarly tradition as well as devotion to medieval texts and medieval textuality cannot but regard such a project as irrational.

The objects of scholarly inquiry (for example, Chrétien's *Perceval*, Marie's *Lais, Aucassin et Nicolette*) belong to the distant past as well as to the present. Yet we are told that in order to comprehend their essential pastness we must look at them in new ways that invite us to ignore our own past, the tradition in which we take part as modern scholars. The newness thus proclaimed must inevitably be unformed and the critical perspective uninformed because what is rejected is precisely the tradition that has taught us everything we know about the Middle Ages. Such is the newness of Bloch's wordplay and Fleischman's application to the *Roland* of structures pertaining to storytelling in New Guinea. This is New, but it is not Philology.

In the *Speculum* volume, it is Siegfried Wenzel's article that most effectively evokes the fourfold field of inquiry valued, *mutatis mutandis* (since Wenzel is an Anglicist and Latinist), by Romance philologists.[36] These may be summarized as: (1) knowledge of medieval vernacular languages and their dialects; (2) textual criticism, knowledge of manuscripts as the written manifestations of literary texts, textual history, and principles of editing; (3) textual analysis and literary interpretation, theory and practice; (4) literary history.[37] Characteristically, a philologist will demonstrate interest in all four areas, with special concern for language and the nature of medieval textuality, as well as competence and, ideally, expertise in most.

Another characteristic of philological scholarship sets it apart from work like Cerquiglini's *Éloge* and the *mises en pratique* of the "New" Philology. Philological writing embraces a rhetoric not of rupture, but of continuity; it seeks not to destroy, not to subvert, not therefore to renovate. The editions and works on textual criticism mentioned before as milestones in the modern history of philology may well have proved to be revolutionary in their time, in the sense that they brought about important changes in perspective, but they did not conceive themselves as fostering a break with the traditions of philological scholarship. They celebrate renewal, not novelty.

In 1872, when he published his first edition of *La vie de saint Alexis*, Gaston Paris was well aware that he was introducing a Lachmannian methodology new to the study of medieval literature but already an established part of classical philological practice in Germany. The point of his exercise was the *recovery*, the restoration and restitution, of linguistic and poetic forms that had been lost in the course of the poem's history. The four versions he had identified are "quatre *moments* bien distincts de notre histoire littéraire" ("Avant-Propos" and 265), to be sure, but the manuscripts are seen as bearing faulty witness to more perfect textual states representing an eleventh-century original and subsequent stages belonging to each of the next three centuries. Establishment of the earliest text was the most difficult, but apparently the most satisfying task for Paris. He could exclaim with positivistic exuberance: "Enfin le poème du XIe siècle a été soumis à un essai de restauration intégrale sur le succès de laquelle auront à se prononcer les juges compétents" ("Avant-

Propos"; "Finally, the eleventh-century poem has been subjected to an attempt at total restoration, the success or failure of which those competent to judge will have to declare"). In a second edition published in 1885, Paris expressed renewed optimism utterly untinged with disappointment: "la connaissance de la phonétique et de la morphologie du plus ancien français a fait depuis 1872 de tels progrès qu'il n'est presque plus un vers de mon texte qui, au point de vue des formes qui y ont été adoptées, me satisfasse aujourd'hui, comme il n'est pas une page de mon introduction grammaticale qui ait gardé, je ne dis pas sa nouveauté, mais sa valeur" (vi; "knowledge about the phonetics and morphology of the oldest French has progressed so much since 1872 that there is hardly a single verse in my text that, from the standpoint of the forms that were adopted therein, still satisfies me today, just as there is not one page of my grammatical introduction that has kept—I do not say its newness, but its value"). Paris does not equate newness and value. Moreover, he especially acknowledges suggestions for different restorations made by Tobler, Stengel, and Paul Meyer (v). Although he is convinced that his latest contribution is superior to the text produced twelve years before, he offers his work in hopes of partaking still further of a collegial effort to recover the truth: "Je ne doute pas que sur plus d'un point *mes confrères en philologie* ne trouvent encore bien à redire, et moi-même je suis loin d'être assuré de tout ce que la lecture de mon texte pourrait faire regarder comme établi pour moi" (vi–vii, my emphasis; "I do not doubt that on more than one point *my colleagues in philology* will still find much to criticize, and I am myself far from certain about everything that a reading of my text might lead one to regard as established to my satisfaction").

As Gaston Paris's student, Joseph Bédier (see p. 181) began his involvement with *Le lai de l'ombre* as a Lachmannian enterprise, published in 1890—an attempt to recover the lost original by a comparison of extant manuscript versions known to him. In 1913, he renounced the comparative method and its goals, having failed to discover his poem's "genealogical tree" (xxxviii–xxxix). He repudiated his earlier work, disclaiming as irrelevant to his project a particular critical methodology. He did so, however, without denouncing the lasting philological values in terms of which he had produced his 1890 edition, nor did he seek to discredit the teachers and colleagues with whom he shared those values. Specifically, he referred, just as his teacher had done, to an ongoing intellectual and scholarly process: "En 1890, je publiai . . . une édition nouvelle, dont je sais aujourd'hui les grands défauts. Si je la mentionne pourtant, c'est qu'elle garde un mérite, celui d'avoir été en son temps l'objet de quatre comptes-rendus qui, étant signés Hermann Suchier, Wendelin Foerster, Ad. Tobler, Gaston Paris, sont donc quatre études très précieuses" (Bédier, *Lai* vii; "In 1890, I published . . . a new edition, the grave weaknesses of which I know. If I bring it up, however, it is because it still has one merit, that of having been, in its time, the object of four critical reviews which, signed Hermann Suchier, Wendelin Foerster, Ad[olf] Tobler, Gaston Paris, are thus four most precious studies"). The sincerity of Bédier's courteous homage shines all the more clearly when these lines are compared with an earlier, more specific confrontation with Gaston Paris. Three years after his Lachmannian edition of *Le lai de l'ombre*, Bédier wrote in *Les fabliaux*:

> L'étude des faits m'a conduit à des conclusions contraires [à celles de Gaston Paris]. Je sens combien elles sont téméraires, se heurtant à une si redoutable autorité. Je ne les exprime pas sans tremblement: je les exprime pourtant. Par là du moins, M. G. Paris me reconnaîtra comme de son école. Parmi ceux qui la forment, il n'en est pas un qui soit à son égard comme le *famulus* du docteur Faust. Tous ont appris de lui la recherche scrupuleuse et patiente, mais indépendante et brave, du vrai: la soumission du travailleur, non à un principe extérieur d'autorité, mais aux faits, et aux conséquences qu'il en voit découler; la défiance de soi, la prudence à conclure, mais aussi, quand il croit que les faits ont parlé, l'honnêteté qui s'applique à redire ce qu'ils ont dit. (22–23)[38]

[Study of the facts has led me to conclusions contrary ⟨to those of Gaston Paris⟩. I am aware of how daring they are, running up against such an awesome authority. I do not voice them without fear and trembling, but voice them I do. In that, at least,

Monsieur G⟨aston⟩ Paris will recognize me as belonging to his school. Among those who make up that school, there is not one who is, with respect to him, like Dr. Faust's famulus. They have all learned from him a way of searching for truth that is careful and patient, yet self-reliant and bold: the scholar's submission, not to any outside principle, but to the facts and to the consequences he sees stemming from them; humility, caution in reaching conclusions, but, once he believes that the facts have spoken, an integrity that strives to repeat what they have said.]

The enduring values Bédier inherited from Gaston Paris—the pursuit of knowledge for its own sake, the primacy of truth, scholarly freedom from forces outside the project at hand, rejection of dogmatism, submission to the facts, the exercise of judgment, self-awareness (and thus mistrust of the scholar's ego), the courageous expression of conclusions judiciously worked out—are likewise evident in his philological endeavor of 1913. The ideal of respectful collegiality is, furthermore, made explicit in Bédier's careful placement of his single-manuscript edition in context with contributions by other philologists, notably Paul Meyer, to whom Gaston Paris had expressed gratitude in 1884, and Gaston Raynaud (xli).

Bédier published yet another edition of *Le lai de l'ombre* in 1928, but the primary purpose of the article where it appeared ("La tradition manuscrite du *Lai de l'ombre*") was to report and to prolong his scholarly dialogue with Henri Quentin. A Benedictine of Solesmes, Quentin was a biblical scholar who had applied principles of Lachmannian methodology in an effort to recover the original Vulgate Genesis ("La tradition manuscrite" 22 and n1). News of his work had caused Bédier again to become "obsessed" (21) with the manuscript genealogy of *Le lai de l'ombre*: "je participe à l'émoi, fait de curiosité et d'espoir, qu'ont suscité dans le monde des philologues les travaux récents de dom Henri Quentin" (21–22; "I share the excitement, born of inquisitiveness and hope, that the recent works of Dom Henri Quentin have aroused in the world of philologists"). With typical courtesy and tact, Bédier emphasized the seriousness of their dialogue—how, in other words, the personal relationship embodied the philological values he had expressed in 1893, those of the *confrérie* Gaston Paris had invoked in 1890. In light of the dialogue's resolution, the fact that Bédier casts Quentin in the role of his "maître" makes an association with the passage from *Les fabliaux* all the more meaningful: "j'ai eu le privilège d'entrer en relations personnelles avec lui [Dom Quentin] dès 1922. . . . Depuis, avec une bonne grâce et une bienveillance que je lui rends en admiration respectueuse et confiante, il a bien voulu, à mon intention, appliquer sa technique à l'étude de quelques vieux textes français, et s'employer par là à mon apprentissage" ("Tradition" 1929, 22; "I have had the privilege to know him ⟨Dom Quentin⟩ beginning in 1922. . . . Since then, with graciousness and good will, which I return to him with respectful and faithful admiration, he has been willing, for my sake alone, to apply his method to the study of several old French texts, and thereby to devote himself to my training"). "La tradition manuscrite" is a record of the "trainee's" progress, and the outcome is well known.

Without announcing a revolution, and certainly without proclaiming his independence, Bédier declared his own mastery in his field of expertise, where the pupil becomes the teacher: the pupil will, in fact, have the last word:

Aussi la méthode d'édition la plus recommandable est-elle peut-être, en dernière analyse, celle que régit *un esprit de défiance de soi, de prudence, d'extrême "conservatisme,"* un énergique vouloir, porté jusqu'au parti pris, d'ouvrir aux scribes le plus large crédit et de ne toucher au texte d'un manuscrit que l'on imprime qu'en cas d'extrême et presque évidente nécessité: toutes les corrections conjecturales devraient être reléguées en des appendices. "Une telle méthode d'édition, a écrit dom Quentin, risque d'être bien dommageable à la critique textuelle." Peut-être; mais c'est, de toutes les méthodes connues, celle qui risque le moins d'être dommageable aux textes. (71, my emphasis)

[Thus the most advisable editorial method is, perhaps, in the final analysis, the one governed by *a spirit of humility, of caution, of extreme "conservatism,"* a forceful desire, carried to the extreme of bias, to give maximum credit to the scribes and to interfere with the text being printed only in case of dire, nearly transparent necessity: all conjectural corrections should be relegated to appendices. "Such an editorial method," Dom Quentin has written, "threatens to be very harmful to textual criticism." Perhaps; but it is, of all the known methods, the one that threatens least to be harmful to the texts.]

What holds our attention in Bédier's closing remarks, where he affirms the editorial experiment undertaken in 1913, is, as well, his reaffirmation of traditional philological values. That Bédier regards the philological enterprise as an ongoing process of transformation and renewal is a point he makes even more forcefully in the article's opening sentence, which serves as the epigraph for the present essay.[39]

More recently, a participant in the Princeton School of textual criticism has stressed the importance that philologists' sense of continuity and collegiality has as a mark of their consciousness of being engaged in an ongoing scholarly process. Karl Uitti suggests that such knowledge is as essential to free, anti-totalitarian philological activity as the study of the textual corpus itself ("À propos" 43–44). I have already given one reason why this is so: it is the accumulated body of modern scholarship that has taught us what we know about the Middle Ages. Uitti's discussion has more profound implications, however, for he regards modern philological practice as taking place in a continuum with ancient and medieval *philologia*. The philological project of a Chrétien de Troyes, for example, was undertaken in harmony with the medieval idea of *modernitas:* Chrétien, as philologist, was involved in a process of transmitting and rewriting ancient texts, in an activity of renewal. Uitti is interested in Chrétien's rewriting of Martianus Capella's *De nuptiis Mercurii et Philologiae* in *Érec et Énide.* Chrétien's *Conte del graal* and Marie de France's *Lais,* as products of *translatio* and transformation, likewise explicitly partake of the philological process, as does *Aucassin et Nicolette* implicitly; Guiot de Provins was involved in a similar practice. When we, as modern philologists, ponder Chrétien's medieval project, we come to understand that we have become engaged in the same process as he. The extent to which we value and are moved by such an insight is the degree of our consciousness of ourselves as philologists and as humanists.

This is why there could never be a *new* philology. What would call itself so has already denied philology's basic principles.

NOTES

1. Nichols, ed., *The New Philology*. The Romance scholars involved are Nichols, Bloch, and Fleischman; the volume also contains articles by Wenzel, Spiegel, and Patterson. Nichols had declared the New Philology two years before as editor of *The Legitimacy of the Middle Ages* (*Romanic Review* 68.1 [1988]), a volume containing papers read at a conference held at the University of Pennsylvania in March 1987. Three articles on Old French topics comprise a section entitled "Text and Manuscript: The New Philology": Bloch, "The Medieval Text— 'Guigemar'—as a Provocation to the Discipline of Medieval Studies"; Hult, "Reading It Right: The Ideology of Text Editing"; and Leupin, "*Raoul de Cambrai:* La bâtardise de l'écriture." Bloch's "The Medieval Text" is reprinted in Brownlee, Brownlee, and Nichols, eds., *The New Medievalism*.

2. The "Procrustean philologist" is an invention of Cerquiglini, in his *Éloge de la variante,* while the monument/document distinction is that between the text perceived to have artistic worth, on the one hand, and, on the other, the text of purely utilitarian value, according to Paul Zumthor's *Langue et technique poétique à l'époque romane* 31–36.

3. Bloch refers to Uitti and Foulet, "On Editing Chrétien de Troyes," which in turn is a response to Hult, "Lancelot's Two Steps."

4. Procrustes figures among the "monstres étouffés et . . . brigands punis" Hippolyte credits to his father's account in Racine's *Phèdre* (I.i. 79–80).

5. Cerquiglini refers to Bédier, "La tradition manuscrite du *Lai de l'ombre*." The 1928 article in no sense "buries" Paris, but is addressed primarily to another Lachmannian, the biblical scholar Dom Henri Quentin, who had commented on Bédier's first single-manuscript edition of *Le lai de l'ombre* (I discuss this in the last section of the present essay). Cerquiglini believes that in 1913 Bédier had simply reprinted his Lachmannian edition of *Le lai de l'ombre* published in 1890: "republiant en 1913 à la *Société des anciens textes français* l'edition (de stricte obédience pariso-

lachmannienne) qu'il avait donnée dans sa jeunesse. . ." (94). In fact, Bédier printed in 1913 the text of his manuscript *A* with a complete set of variants; the manuscript used in 1928 is *E*, with rejected readings only.

6. U. T. Holmes, Jr.—a philologist, certainly, but no Procrustes!— taught his students, including me, both to respect the stemma (based not on Lachmannian "errors," but on common lessons) and, following his own teacher Bédier, to value the earliest and the "best" copy; in the editorial project he championed minimal intervention. Such values are exemplified in his edition of *Adenet le Roi's Berte aus grans piés*; see also his review of Ham, *Textual Criticism and Jehan le Venelais*, where Holmes expresses concern that the Bédierist approach might grow to be "anachronistic" in the wake of thoughtful, moderately Lachmannian work like Ham's. Another edition, this one minimalist in the extreme, was produced by Holmes's student Nancy V. Iseley: *La chançun de Willame*. This edition of a difficult work preserved in a single Anglo-Norman manuscript illustrates both the virtues (as a commented, quasi-diplomatic edition with resolution of abbreviations, modern punctuation, etc.) and the vices (as a failure to account for the ways Anglo-Norman usage distorts our perception of the metrics) of such an enterprise.

7. Another single-manuscript edition, this one of the text of manuscript Bern 354, has subsequently been published by Charles Méla: *Chrétien de Troyes, Le conte du graal ou le roman de Perceval*.

8. Micha, *Tradition* 169–209, 233–53. See also Pickens, ed., *Chrétien de Troyes, The Story of The Grail (Li contes del graal)*, or *Perceval* xxx–xxxii.

9. Roques, "Le manuscrit fr. 794 de la Bibliothèque nationale et le scribe Guiot"; see also the introductions of his editions of *Érec et Énide* xxxvii–liii and *Cligés* xix–xx. On Guiot's good copy of Wace's *Brut* see Woledge, "Un scribe champenois devant un texte normand: Guiot copiste de Wace." As Woledge notes (1139–40), both Roach and Frappier disputed the primacy of Guiot's *Perceval* text; for negative critical assessments, see Reid, "Chrétien de Troyes and the Scribe Guiot," and Hunt, "Chrestien de Troyes: The Textual Problem." Prior to Micha's *La tradition manuscrite*, the prestige of Guiot's *Perceval* text was enhanced by Baist's privately printed edition, *Crestien's von Troyes Contes del Graal (Percevaus), Abdruck der Handschrift Paris, français 794*; by Hilka's completion of Foerster's series of critical editions of Chrétien based on Guiot; and by the discovery of the Annonay fragments (Pauphilet, Flutre), the earliest witness to a Chrétien text that is very close to Guiot's source.

10. Cerquiglini does not mention Potvin's monumental edition of the Mons manuscript (now called *P* in his honor) containing Chrétien's text, the continuations, and minor related texts.

11. As Cerquiglini was writing, only the "Procrustean" philologist Hilka had committed the worse crime of subjecting Guiot's text itself to the stretching and cutting of the editorial process. See Pickens, ed., *Chrétien de Troyes, The Story of the Grail*, an edition based on *A*, and Pickens, "Toward an Edition of Chrétien's *Li contes del graal*: Hilka vv. 1869–2024." See also Keith Busby's critical edition based on manuscript *T*, prepared for the series of Chrétien's complete works sponsored by the Vinaver Foundation (Tübingen: Niemeyer, 1993).

12. "E cil gard qui l'orrat [i.e., the *Cumpot*] / E qui bien l'entendrat, / Que s'il digne le veit, / Qu'il a escrivre seit, / Que aprof le patrun / Recoillet sun sermun. / S'il issi nel volt faire, / Que li seit a contraire, / Prei lui pur Deu amur, / N'i metet sun labor, / Car suvent par les mains, / Par malveis escriveins, / Sunt livres corrumpud / E en neise perdud" (149–62, British Library Ms. Cotton Nero A.V, my transcription; "And he who hears it [the *Cumpot*] and understands it well, if he finds it worthy, and if he starts writing, may he take care to set down its text according to the exemplar. If he is unwilling to do this, if it bothers him, I beg him for the love of God not to devote his effort to it, for often by hands, by bad copyists, are books corrupted and lost in hubbub"). By contrast, worthy readers ("mestre," 163) are given license to introduce changes after an attentive hearing: "Ne targez, / Mais ma raisun oiez; / Prei vus de l'esculter / E puis de l'amender" (173–76; "Do not delay, but hear my discourse; I pray you, listen to it attentively, then improve it"). See also Pickens, "Jaufré Rudel et la poétique de la mouvance."

13. Cerquiglini here follows Bédier, "Tradition" 28 (my page references are to the 1929 pamphlet).

14. Guiot's text is, indeed, highly idiosyncratic—and interestingly so in its emphases and characterizations as well as in its language. Cerquiglini could have profited from David F. Hult's arguments for the primacy of Guiot's *Lancelot* text ("Lancelot's Two Steps"), which appeared two years before *Éloge* was published, although the response by Karl D. Uitti and Alfred Foulet ("On Editing Chrétien") and Hult's subsequent reply ("Steps Forward and Steps Backward") were printed too late for him to have taken them into account.

15. See above n. 8; also Pickens, "Towards an Edition" 55–57. Dating and dialect are of primary importance in the Bédierist project.

16. Plà's chansonnier is Vatican Ms. Barb. Lat. 3965 (Jeanroy *e*, Brunel 331). Lacurne de Sainte-Palaye possessed many volumes of troubadour and trouvère texts that are housed in Paris, Bibliothèque de l'Arsenal Mss. 3092–98 (cf. Jeanroy S[a], Brunel 132), 6361, etc.

17. Also see Zumthor, "Du nouveau sur la poésie des troubadours et trouvères" and "Intertextualité et mouvance." For more recent associations with textual orality and "vocality," see his *La lettre et la voix* 160–68.

18. Cerquiglini dismisses the significance of Zumthor's 1972 contribution because in subsequent discussions of *mouvance*, especially since 1984, Zumthor has increasingly associated it with what he perceives to be the essential orality of vernacular textuality. This shift in Zumthor's critical perspective does not diminish the fact that the only records of textual change, whatever the presumed origin of the impulse in the Middle Ages, are *written* records.

19. Pickens, ed., *The Songs of Jaufré Rudel*; see also "Jaufré Rudel et la poétique de la mouvance." Noomen and van den Boogaard, eds., *Nouveau recueil complet des fabliaux*, likewise justify their multi-text format in terms of Zumthor's discussions of *mouvance* (1:ix).

20. In some of these editions textual change is regarded as a hindrance to our perception of medieval textuality rather than its essence. Among many well-known examples, some mentioned by Cerquiglini (112), are Roach and others, eds., *The Continuations of the Old French Perceval of Chrétien de Troyes*; Marie de France, *Le lai de Lanval*, ed. Jean Rychner (rather than fully edited, a quasi-diplomatic transcription, with resolution of abbreviations, of the four manuscript texts, accompanied by an established text); Régnier, ed., *Les rédactions en vers de la Prise d'Orange* (like Roach's *Continuations*, critically edited texts of each redaction); Stuip, ed., *La chastelaine de Vergi* (an established text followed by quasi-diplomatic editions of the ten manuscripts from the thirteenth and fourteenth centuries); Dembowski, ed., *La vie de saint Marie l'Égyptienne*; Lepage, ed., *Les rédactions en vers du Couronnement de Louis* (same format as Régnier's *Prise d'Orange*); Noomen and van den Boogaard, eds., *Nouveau recueil complet des fabliaux*; Keller, ed., *La vie de saint Marguerite* of Wace; Speer, ed., *Le roman des sept sages de Rome*. We recall that Gaston Paris's 1872 edition of *La vie de saint Alexis* accounts for every version of the poem known to him, although, to be sure, the editor attempts to restore the text of each to an idealized earlier state.

21. For example, Mortier, ed., *Les textes de la Chanson de Roland*; Roach, ed., *The Didot Perceval*; Jenkins and others, eds., *La seinte resureccion*.

22. Compare *Éloge* 73–110 with Foulet and Speer 1–28.

23. Foulet, "On Editing Chrétien's *Lancelot*" and "On Grid-Editing"; Uitti and Foulet, "On Editing Chrétien." Foulet had taken part in the Princeton *Roman d'Alexandre* project (ed. Armstrong), editing volumes 3 (1949) and 6 (1976) alone, and coediting volumes 4 (1942) and 7 (1955).

24. Speer, "Wrestling with Change: Old French Textual Criticism and *Mouvance*, " "Textual Criticism Redivivus," "Editing the Formulaic Romance Style: The Poetics of Reception in the *Roman des sept sages*," and "Editing Old French Texts in the Eighties: Theory and Practice."

25. Armstrong et al., eds., *The Medieval French Roman d'Alexandre*. See also Ham, "Textual Criticism and Common Sense," and Dembowski's discussion in this volume.

26. Cerquiglini and others, "L'objet 'ancien français' et les conditions propres à sa description linguistique" (191–92). The authors do not refer directly to the *Lanval* manuscripts, but have consulted Rychner, *Le lai de Lanval* (191). In fact, the purpose of the demonstration is to criticize Rychner for following one of Bédier's editorial conventions, referred to imprecisely as "une certain théorie des parties du discours" (192), and showing modern word divisions rather than reproducing the (somewhat erratic) patterns inscribed in an unspecified manuscript.

27. Enclitics are said to occur in *H* (British Library, Harley 978) and proclitics in *C* (British Library, Cotton Vesp. B XIV) "pratiquement toujours" (192). However, exceptions are not shown. In *H*, all the examples inventoried involve *le* (pronoun and definite article); exceptions constitute an interesting counter-pattern, in that other pronouns (*me, se*) and the negative particle *ne* occur as proclitics: "Asez le mad hume dit" (v. 279), "ne socit" (346), "ne seschaufast" (584), "un sul ke nait iugie" (627). In *C*, some passages are indeterminate: e.g., "De ce ke la out si auilee" (306), "kil lad pleui" (400), "Pur la reïne ke les atent" (470); meanwhile, enclisis is evident elsewhere: "nel auum amene" (233), "nel apele" (443), "veu nes out" (525), "nil nes amout" (526). The sampling reappears in Cerquiglini's *Éloge* (45–46, without reference to "L'objet"); Bloch also refers to it. Fleischman recognizes the original source; Bloch knows only *Éloge*, where "The problem ['of variant versions of identical words'] is brilliantly discussed" ("New" 46 and n32).

28. For example, Fleischman applies to the study of epic texts written in Old French principles based on oral usage in modern English and New Guinean Pidgin storytelling ("Philology" 34–35), using the concept of overlay developed by Grimes in "Outlines and Overlays." Elsewhere, her discussion of *Aucassin et Nicolette* (23, 35–37) assumes that the Picard work manifests an exemplary Old French prose—yet *Aucassin et Nico-*

lette is *sui generis;* it is comically parodic, therefore self-consciously literary, and its highly charged prose is meaningfully constructed to reflect the verse text with which it alternates. See Brownlee, "Discourse as *Prouesces"*; Ménard, "La composition d'*Aucassin et Nicolette"*; Smith, "*Aucassin et Nicolette* as Stylistic Comedy"; and especially Vance, "*Aucassin et Nicolette* as a Medieval Comedy."

29. Homophonous *lai* "signifies that which is left over—not only fluvial deposits and manure, but any excess, including the idea of a testamentary *legs* (see the *Lais* of François Villon). All of which suggests a link between the concept of a vestigial mark and the *Lais* as a written trace of preexisting song" (47–48). Bloch is right to associate *lais*, "trace," with the prosodic term *laisse* and the verb *laissier* (to which he refers, oddly, in the Old Provençal form *lassar*), but *lais*, "trace," and *lai*, "song," are not homophonous: the root-form of "trace" bears articulated /s/ and thus the vowel is always open; "song" has no radical /s/ and the vowel is close. Furthermore, it is unduly confusing to associate *lais*, "trace," as in Villon's title, with modern *legs*, where orthographic g links the word to Latin *lego* and *legatem* via a false etymology that has influenced current pronunciation.

Problems continue: "The notion of the *lais* as a residue or mark connects such a legacy to the legitimation of a place or *locus* (OF *leu*) from which to speak or from which poetry becomes possible. 'La, lai, lay, adv., se dit d'un lieu qu'on désigne d'une manière précise,' specifies Frédéric Godefroy. . ." (48). With respect to the adverb *la/lai*, "there," the palatal element arose from final Latin /k/ (Pope §357), and the resulting diphthong /aj/ is precisely the kind that did not level to /e/ and often persisted well into the Middle French period (Pope §530). In Marie's usage it is the simplified form /la/, not /laj/, that dominates, as is suggested by the rhyme *surjurna : la* (*Milun* vv. 331–32, ed. Rychner), cf. analogous *ça : ja* (*Fresne* vv. 109–10).

30. The *lai* associations recur in articles by Bloch published in two other Nichols projects: "The Medieval Text" and "The Lay and the Law." In the latter, Bloch's "purpose is . . . to link (*lassar*) the notion of *lai* as written residue to the question of the law, and, finally, to show . . . the extent to which a certain medieval (and also peculiarly modern) notion of poetry is implicated in what seems to be an obsession with transgression" (182). The double number of *Stanford French Review* in which this article appears is a special issue coedited by Nichols, Kevin Brownlee, and Marina Scordilis Brownlee.

31. The author of the *Lais* is traditionally identified from the signature of a collection of *Fables* translated from English that is found in the same Harley manuscript as the complete collection of *Lais:* "Marie ai num, si sui de France" (Epilogue 4, ed. Warnke). In the *Lais* the name "Marie" occurs only in the *Guigemar* prologue; in the general Prologue, the only words referring to the narrator are adjectives of intriguingly indeterminate gender: *lie : surquidie* (vv. 53–54; see Rychner's variants, 194), which could be masculine *lié : surquidié* or feminine ("Picard form"). Baum argues against both attributing the *Lais* to the author of the *Fables* and ascribing authorship of the whole collection of *Lais* to the woman who signed *Guigemar.*

32. Attempts to identify Marie with women who were alive in the third quarter of the twelfth century are summarized by Burgess (32–34).

33. David Hult, in "Lancelot's Two Steps," also mentions multi-text editions. But he commends them as a means of conveying to the reader the products, if not the processes, of medieval textual change (852). In "Reading It Right," Hult elaborates: ". . . the special skills of the editor are necessary in order to mediate between the dispersion and frequent inscrutability of manuscript exemplars and the needs of the literary specialist. But instead of hiding or simply reducing the multiplicity of readings, the editor should attempt to make them available so that new approaches, new forms of reading—hopefully more appropriate to the medieval artifact—can be tested" (87–88). Hult values books. Moreover, he sees in what he takes to be "The [ongoing] struggle between Bédierists and Lachmannians, between scribes and authors," a "creative moment" that "both precedes and accompanies the interpretive voice" (88).

34. Uitti discusses his principles and method in "Poetico-Literary Dimensions and the Critical Editing of Medieval Texts."

35. Peter Robinson of Oxford University has developed a computer program called Collate with the potential to provide machine-assisted analyses of manuscript data, entered both manually and by scanning photographic reproductions of manuscripts, and to produce critical editions of texts found in multiple sources along with various apparatus. Practical applications for texts of more than a few lines have yet to be demonstrated. Significantly, Collate is designed to produce a single critically-edited text, not to celebrate *mouvance/variance*; unlike Uitti's project, it is not intended to account for all details of the *mise en page.* Collate was announced and publicized after the present essay had been completed.

36. Wenzel, "Reflections" 11–12. Wenzel's contribution precedes the Romance scholars' articles and thereby establishes a critical perspective for reading—and judging—them. Wenzel does not pretend to understand what might constitute a "New" Philology.

37. Not to be excluded from a broad definition of the field are related areas of knowledge such as Latin language and literature, ancient and medieval, and the histories of music, art, architecture, philosophy, science, the curriculum, and political, social, religious, and educational institutions, that can form the bases for interdisciplinary studies.

38. Quoted by Uitti, "À propos de philologie" 43–44; see also Uitti's "Introduction" in *Trends in Romance Linguistics and Philology*, especially 14–15, and his "Philology: Factualness and History."

39. In another seminal article, "De l'édition princeps de la *Chanson de Roland* aux éditions les plus récentes," Bédier returned to his editorial approach as illustrated in his definitive edition of the Oxford *Roland* (1937). His concern for philological continuity and collegiality is evident throughout. One example will serve to illustrate: "Le maître à qui nous devons des éditions impeccables de l'*Historia septem sapientum*, de *Perceval*, d'*Athis et Prophilias*, Alfons Hilka, avait scruté la tradition manuscrite de trop de textes latins et français pour ne pas s'être convaincu dès longtemps que la critique ne doit jamais viser aussi haut [c'est-à-dire, à mettre en pratique le principe de Léon Gautier: 'Quand on entreprend de publier une chanson de geste, il faut se proposer d'en reconstruire le texte original']" (64:521; "The master to whom we owe impeccable editions of the *Historia septem sapientum*, of *Perceval*, of *Athis and Prophilias*, Alfons Hilka, had scrutinized the manuscript tradition of too many Latin and French texts not to have become convinced long ago that textual criticism must never aim so high [that is, to put in practice the principle of Léon Gautier: 'When one undertakes the edition of a chanson de geste, one must attempt to reconstruct the original text']"). Bédier refers to Hilka's "moderately Lachmannian" edition, *Das altfranzösische Rolandlied*.

IS THERE A NEW TEXTUAL PHILOLOGY IN OLD FRENCH?

PERENNIAL PROBLEMS,

PROVISIONAL SOLUTIONS

Peter F. Dembowski

To the memory of my teacher at Berkeley,
Edward Billings Ham (1902–1965)

At this time of epoch-making changes in the political ideologies of the world, it is only proper that the conference on "The Future of the Middle Ages: Medieval French Literature in the 1990s" asked an important question: How are the economic and political changes taking place in Europe and elsewhere going to affect the study of medieval French literary culture? The question is important from at least two points of view. First, the gradual development of economic unity in Western Europe will make ethnocentric and nationalistic approaches, at least in that region, less and less likely. As medievalists working in French we know that many past academic and scientific debates were, if not caused, at least enhanced by prevailing national feelings. This certainly was true in regard to the subject at hand: from 1870 until the end of the Second World War, French debates concerning Old French texts in general and text editing in particular were deeply influenced by Franco-German national and cultural antipathies. Second, and more important, the dramatic deemphasizing of ideology by Central and Eastern European regimes (both in the elucidation of past events and in the choice of present actions) will doubtless not only renew debates concerning the history of medieval studies, but will probably also affect our discussions of the main problems in medieval studies. It is highly possible and desirable that the epoch-making changes in the application of ideology to political life will diminish reliance on ideological bias or on other forms of deductive imperatives in our doctrine. We are not yet free from such reliance.

The conference held at the Newberry Library in March of 1990 was preceded, in January 1990, by the publication of a special issue of *Speculum* entitled *The New Philology*. Edited by Stephen G. Nichols, this issue addresses itself not so much to the future of the Middle Ages as to the present state of medieval studies. The three *Speculum* essays of interest to our subject preempted, so to speak, the discussion of some of the main points addressed by the conference. And since two of the authors, Nichols and R. Howard Bloch, were also invited to participate in the conference, it will be proper to discuss what I wish to call henceforth textual philology, that is, the complex body of linguistic and literary insights used in the art and science of editing Old Provençal and Old French texts,[1] by addressing myself to certain points raised in the special issue.

The issue opens with a brief note by Luke Wenger, the editor of *Speculum*, who asks "whether medieval studies have become irrelevant," whether "medievalists speak a (conservative) language of their own, addressing antiquarian concerns of interest to no one but themselves," whether "there is . . . a breach between medievalists and their colleagues in other fields of the humanities," whether "it [this breach] is the creation of the modernists, cultivating theoretical elaborations and ignoring history." Wenger believes that "impertinent questions of this kind are sometimes worth asking." I too believe in asking questions, impertinent or not, but I am afraid that from the point of view of Old Provençal and Old French textual philology, these questions have not received pertinent answers.[2] They serve rather as deductive imperatives for a general critique of philology.

It is regrettable that Nichols, in a debate whose theoretical background is French, did not seek the collaboration of persons actually involved in Old French or Old Provençal textual philology, particularly so because that philology has its own particular history. The textual philology applied to Latin, Germanic, Italian, and Spanish medieval texts has remained relatively free from both *querelles bédieristes* and (stemming from them) *boutades foucauldiennes*, which, as we shall see, animate much of what Nichols and his collaborators have to say about textual philology.[3] It is certainly good and profitable to raise embarrassing questions (and, if one wishes, in the language of Michel Foucault, to "inquiéter tous les positivismes"), but it would be more in keeping with old-fashioned Anglo-Saxon tradition to present both sides of the eternal debate between the "old" and the "new."[4]

In his leading article, "Introduction: Philology in a Manuscript Culture," Nichols sees a crisis in philology, but talks about it in terms not of something new, but rather of something that goes back to the disputes which took place, as he says, in the second half of the nineteenth century. (Actually the Bédierist arguments lasted well into the 1930s.) At the outset of his article, he cites with approval the concluding observation from Bernard Cerquiglini's recent monograph: "Or l'écriture médiévale ne produit pas de variantes, elle est variance. La récriture incessante à laquelle est soumise la textualité médiévale, l'appropriation joyeuse dont elle est l'objet, nous invitent à faire une hypothèse forte: la variance n'est jamais ponctuelle" (Nichols 1, citing Cerquiglini, *Éloge* 111; "Medieval writing does not produce variants, it is itself variance. The ceaseless re-writing to which medieval textuality is subjugated, its joyful appropriation by variance, invite us to propose a bold hypothesis: variance is never punctual [limited to a point]"). It is clear that Nichols's views on philology and on "manuscript culture" are largely informed by Cerquiglini's work. Nichols transplants a statement from a larger French *querelle*—which, I suspect, has more to do with defending the validity of Foucauldian assertions and methods than with philology or its history[5]—into the North American continent without bothering to survey the terrain around him. For whatever "philology" signified to Erich Auerbach, René Wellek, or Leo Spitzer, and whatever it signifies to the authors in this special number of *Speculum*, the term must include textual philology in all its theoretical and practical aspects.

Nowhere in his article does Nichols mention any actual textual editions published in the last twenty years either by European editors or by those working on this continent. He does not ask himself the question about his own field: What is the actual state of the theory of the Old Provençal and Old French textual philology on this continent? Rather, he depends heavily on the guidance of Cerquiglini, with whom he seems to share the sense of drama and the accompanying anxiety over the eternal struggle between the old and the new.[6]

The difficulty in reading Nichols—and in reading Cerquiglini— lies chiefly in his broad generalizations on the one hand and the lack of precision on the other. There is a strong Manichean dichotomy in Nichols's reasoning: "Medievalists are frequently viewed by modernist colleagues as hostile or indifferent to contemporary theory. In such strictures, philology often figures both in the attack and on the defense: the modernists oppose theory to philology; the medievalists cite philology as a sufficiency that either precludes the need for theory or renders modern theories anachronistic in a medieval context" ("Introduction" 1–2). Nowhere does he attempt to define what "modernist," "medievalist," "contemporary theory," "modern theories," and, above all, "philology" mean in his essay. He does not cite any works of contemporary scholars which could illustrate his dichotomies of medievalist versus modernist, theory versus philology, old philology versus new philology.[7]

Suzanne Fleischman's essay, "Philology, Linguistics, and the Discourse of the Medieval Text," also fails to survey the field of textual philology. It opens with a repetition of Nichols's alarmist position: "Philology . . . has come to be equated in the minds of many with desiccated and dogmatic textual praxis" (19). She believes that "the 'crisis of philology' . . . is still very much at hand" (19), and concludes "that we might ultimately reformulate philology's role in the field of medieval studies, adapting its praxis to the challenges of postmodernism" (37). But aside from the prefatory and concluding claims of agreement with Nichols, her article treats problems which have little to do with his preoccupations.

Fleischman wishes to revitalize philology through linguistics with its emphasis on the spoken idiom. She is right in regard to textual philology. A bad linguist, or at least a bad language specialist, will always be a bad editor. But the badness of bad editors working in the present time is not necessarily due to their perpetuation of nineteenth-century errors; more probably they are bad editors because they are uninformed and/or careless scholars.[8]

Fleischman cites Cerquiglini's thesis about variants and agrees with him that "medieval literary aesthetics . . . until the end of the thirteenth century was founded on an 'écriture de variance,' which the prevailing methodology of textual criticism has served to camouflage" (25). I think that if she had examined not so much the theoretical disquisition of Cerquiglini, but rather the actual practice of modern editors, she would have found that many good practical textual critics working in the field of Old Provençal and Old French know all about *mouvance,* and they do not want to camouflage it, just as they do not wish to camouflage other difficult problems in editorial practice.

Fleischman's essay, which in the main deals in a perfectly acceptable way with the syntactical questions of Old French literary language, and above all with the problem of verbal narrative tenses (which is the subject of her recent study), is marred by the use of Cerquiglini's highly inflated language of the *querelle,* in which he associates Gaston Paris (1839–1903) with the "dinosaurs of science" and caricatures the typical practitioner of philology as "Monsieur Procuste, philologue." Such tactics of exaggeration and divisiveness (perhaps explainable in Cerquiglini's *querelle*-centered language) are counterproductive to understanding the present state of medieval studies in this country or to affecting their future for the better. The points that Fleischman makes about "orality" and "discourse" in Old French are well taken. They do not require the rhetoric of "us" versus "them," of "modern linguists" versus "Gaston Paris and the dinosaurs," of "new" versus "old."

This rhetoric is attacked by R. Howard Bloch. In his "New Philology and Old French" he explicitly disagrees with the very basis of the "old" versus "new" rhetoric used by Nichols and Fleischman.[9] Bloch does not denigrate any "dinosaurs" working in the field of textual criticism. His essay, however, touches upon the problems encountered by a modern editor. "New Philology," as used by him, refers to developments which have occurred since the late 1950s. He dates the "New Philology" to "a certain unsettling rethinking of medieval literature" (38), and more specifically to the appearance in 1949 of Robert Guiette's short essay "D'une poésie formelle en France au moyen âge," and, in 1963, that of Paul Zumthor's *Langue et techniques poétiques à l'époque romane.* Whether such an exact periodization can ultimately be justified is an open question. I agree, nevertheless, with Bloch, *grosso modo,* on the gist of his sketch of the history of attitudes towards the Middle Ages and medieval studies.

But later in his essay, Bloch enters more directly the domain of textual philology. While discussing the difficulties in the manuscript of the *Serments de Strasbourg,* he rightly warns his readers against facile and overconfident interpretation of the graphic details of this difficult text. But he overstates his case:

> Put in the simplest terms, the closer one reads the medieval text, the less it is possible to maintain the positivist position of literary transparency, which would make the establishment of the meaning of a poetic work, or even of a particular passage, merely a question of "figuring out" what the letters on the page or parchment, to invoke Gaston Paris's phrase once again, "fully and clearly say." For there is nothing in the Old French text, as the positivist holds, that guarantees the coincidence of meaning with intention, nothing that suggests that the Old French language, with its plethora of divergent spellings for the same word and the homonyms for different words, is not every bit as deceptive to the eye and to the ear as the works of Mallarmé or Proust are assumed to be—nothing, in short, that leads to the conclusion that the language of medieval poets keeps its promise to mean what it says, to be true. On the contrary, the more we try

to read it literally—or at the level of the letter—the more we become convinced of the very impenetrability, of the impossibility of reducing its pregnant plays of the letter to univocal meaning, or for that matter, of the impossibility of ever exhausting the semantic resonances of certain key syllables and words. (46–47)

I am not sure who this "positivist" is. Who is this Other who still believes in univocal meaning?[10] Furthermore, in this paragraph Bloch raises at least four different but interconnected issues, all of which touch upon Old Provençal and Old French textual philology.

First, the problem of the *truth* of any literary text is often, we know, imponderable. Without entering into any complex epistemological arguments, let me be simply pragmatic. I believe that in philology (as in any other significant human activity) it is important to act as if truth were (sometimes) reachable. To put it in a negative way, I believe that to abandon the criterion of truth—because it is often difficult to ascertain—is always harmful to any textual-philological and literary-critical enterprise. Without believing that truth is to be strived for, the critic becomes either ideological (substituting ideology for truth), cynical, or simply ludic.

Second, any good reader of Old French literature knows that the interpretation of, for example, *Érec et Énide*, can and should be as difficult to perform as an interpretation of Mallarmé or Proust. Our conclusions about the meaning(s) of many passages are and will always be provisional. The difference between the interpretation of Old French and Modern French lies in a more technical domain. The latter, with its imposed unified spelling (one sees that *pays* has two syllables and *paix* one) and its appeal to modern *bon usage* (one knows that *-ie* in *prier* normally represents a hiatus, and *-ie* in *Bédier* a diphthong), offers far fewer possibilities of varied readings than the former. The difference here is in degree but not in kind.

Third, both Old French and Modern French are languages, that is, systems, in which certain things are fixed. There is no need to protest against the "positivist position of literary transparency" (whatever it is at the present time). Had Bloch been more involved with textual philology, the work which forces one to manage (but not to ignore) the *mouvance*, his point about infinite divergency of meaning (like Cerquiglini's infinite divergency of variants) would have been better put. He would have known that certain things are truly (orally) contrastive and that an editor is, in certain readings at least, guided by the concrete testimony of the old text. As Rupert Pickens demonstrates in this volume, Bloch's treatment of what he calls "homophony" is simply and demonstrably wrong. Bloch should have followed Fleischman's advice to become more oral, that is, more linguistic.

My fourth point stems from the third. Even if we cannot discern what a given word or group of words means, we can very often state with reasonable certainty what they cannot mean: in philology, truth is often elusive but error is frequently obvious.[11] Bloch's disregard of discernible and demonstrable linguistic principles does not really invalidate his main thesis about the important problem of polysemy,[12] but it weakens the bearing of this thesis. The points that Bloch makes about the meaning of Old French texts, here and in other studies such as his essay on *Guigemar*, would have been more persuasive if they conformed to verifiable linguistic elements. Many spellings, as well as rhyme and metre, can and in fact should be used by good editors in arriving at the meaning of the text. There is no need to be haunted by the spectre of positivism and to brand such editors as positivists. There is no need to insist that nothing can be semantically ascertained in the medieval text.

But if, indeed, there is nothing ascertainable ("true," at least provisionally) in Old French or Old Provençal texts, then any work of an editor would be *ipso facto* positivistic, that is, "absurd and rigidly superannuated." Such, happily, is not the case.

I believe that the spirit which animates the three *Speculum* articles does not help us to grasp the situation in textual philology. While holding contradictory views on essential matters concerning medieval language and medieval writings, the three authors seem to accept as binding Cerquiglini's consideration of philology as not only a simplistic but also an outmoded tool of research.

PETER F. DEMBOWSKI

How does such a view compare with the actual situation of textual philology? Speaking here chiefly about the activities of North American colleagues, I agree with Siegfried Wenzel in believing that textual philology is alive and well. Without going into ancient history, one may say that the last twenty years have seen many thoughtful and often very successful editions or reeditions published by scholars working on this continent. This activity continues: thus, just to mention the projects which immediately come to my mind: Larry Crist and Robert Cook have just completed *Baudoin de Sebourc* for the Société des Anciens Textes Français; Cook is preparing the *Roland* in manuscript V^4 and *La chanson d'Antioche*; Crist, *Hugues Capet*; Nigel Thorp, *La chanson de Jerusalem*; Emanuel Mickel, *Les enfances Godefroi*; Jan Roberts, *Godefroi de Bouillon*; Peter Grillo, *The Jerusalem Continuations*; Keith Busby, Chrétien's *Perceval*; Rupert Pickens, *Perceval* (following different editorial principles); William Paden, *Les vers de la mort* of Hélinand de Froidmont. James Wimsatt and William Kibler have recently published Machaut's *Le jugement du roi de Behaigne* together with his *Remede de Fortune,* and Carleton Carroll, Chrétien's *Érec et Énide.* Karl Uitti, having published (with Alfred Foulet) *Lancelot* in the Classiques Garnier, is preparing *Yvain,* and I myself, having completed a new edition of *Jourdain de Blaye* for the Classiques Français du Moyen Âge, am working on *Érec et Énide* as well as *L'estrif de Fortune et Vertu* by Martin Le Franc.

Neither have the more theoretical aspects of textual philology been neglected on this continent. While reading Cerquiglini's essay one may erroneously conclude that nothing has really happened in the discussion of the theory and practice of textual philology since 1940. It is simply not true that the struggle between the incorrigible Lachmannians and the radical Bédierists still occupies the central stage of textual philology, nor is it true that a strict adherence to the Bédierist position dominates the whole field of this activity. I have tried to outline the main points of Bédier's theory and practice in editing Old French texts in my article "The 'French' Tradition of Textual Philology and Its Relevance to the Editing of Medieval Texts." It is important to note that his views were not universally accepted.

Thus, more than thirty years ago, Edward B. Ham (sse p. 185) published an essay under the revealing title "Textual Criticism and Common Sense." The paper was ostensibly directed to the "graduate student looking for a dissertation in the editorial field" (198), but the theoretical implications of this "anti-theoretical" and fundamentally eclectic statement are still valid for all editorial ventures. The "common sense" in Ham's approach stems not only from his own mental make-up and experience in textual philology,[13] but also from his mistrust of theories, especially if they precede practice. At the outset of his paper he wrote that he wished "to counteract some of the needless complications which textual theorists have been multiplying in recent decades" (198–99). Like his much admired predecessor, A. E. Housman, Ham does so not with cries of despair and deprecation of past masters, but rather with gentle humor, securely based on the knowledge that a reasonably good edition is possible.

What I believe is the most important of Ham's contributions is his clear view that every editorial enterprise is *sui generis*. Thus, rather than espouse this or that editorial doctrine and follow its supposedly logical development in the establishment of manuscript relations, the editor should simply start by carefully transcribing and collating the manuscripts and thus learning the practical facts. In the presentation of manuscript relations, he should follow good practical models rather than any theoretically slanted "universalizing doctrine."[14] For Ham, each case has a good model:

> Old French offers excellent models to match the particular situation created for any poem which he [the student editor] is likely to have selected. For instance, Bédier's *Roland* for brilliant "best manuscript" conservatism; Roach's *Perceval*-continuations for problems posed by a multiplicity of manuscript traditions; Emmanuel Walberg's bestiary (Philippe de Thaün) for the three-manuscript poem; Henry's *Adenet* for the use of "controller" manuscripts; Mrs. Grace Frank's *Passion d'Autun* for the two-

manuscript situation where the versions are poor and dissimilar . . . ; the *Aucassin* editions by Suchier and Roques, where only one manuscript has survived; and so on. (200)

This advice is still valid in principle. I would replace Bédier's *Roland* with volume 1 of Cesare Segre's edition of *La chanson de Roland*,[15] and I would also propose good models for certain prose texts (the edition of which Ham did not discuss), such as Roach's *Didot Perceval*, but I would above all stress the practical and eclectic approach advocated here by Ham. We are very far from the nightmarish "Monsieur Procuste, philologue" and his accompanying dinosaurs.[16]

The same spirit of simple tolerance and respectful understanding of past errors and past achievements[17] informs another work, the most important theoretical and practical statement on Old French textual philology to date: Alfred Foulet (see p. 186) and Mary B. Speer's *On Editing Old French Texts*. The work opens with a succinct chapter offering "A Historical Orientation." It is divided into four chief sections, the titles of which reflect the authors' concept of the history of our enterprise in the last one hundred and fifty years: "The Empirical Period," "The Scientific Period," "Crisis of Confidence," and "Towards a New Consensus?" The scientific period corresponds *grosso modo* to the reign of "Lachmannism," the crisis of confidence to the period of the "Bédierist" debates.

The bulk of *On Editing* is a practical manual. It develops and systematizes the strictly practical but terse (and sometimes confusing) "Établissement de règles pratiques pour l'édition des anciens textes français et provençaux" presented to the Société des Anciens Textes Français by Mario Roques in 1925. It would be fair to say that this American manual reflects an optimistic, tolerant and profoundly commonsensical view of the hoped-for "new consensus." It advocates, if not explicitly at least implicitly, the eclecticism advocated by Ham. The authors illustrate the variety of possible approaches to editorial practice by citing various editions published since 1950 (35–38). Their conclusions stress the inappropriateness and impossibility of a "purely mechanical system of editing" (38). They insist that "the editor's informed judgment or subjectivity must play a crucial role in each stage of the editing process" (38). They underscore the duty of the editor to choose the proper method and "to inform the reader as fully as possible about his attitude and justify any debatable decision he may make" (39). One can disagree with this or other advice given by Foulet and Speer; one can disagree with any one of their numerous practical prescriptions;[18] but it seems to me unthinkable to speak about a crisis in the study of philology and manuscript culture without mentioning this work.[19]

On Editing addresses itself chiefly to the practice of textual philology. The term "practice" is essential. Anybody has the right and duty to criticize the products of editorial philology, but I agree with the editor of the special issue of *L'esprit créateur*, Karl Uitti, when he states: "The experience of editing a text, or texts, lies in the core of whatever may be affirmed or denied in respect to the 'theory' of textual criticism; and this experience is founded on one's appreciation of the pertinent issues—the reality—raised by the text" (*Poetics* 7). In other words, a given text conditions basic editorial decisions.

Let me close my remarks with a few practical points culled from my own experience. In editorial practice (as in literature itself) it is not always possible—or even desirable—to maintain logical consistency. This point has not been sufficiently stressed in the old *querelles,* or, paradoxically, in the essay of Cerquiglini, who, to my mind at least, seems unable to conceive of practical and eclectic solutions to the real problems raised by Bédier. Thus he presents not a solid argument, but "une hypothèse forte," a *boutade.*

It is perhaps "joyeux" to proclaim that "l'écriture . . . est variance," but experience shows us that many texts in Old French, even those copied before 1300, simply cannot be classified in the category of essential *mouvance.* Thus my own experience with the *Vie de sainte Marie l'Égyptienne* in its five versions, *T* (six manuscripts), *X* (seven manuscripts), *O* (eight manuscripts), *Z* (three manuscripts), and *U* (five manuscripts), most of them copied in the thirteenth century, convinced me that it is possible to produce a text (if not *the* text) of each version, based on the "best" or "least bad" manuscript containing it, with a listing of variants which enables a careful reader to realize what is going on in other manuscripts, that is to say, to control the anxiety of *mouvance.*

In editing various versions of the *Égyptienne* I observed the best-manuscript principle, but the choice of this manuscript had little to do with a more logically consistent search for the original. What usually entered into consideration was not so much the desire to establish a genealogical stemma of manuscripts—although certain relations between manuscripts become immediately obvious—but rather to select the most complete and most coherent text from among the relatively older manuscripts. This solution is not an ideal one, but, as we should realize better now, ideal solutions are to be found mostly in the heads of ideologists. It is neither, I hope, mechanistically positivist nor capriciously subjective. And it has been explained to the reader.

I can very well imagine that there are situations where it is practically impossible to report the *mouvance* so fully as to contain it. There are situations in which recording of variants would be too onerous, and consequently impractical for the reader. In such a case a synoptic edition might be the only solution. An excellent example of such an edition is Rupert Pickens's *The Songs of Jaufré Rudel,* in which he reproduces seven poems, each in several (from five to twelve) variant versions. But, of course, longer works lend themselves less to such a treatment. We must consider the purely economic factors while contemplating such editorial ventures. It would be very difficult to publish now a synoptic edition of a *chanson de geste* of some 5200 verses in which four versions were printed in four parallel columns, with a prose version at the bottom of the page. But even in such an edition not all is *écriture de variance;* not all the manuscripts present a *mouvance* justifying a separate text.[20]

In the concluding paragraphs of his work (*Éloge* 115–16), Cerquiglini suggests that the computer will resolve the problem of the unsteady text(s). The computer revolution is certainly with us, although, as Pickens points out in this volume, it is still too early to assess its whole impact on textual philology. But the shifting texts subject to *mouvance* are not the only problem for a modern editor. Many important texts are preserved in a single manuscript. Here, without any actual *mouvance*, the editor is confronted with a *mouvance* which is virtual, that is, with scribal errors. After a hiatus of some twenty years, I have corrected more errors in the second edition of the single-manuscript text of *Jourdain de Blaye* than in the first. The reasons for the corrections are practically the same as the reasons for rejecting the readings of the "best" manuscript in the multi-manuscript situation. In a one-manuscript edition correcting is in a way more difficult to carry out, because the editor lacks the comfort of sharing with other manuscript(s) the responsibility for emendations.

The manuscript of *Jourdain* was apparently copied by a careful scribe who understood what he was copying. In verse 3140, however, he made an obvious error, as I realized in my second edition: "Et maronniers qui la mer ont guïee" ("And the seamen who have guided the sea"). In the first edition I let this reading stand, hoping for a future positivist solution—that is, I hoped that someday, someone would find a confirming reading of *guïer la mer* in the meaning "to serve as pilots." No such meaning has come to my attention in the last twenty years. I therefore adopted the correction suggested by a reviewer of Hofmann's edition: "qui la nef ont guïee." I now believe that *la mer* is a mechanical scribal error made by anticipating *En mer* in the following line.

In verses 1183–84 the manuscript offers another typical problem:

> Reniers garda parmi mer et par l'aigue,
> Si a veü douz estoires en l'aigue.

> [Renier scanned the sea and the water
> And saw two ships on the water.]

In the first edition, mindful of the dangers of intervention, I retained the reading of the manuscript, like my predecessor.[21] Later, I realized that *rimes du même au même*, that is to say, both homophonic and synonymic rhymes, are rare in our *chanson*. This literary judgment, rather than any positivist desire to restore the original or the "true" reading of the text, convinced me to emend verse 1183 to:

Reniers garda par mer et par palaigre.

[Renier scanned the sea and high sea.]

It is fair to say that my anti-interventionist attitude (which I maintain to this day, since we must respect the texts as much as possible; they are archeological monuments, so to speak, of the collaboration between the poet and the scribe) was somewhat mollified here by the fact that verse 1122 reads:

Najant s'en vont par mer et par palaigre.

[They navigate on the sea and the high sea.]

But some readings are evidently impossible to correct with any degree of objectivity, that is, shareable agreement:

Jordain noz ont diable ramené
Cui je cuidai avoir le chief copé,
Mais or le ront diable si siré. (vv. 3813–15)

[The devils have brought us Jourdain
Whose head I thought I had cut off,
But now the devils have again so *siré*.]

This *si siré:* (1) does not make sense, (2) does not correspond to any *si siré* elsewhere in the manuscript, (3) does not seem to stand for *si tiré, si viré, si finé* (all suggested by Hofmann), (4) might be an error for *suscité* (suggested by Hofmann's critic). But this reading cannot be accepted on broader cultural-semantic grounds: all the known (positivism again!) medieval uses of the verb *(res)susciter* ultimately refer to divine action. Can devils do it? Here the editor of a single manuscript is in a real quandary. He must simply inform his readers about this quandary.

Even these humble but real examples taken from a one-manuscript edition show that the problems of medieval textual philology lie not so much in choosing one or another absolute position. It is practically impossible and theoretically wrong, I believe, to declare oneself an interventionist or a non-interventionist and proceed logically from one of these positions.

Each situation requires a new decision. Practice makes each new situation a little less new, but the principle still stands that the editor's informed judgment must be applied non-mechanically to each textual difficulty.

Let us turn to an important multi-manuscript editorial situation, in which it is possible to indicate the extent of the *mouvance* with a listing of variants. I have in mind the *Érec et Énide* of Chrétien de Troyes. (Some of what follows here draws upon my "De nouveau: *Érec et Énide*, Chrétien et Guiot.") Serious editorial problems in this work lie not so much in the listing of abundant variants, but in establishing a good text. It is preserved in seven manuscripts: *B, C, Ch, E, H, P* and *V* (and four fragments). Two of the manuscripts are particularly important for our purpose here: *C*, the Guiot manuscript (Paris, Bibliothèque nationale fr. 794), and *H* (Paris, Bibliothèque nationale fr. 1450).[22] They are both collective, that is, they contain other romances by Chrétien. Foerster used *H* as the base of his edition. He corrected the text freely and supplied many variant readings from the other manuscripts. Roques chose *C*, followed it as closely as possible, supplied a short list of rejected readings in *C*, and offered some variants from *H*. As is well known, Roques's edition of *Érec et Énide* is probably a better illustration of both the strength and the weakness of Bédier's principles than is Bédier's own *Roland*.[23] I do not wish to repeat here what the late Alfred Foulet said in his "On Grid-Editing Chrétien de Troyes."[24] Briefly, while advocating a position of "controlled interventionism," he champions the use of *C* as the base, but with greater attention given to the poet Chrétien than to the scribe Guiot. The first, whatever stands behind this name,[25] was a very capable craftsman and very gifted narrator. The second was evidently a good copyist, but he sometimes did not understand certain principles of versification which a good poet would understand.

We are here at the heart of what I consider to be the modern problem of interventionism. No one wishes to publish a composite edition, to emend the text with the aim of reconstructing an unobtainable original. What is desired is not the *Urtext*, but a good text. The editor, fully conscious of all the implications of the theoretical disputes concerning textual philology, should strive to produce a text based on a "good" (or a "least bad") manuscript (in this case Guiot), and emend it with the help, if possible, of a *varia lectio*. Editorial interventions should take place when the base manuscript does not make sense, or makes less sense than the other manuscript(s), or when it violates the rules of versification which a good poet would have followed. There is nothing absolute about these principles. They are, I hope, neither positivistic nor capricious. They are based broadly on literary criticism. The critical-esthetic assumption underlying them is that Chrétien's texts are composed by a good poet, that is to say, by a careful narrator and a good versifier.

Four examples of such emendations should suffice here. Like practically everything else in Chrétien, they have been studied before; see, for example, the textual investigations of T. B. W. Reid, or the recent edition of *Érec et Énide* by Carroll. In the first example, Roques maintains the rhyme *du même au même:*

> l'eve lor done en deus bacins;
> tables, et napes, et bacins . . . (vv. 495–96)

> [he gave them water in two basins;
> tables and tablecloths and basins . . .]

He attempts to justify it in a note by suggesting that this rhyme "pourrait s'expliquer par la légère différence entre les 'bassins' à laver et les 'bassins,' plats creux pour le service de la table . . ." (215). Other manuscripts offer a clearer reading from the narrative point of view, a reading which does not repeat the same word in the rhyme and which I have adopted:

> l'eve lor done en deus bacins;
> tables et napes, pains et vins . . .

> [he gave them water in two basins;
> tables and tablecloths, bread and wine . . .]

A common occurrence of *mouvance* in the manuscripts of *Érec et Énide* consists of rhymed couplets which are missing in *C.* Thus we read in Roques:

> . . . dui vaslet
> qui portoient et pain et vin
> et cinc fromages de gaïn. (vv. 3120–22)

> [. . . two servant boys
> who were carrying bread and wine
> and five fat cheeses.]

Guiot does not give the reader any idea why the servants are there or for whom they carry bread, wine and fat cheeses (*de gaïn*). All six other manuscripts add two more lines (virtually identical) which explain realistically that the food was destined for the hay-makers working for a local count (I cite manuscript *H*):

> As prez le conte Caloain
> a ceus qui fauchoient son fain.

> [to the meadows of Count Galoin,
> for those who were mowing his hay.]

In addition to explaining the reason for mentioning the food, other manuscripts give us the name of the count. Caloain (*H*) or Galoain (other manuscripts) is going to play an important role in the story, but his name is never mentioned by Guiot.[26] Roques (232) objects to the additional couplet on the grounds that it would give four identical rhymes. He is wrong, since in *Érec et Énide* forms in -*in* rhyme only with others in -*in*, and forms in -*ain* rhyme only with others in -*ain*. The word *gaïn* (which should perhaps be spelled exceptionally *gäin*) represents the -*in* rhyme. Furthermore, the sense of the episode (food, for whom?) and the coherence of the whole story (who is this wooer of Énide?) require that the base manuscript be emended here by the addition of the missing couplet. By not adding it Roques sacrificed a clear sense and coherence in this romance on the altar of theoretical consistency.

We see a similar, but less obvious case next. Our hero begins a new adventure:

> Érec s'an vet toz esleissiez
> une voie antre deus pleissiez.
> Au desbuschier d'un pleisseïz

troverent un pont torneïz . . . (vv. 3653–56)

[Érec rides full speed
along a path between two hedges
At the end of the enclosed part of the wood
they found a drawbridge . . .]

The narration is not smooth. We do not know whether Énide is present at the drawbridge. He leaves the enclosed forest (*pleisseïz*) too abruptly. We are not prepared for the sudden appearance of the drawbridge. And we are certainly not ready for the plural form of the verb (*troverent*). Neither *C, H,* nor *E* contains the additional verses which are preserved in four other manuscripts. There, right after *pleissiez* (verse 3654), we read in *B, Ch, P,* and *V:*

Il et sa fame devant lui.
A esperon an vont andui.
Tant ont erré et chevauchié
Qu'il vindrent an un pré fauchié.

[He and his wife in front of him,
They both ride spurring.
They traveled and rode so much
that they came to a mowed meadow.]

These four verses could represent either an original reading, that is to say, a lacuna common to *C, H,* and *E,* or an addition common to four other manuscripts. We shall probably never be able to prove either of these possibilities.[27] The agreement of *C, H,* and of *E* (which belongs to a different family than *C* and *H*) speaks in favor of a common interpolation. But these lines, which offer more narrative details and a better syntax (plural verb), could, perhaps, be included in the text of *C.* Most importantly, however, the addition or non-addition of these lines must be clearly acknowledged in the critical apparatus. No camouflage!

My final example concerns the closing of the romance. Unlike the preceding example, there is no syntactical indication here that the missing lines should be restored. But there is an abrupt change of tone. *Érec et Énide* ends with an apotheosis, with the crowning

of the now-reconciled couple. We are at the feast, and the tone is
both solemn and joyful:

> Des mes divers don sont servi,
> ne por quant se ge nel vos di,
> vos savroie bien reison randre;
> mes il m'estuet a el antendre. (vv. 6875–78)

> [Of the various dishes which were served,
> if, however, I do not tell you
> I would be able to give you an account,
> but I must attend to something else.]

The last line of *C* and of Roques's edition makes the closing of the
romance abrupt, jarring and whimsical; this "but I must attend to
something else" reads as if the poet has suddenly lost interest in
his story. Furthermore, the *mouvance* here is not simply confined
to the base manuscript. As in the previous case, the editor faces
either a common error or a common addition. The restoration of
the sixteen lines omitted by *C* and *B*—but preserved by three
manuscripts, *H*, *E*, and *P*, belonging to two different groups (while
Ch and *V* offer shorter and different epilogues)—is necessary to
the solemn tone of the ending of the romance. Roques printed
them (according to *H*) in the notes as an important variant. The
editor who is mindful of the general literary nature of the whole
poem, who is appreciative of the esthetic of the text, should add
the following (edited) lines that close the solemn occasion in a fit-
tingly solemn manner:

> que a raconter le mangier:
> asséz en orent sans dangier,
> a grant joie et a grant plenté
> servi furent a volenté.
>   Quant cele feste fu finee,
> li rois departi l'assamblee
> des rois et des dus et des contes,
> dont asséz estoit granz li contes,
> des autres genz et des menues
> qui a la feste sont venues.

PETER F. DEMBOWSKI

Mout lor ot doné largemant
chevax et armes et argent,
dras et pailes de mainte guise,
por ce qu'il iert de grant franchise
et por Érec qu'il ama tant.
Li contes fine ci atant.[28]

[besides telling you about the food:
they had plenty without fail,
with great joy and great abundance
they were served as much as they wished.
When the feast came to an end,
the king dismissed the gathering
of kings, dukes, and counts,
whose number was very large,
and of other people and lesser ones
who came to the feast.
Generously he had given them
horses and arms and money,
clothes and various silks,
because he was of great generosity
and because of Érec whom he loved so much.
The story ends here.]

Does the above discussion of some theoretical issues and practical examples furnish a proof that there exists a new textual philology? The answer depends on what is meant by this adjective. If
"new" means, as the discussions in the special issue of *Speculum*
seem to indicate, something "good," that is to say "progressive,"
and capable of "adapting its praxis to the challenges of postmodernism"—as opposed to something "old," that is to say "bad,"
"desiccated," "dogmatic-positivistic," etc.—then the answer is
no. But if by "new" we mean recurring, actual practice, which is
always a mixture of past experiences and present improvements,
then the answer is yes. There is a new textual philology which
consists of renewed efforts to understand and to improve upon the
practice of our predecessors. Such textual philology is always old

because it addresses itself to perennial problems of making a book out of a manuscript or manuscripts. But it is also always new because it searches for solutions which are at least provisional, if not true.[29]

NOTES

1. This term is perhaps preferable to the more commonly accepted "textual criticism" simply because "textual philology" implies also its application to those editions which are not *sensu stricto* "critical."

2. Wenger's questions were answered in the affirmative in the same issue by Spiegel and Patterson. Though they are critical of the marginalization of medieval studies, they address themselves to neither "new" nor "old" philology in the stricter sense of this term.

3. The only contributor who is an experienced editor, Siegfried Wenzel, simply and firmly disagrees with Nichols's basic assumptions. Wenzel's article is most sensible and should be read by all who wish to know about textual criticism. But, precisely, Wenzel does not deal with Old French. He edits Latin and Middle English texts. He concludes that "whether old or new, it would seem that philology is very much alive and has a surprising amount of blood in it" ("Reflections" 18).

4. As is always the case, there are, of course, more than two sides in this debate.

5. *Éloge* was published in a series organized by Foucault and opens with the following dedication: "Michel Foucault a souhaité ce livre, qui est dédié à sa mémoire" ("Michel Foucault wished for this book, which is dedicated to his memory"; 13).

6. I am sure that Nichols's conviction that "medieval philology has been marginalized by contemporary cognitive methodologies, on the one side, while within the discipline itself, a very limited and by now grossly anachronistic conception of it remains far too current" ("Introduction" 1) would have been attenuated if he were a practicing textual critic. His experience with the nitty-gritty of textual philology is limited. He published (with the assistance of five other persons) *The Songs of Bernart de Ventadorn*, 1962. This edition reproduces the text established by Appel (1915) and supplies an English translation and notes.

7. Such dichotomizations can be useful for the rhetorics of a *querelle*, but they have little connection with the reality of the academic situation. Without even talking about such towering figures in both philology and theory as Cesare Segre and Paul Zumthor, it is not difficult to cite con-

PETER F. DEMBOWSKI

temporary American medievalists who work in Old French and who are not inimical to (various) modern theoretical insights. Suffice it to cite here Peter Haidu, Donald Maddox, Eugene Vance, and Evelyn Vitz, among others.

8. Elsewhere, Fleischman's needless polemic gets the better of her. She dismisses Kibler's *Introduction to Old French* and Ménard's *Syntaxe de l'ancien français* as works of "grammarians or early language 'specialists,' not linguists . . . largely unreflective of developments in linguistic theory and methodology" ("Philology" 27–28). It is far easier to dismiss these certainly useful pedagogical tools than to write a better one.

9. "Use of the labels 'new' and 'old,' applied to the dialectical development of a discipline, is a gesture sufficiently charged ideologically as to have little meaning in absolute terms—before and after, bad and good—that it affixes. On the contrary, to the extent that calling oneself 'new' is a value-laden gesture which implies that something else is 'old' and therefore less worthy, it constitutes a rhetorical strategy of autolegitimation—with little recognition, of course, that the process itself of declaring oneself 'new' is indeed very old" (Bloch, "New" 38). Even stronger disagreement with Nichols is confined to the footnote on the same page: "Please note that I do not consider myself a 'New Philologist,' or a 'new' anything, except perhaps a new man; and since part of a new man implies a certain obligatory return of the subject, and since the phrase 'New Philology' bothers me, I therefore place it in quotation marks." But somehow these quotation marks have been removed from the title of Bloch's essay. Modern *mouvance* camouflaged!

10. Even the much maligned Gaston Paris was fully aware of the enormous difficulties of semantic opacity and of the literary consequences of that opacity. In his review of Foerster's edition of *Érec et Énide* he glossed the famous outcry of Énide directed at her husband, "Tant mar i fus!" as follows: "Locution intraduisible, qui signifie à peu près: 'Quelle triste destinée que la tienne!' " (159)—an untranslatable saying. which means approximately: "How sad is your destiny!" His interpretation is certainly not that of an absurdly rigid positivist. It is not even overly pedantic, for it actually approximates a variant of the manuscript *B* (*mouvance!*), which Foerster prints here as "Con mar i fus!" (v. 2507).

11. Ever since Henry D. Learned's short article, "The Eulalia MS. at Line 15 Reads *aduret*, not *adunet*" (1941), the reading *Ell' ent adunet lo suon element* has been simply erroneous. Ever since this purely paleographical demonstration, all attempts to interpret *adunet*, e.g., "Elle concentre donc toute son énergie," have been simply wrong. (See pp. 188–89.)

12. Just so, Cerquiglini's ill-chosen insistence on the *absolute* character of variance does not invalidate his general concern with the problem of *mouvance* and with illegitimate attempts to camouflage its existence. For a serious critique of Cerquiglini's essay, see Vàrvaro's review.

13. Ham, himself a student of a highly eclectic and influential editor, Edward C. Armstrong, published good critical editions of *La venjance Alixandre,* 1931; *Five Versions of the Venjance Alixandre,* 1935; *Girart de Roussillon,* 1939; *Renart le bestorné,* 1947. At the time of his death, he was working on an edition of the Provençal *Flamenca.* Besides these editions, Ham published many articles on manuscripts and on textual philology, as well as an important monograph, *Textual Criticism and Jehan le Venelais.*

14. This ideal of universalizing from a good example has, I believe, been the main cause of the editorial quarrels of the past. Thus, Bédier spoke ostensibly about specific cases of editorial enterprise. In his three-part essay, "De l'édition princeps de la *Chanson de Roland* aux éditions les plus récentes: Nouvelles remarques sur l'art d'établir les anciens textes," while discussing only the text(s) of *Roland,* he generalized the principles of textual philology. His generalization can be seen explicitly in the subtitle of his work, as well as in the conclusion (519); implicitly this generalization informs all his work.

15. Segre's first, Italian, edition was dedicated to the memory of Theodor Müller, Edmund Stengel and Joseph Bédier; the new French edition, to Albert Henry, Jean Rychner and Georges Straka. Rather than denigrating past scholarship, Segre thus celebrates the tradition, the communal ties to the past. Rather than stressing the differences, he sees in them a common and continuous effort to solve the real difficulties.

16. On the more theoretical level, Ham ("Textual" 200) advises us to read Bédier on the *Lai de l'ombre,* Fourquet's critique in "Le paradoxe de Bédier," Roques's criticism of Fourquet, and Fourquet's reply to Roques. Ham is not alone in the English-speaking world in discussing the theory and practice of textual philology. Thus, for example, Frederick Whitehead, Cedric E. Pickford, and T. B. W. Reid ("Right to Emend") addressed themselves to the assessment of Bédierism. Christopher Kleinhenz has republished a series of important essays by English-speaking textual philologists, as well as by non-Bédierist Italians (*Medieval Manuscripts and Textual Criticism*). More recently an issue of *L'esprit créateur* edited by Karl Uitti presents a gamut of contemporary and chiefly practical problems of textual philology under an obviously new heading of *The Poetics of Textual Criticism.*

PETER F. DEMBOWSKI

17. Such is the hallmark of exact science. Modern biochemists do not denigrate the accomplishments of their nineteenth-century predecessors; they correct them.

18. Even in the most concrete aspects of editorial work, there are problems which defy ideal solutions. Foulet and Speer completed and systematized Roques's advice concerning the use of diacritical marks. The principles guiding the often tricky use of the *tréma* are presented with model clarity (69–73). But even there one finds, as a result, certain frustratingly diverse graphic representations of cognate words coexisting in the same text, such as *söef/souef; oblïent/oblia; enscïent/ensciant*. This situation arises from systematic application of the rule that the tréma should be used only where the opposition hiatus/diphthong was possible in Old French; since *oue, ia, ian* were always bisyllabic, there can be no need to mark them.

19. *On Editing* was praised in Europe (see, for example, the laudatory reviews by Régnier and by Thiry), but I agree with Foulet and Speer that any "new consensus" in France is perhaps less discernible: ". . . it is curious to observe that the more adventurous and judgmental methods for handling texts in the post-Bédier period have often been practiced by scholars from outside the hexagon of France. Perhaps the French love of system and clarity favors the best-manuscript edition as the only logically consistent method left to us" (38).

20. I speak here of Wahlund and von Feilitzen, eds., *Les enfances Vivien*. But inside their synoptic edition, there are are three "normal" editions. Text *C* is published according to a base manuscript with the *varia lectio* printed at the bottom of the page. The same applies to text *D* and to the prose version. Contemporary editors follow similar procedures. In his edition of *Les rédactions en vers de la Prise d'Orange*, Régnier prints the *AB* version as one text, followed by the texts of *C* and *D*. A similar solution was adopted by Lepage. For the discussion of such partially synoptic editions and their usefulness for stylistic and linguistic investigations, see Heinemann.

21. Contrary to what one should expect from a "dinosaur," Konrad Hofmann (to whom Wendelin Foerster dedicated his edition of *Érec et Énide*, and after whose name he established the siglum *H*) was a noninterventionist, at least in the one-manuscript situation.

22. There is confusion even in the use of the sigla: *C*, as designated by Foerster, is Roques's *A*; Foerster's *H* is Roques's *R*. Micha retained Foerster's sigla (*La tradition manuscrite des romans de Chrétien de Troyes*).

111

23. The same applies to other Guiot-based editions: Roques's *Yvain* and *Lancelot*, Micha's *Cligés*, and Lecoy's *Perceval*.

24. See also Foulet, "On Editing Chrétien's *Lancelot.*"

25. Cerquiglini does not help by suggesting that this name is a result of "une admirable stratégie médiévale: le nom . . . de Chrétien de Troyes (de la culture antique—Troie—à la foi révélée) dit l'ambition culturelle du Moyen Âge, à savoir la *translatio studii*" (57; "an admirable medieval strategy: the name . . . of Chrétien de Troyes [from the culture of Antiquity—Troy—revealed to faith] expresses the cultural ambition of the Middle Ages, that is to say the *translatio studii*"). Obstacles to this hypothesis include the final -*s* in *Troyes* (a little positivistic problem) and the fact that the name of the poet was used by other writers as if it were a real name of a real person. Thus, for example, the author of the *Roman de Hunbaut* defends himself against accusations of plagiarism: "Ne dira nus hom que je robe / Les bons dis Crestïen de Troies. . . ." ("No man shall say that I steal / The good stories of Chrétien de Troyes"). (See Winters's interesting comment on these lines, pp. xxii–xxiii.) Similarly: "Mais de çou ne parole pas Crestiens de Troies ne li autre troveor qui en ont trové por faire lor rimes plaisans . . . (Roach, ed., *Didot Perceval*, 220 ("But about this Chrétien de Troyes does not speak, neither do the other troubadours who wrote about it to make pleasant rhymes"). Crestïen (de Troyes) is also mentioned in various *Continuations de Perceval*, as well as in *Le chevalier a l'espee*, *Le roman de Claris et Laris*, and *Le roman du Hem*.

26. A similar situation exists in *Yvain*, in that the name of Laudine is nowhere mentioned in the Guiot manuscript. Quite inconsistently, Roques refers to "Laudine" in his introduction and in his index of names.

27. Roques does not mention this omission (or addition) in his notes.

28. I offer the sixteen-line epilogue according to manuscript *H*, corrected by *P* and *E*. The spelling has been modified to fit the graphic habits of manuscript *C*. In *H* the last line reads "Huimais porés oïr avant" ("Now you can hear further"), referring to *Perceval*, the text of which immediately follows the text of *Érec et Énide*.

29. In preparing this paper I profited greatly from the correspondence that I have recently had with my colleagues, all of whom have been engaged in the editing of Old Provençal or Old French texts. I wish to thank, therefore, Keith Busby, Carleton Carroll, Noel Corbett, Larry Crist, Edward Heinemann, William Kibler, William Paden, Rupert Pickens, Mary Speer, and Karl Uitti for their generous advice.

PETER F. DEMBOWSKI

PHILOLOGY AND ITS DISCONTENTS

Stephen G. Nichols

> . . . the textual condition
> is a scene of contest and interaction
> . . . that involves many people. The actions
> of these persons, while always collective, are not
> always consciously or willfully cooperative.
> —Jerome J. McGann

Philology seems capable of stirring passions even when evoked positively. One would have thought that my affirmation of philology as "the matrix from which all else springs" ("Introduction" 1) might have been taken in the spirit proffered as an invitation for dispassionate discussion to bridge what I and others perceived as a "widening gyre" among philology's various sub-disciplines. Faint hope! As attested by some of the articles in this volume, or by recent symposia held at the Modern Language Association, Kalamazoo, the Medieval Academy and elsewhere, we did stimulate passionate polemic, but little dispassionate discussion. Is it too late in the day to examine some of the possible causes for these philological discontents?

Drawing upon some recent discussions inspired in part by the "new philology" debate, I will try to address some of the larger questions they suggest in a manner that I hope will be seen as an example of dispassionate discussion. The material I have chosen parallels issues raised in this volume, and in some instances the substance of other contributions, in the spirit of engaged intellectual discussion. By way of conclusion, I will offer a modest methodological proposal for a philology of textual studies based on a pragmatic approach to representation in a manuscript culture.

PHILOLOGY AND/AS THE TEXTUAL IMPERATIVE

A curious thing happens to discussions of philology in the United States, at least to discussions of Romance philology. Not infrequently, they have a way of turning into discussions of text editing and textual studies. Rather than focusing on the historical context of medieval literary production to determine the place and nature of verbal and visual representation broadly conceived—the philological culture of the period, as it were—emphasis falls on the crucial matter of editing texts. I say crucial because editions are indeed one of the principal ways that medieval literary artifacts survive into our time, and editing is certainly a major vehicle for institutionalizing them within the academy. It is not the centrality of textual studies and text editing—which I take to be a given—that concerns me here, but only the breadth (or narrowness) of the center.

For if editing provides a major route for keeping texts alive, it is certainly not a way sufficient unto itself, as many colleagues are quick to recognize. Still, many remarks—"The editing of texts is the most important thing that medievalists do" (Pennington)—stress the centrality of text editing as a privileged way to be a philologist, an assumption that merits investigation.[1] Text editing has seemed so clearly a principal preoccupation of philology—indeed a commonsense response to the question, What does a philologist do?—as to have seemed self-evident. The way in which practical responses to this question have structured debates on text editing may be seen in Alfred Foulet and Mary Speer's *On Editing Old French Texts*.[2] But in looking at these debates, one discovers an accumulation of conventional wisdom about the relationship of philology to text editing that merits scrutiny. The appeal to practicality that provides the authority for the formulations—the premise that practical experience is the best way of

STEPHEN G. NICHOLS

"doing" philology—constitutes an assumption that may be investigated like any other hypothesis.

American editors of the last several generations certainly stress a thoroughgoing empirical approach to the question of text editing. Karl Uitti affirms that "The truth of textual criticism resides in the practice of editing, and in the setting up of hypothetical criteria in order to deal with the text(s), or type of text, that one proposes to edit as accurately as possible on its own terms" ("Preface," *Poetics*, 7). With admirable succinctness and impartiality, Mary Speer sums up "good Old French editing":

115

> not as anti-theoretical in an antagonistic sense, but as empirical, properly focused on the concrete realities of one or more manuscript traditions and therefore skeptical—in an informed way— towards general theories of any kind. Editors can never afford to ignore theories about the nature of texts, any more than they can suppress textual data. But their primary allegiance is to the text, and they must devise for each text ways of presenting to the reader that text's textuality. I would also emphasize that the editorial enterprise, unlike modernist theory, is both communal and open-ended. All textual critics must reckon with the work of their predecessors, honestly and honorably, in a community of scholarship that transcends time, and they are in turn obligated to leave a meticulous record for their readers and successors. An edition is always an interpretation of a text, a provisional working hypothesis about its nature and its poetics. . . . Close reading, probing, inductive and deductive evaluation of data, rereading, comparing with other texts, local theorizing, presentation of results, rereading, rethinking, revision—these are the processes by which the slow art of editing proceeds in the hope of getting closer to the truths about individual texts. ("Editing Old," 24–25)

Elsewhere in the same article, Mary Speer uses the term "editorial-practitioners" as a means of differentiating practice from theory, that is, those who produce editions from "non-editors" (8) who theorize the process without actually doing it. This distinction has been a cornerstone of the Anglo-American school of editing at least since World War II, according to Jerome

McGann (in *A Critique of Modern Textual Criticism* and *The Textual Condition*, especially chapter 2), and Mary Speer's elegant formulation demonstrates how very much alive and flourishing it is among Old French philologists. Its force, as articulated for example by Karl Uitti or Brian Woledge, lies in the promise of producing a text that comes as close as possible to the author's original. So Woledge: "With [T. B. W.] Reid's corrections, Wendelin Foerster's edition of 1912 . . . is the nearest we have yet got to the original text of Chrétien's *Yvain*" ("Problem" 254). And Uitti: "For our purposes Guiot furnished an excellent starting point, a means to reach and to set down, in a modern critical format, a text closer than any now extant (including Guiot and other thirteenth-century versions) to Chrétien's lost original. Our edition thus represents a revision of Guiot—a revision carried out in terms of what we believe Chrétien wrote, a text, I repeat, not given in complete form by any single medieval redaction" ("On Editing" 291).

It is not my point to take issue with these positions. We have to assume that Chrétien did indeed have an original version of his romances, and that attempts to recover as much of each version as possible require dedication, uncommon sensitivity, and hard work. Not a task for the faint of heart. Nor do I want to suggest that empirical text editing somehow fails to grasp the elusiveness, the indeterminacy of the medieval text. On the contrary, no one feels more keenly the frustrations of the text in flight from definition than the text editor, be it at the level of determining a reading, establishing a contextual glossary, or pondering an example of unorthodox syntax: is it an important stylistic trait of the author or a scribal *écart*? It requires courage to assert the former, especially if the bulk of the manuscript tradition has elected a more normative reading.

Tools have been proposed in recent years to assist in resolving such questions. The Foulet-Uitti "editorial grid" (*grille éditoriale*) provides an ingenious attempt to map the matrix of poetic, semantic, syntactic and other traits constitutive of symbolic language in manuscripts to provide a physiognomy of an author's style that can serve as a guide in making difficult editorial decisions.[3]

I do not want to leave the impression that all text editing today seeks to reconstruct a single authorial text. While there may be important voices raised in defense of this ideal, a variety of other editing approaches exist. Mary Speer's overview of current trends in text editing, already cited, details various projects, such as the synoptic edition illustrated by the *Nouveau recueil complet des fabliaux* directed by Willem Noomen and the late Nico van den Boogaard, that attempt to mediate between manuscript versions and an authorial text. To date, however, truly synoptic editions or other attempts to represent different manuscript versions of a work or works in a single edition have been hampered by the cost of producing printed editions of this sort and the difficulty of using them.[4]

PHILOLOGY AND/OF THE MANUSCRIPT CULTURE

My point does not intersect these concerns so much as parallel them in a complementary manner. From the standpoint of text editing so conceived, the manuscript represents something like an irritating obstacle to the recovery of a satisfactory text, either of the author's lost original or of something more than any one manuscript version. In a word, I want to consider the medieval artifact itself, the manuscript as an historical document whose materiality constitutes precisely what the ideal text cannot be in Uitti's view (quoted above): a medieval event. I am not here arguing the superiority of scribal alterations over a critical text, a position ascribed to me by Mary Speer ("Editing Old" 24 n23). I am suggesting that the manuscript, each manuscript, like the critical edition, is also the product of a collaborative effort in its own time, an effort of production that tells us not simply about the reception of and public for the works it contains, but more importantly *contextualizes* those works in material culture.[5]

Rather than seeking to recover the lost voice of a single author, we need an approach that focuses on the poetic text as one of several discourses within the manuscript. Such a theory would consider the manuscript as a complex system of expression and study its networks of meaning production. It would assume that scribe, illuminator, rubricator—the one and the many whose work focuses on the poetic text—are aware of their posterior status vis-à-vis the verbal narrative and of their interaction with one another's discourses.

To propose a philology of the manuscript goes beyond simply including information in the critical edition about "illuminations, capital letters, rubrication, scribal punctuation, redactional poetics, musical notation, and other works in the codex," although I agree with Mary Speer that such facts should be noted ("Editing Old" 43). Taking as its goad E. R. Curtius's critique of medieval philologies as disciplines dissociated from "the basic foundation of history" (*European* 520), this philology views such textual supplements as agents of historical mediation between the text and the manuscript culture which propagated it.

The philology of the manuscript or material philology must focus on the dynamics of the expressive systems within the manuscript viewed as cultural artifact. Linguistics, paleography, anthropology, history, history of art, sociology, philosophy, esthetics, and literary history (to name but the most obvious disciplines potentially implicated) can all be involved to some degree, depending on the work and manuscript studied. The more complex the manuscript as an artifact, the more extensive the possible subjects for study.

As a description of a series of interactions with a prior work, the manuscript will show evidence of the horizon of knowledge and expectation brought to bear by the producers of the manuscript. Material philology will study and analyze these factors not only to identify them, but also to demonstrate the way they interact to produce text and supplementation. I offer "supplementation" as a useful theoretical term for the many forms of accretion to medieval texts in the space of the manuscript. The interpretive process *per se*, at least as traditionally understood, will play a smaller role than the task of, first, identifying the different constituent elements at work in the description and, then, showing how they interact to make what kinds of meanings.

By making manuscript supplementation the subject of study in its own right, one may hope to glimpse how social, economic, political, artistic, legal, theological, and other historical factors

STEPHEN G. NICHOLS

affected the fate and meaning of literary texts during the Middle Ages (see Nichols, "Commentary"). As Curtius hoped, such an agenda requires enlarging the center of philology to include not only the conceptualization of an ideal text, but also a willingness to extend the same effort to conceptualize the representational space of the manuscript as what I have elsewhere called the "manuscript matrix."

By manuscript matrix I mean nothing more nor less than the historical fact that medieval texts were written in a manuscript format which is both multivoiced and temporally open-ended, in the sense that it is continually being re-represented and redefined, often over several centuries as in the case of popular works like the *Roman de la rose*. The manuscript matrix betokens an historically determinate representational space unlike any that has existed since the advent of print culture; it is a space of radical alterity very different from the conception of textual space propounded by the critical edition. Manuscripts involved continuous supplementation: scribal recension, rubrication, decoration and / or illumination. Their margins invited commentary, either planned or spontaneous. Manuscripts were copied and recopied so that the form of a work was continually subject to change in conformity to evolving tastes and methods of "book" production. Perhaps nowhere else was the Aristotelian precept frequently repeated in the Middle Ages—*Omne quod movetur ab alio movetur*—so applicable as in medieval book production.

Although often products of scriptoria where conventions and formulas for facilitating production imparted a degree of uniformity, circumstances of patronage and function made each manuscript a unique witness to its historical context, particularly the context of production. It is not only the text that bears witness, though the kinds of textual modifications editors grapple with are indeed significant. One thinks, for example, of the scribe Guiot of Bibliothèque nationale fr. 794, who transcribed Chrétien de Troyes's manuscripts, all the while suppressing certain of the author's signature poetic traits.[6] Does his apparent distaste for rhetorical ornamentation bespeak a shift in the esthetics of narrative verse? Could it reflect a growing discomfort in the thirteenth century with the verse form as a narrative vehicle, in the face of a growing preference for prose?

Besides intervening in the "author's" text, the manuscript matrix encourages supplementation as a contextualizing gesture. Annotation and commentary, for example, are two fundamental components of medieval manuscripts that we may generically term supplements to the text. Internal additions interpolated in the text; formal elements for ordering the text on the manuscript page such as rubrication, historiated or decorated initials, illuminated miniatures, *bas de page* paintings, marginal decoration; and, finally, glosses of various sorts are all supplementation. Supplementation was usually informative and almost always a device for adapting the work to a particular set of circumstances, whether to the taste of a patron whose wishes had to be carried out or to the intellectual agenda of scribe or illuminator. For example, the J. Pierpont Morgan Library's MS M332 in New York is a sumptuous presentation manuscript by Jean Boutefeue made in Paris about 1410 that illustrates deftly how supplementation configures the alterity of medieval bookmaking. Bespeaking royal patronage (it contains a miniature [see p. 190] showing Jean de Meun presenting his book to the king of France, Philippe le Bel), M332 contains the Latin text of Boethius's *De consolatione philosophiae* with a facing French translation by Jean de Meun. Both the original Latin text and the facing translation are surrounded on each folio by a Latin commentary on the *De consolatione* by William of Conches. Each book of the treatise in this manuscript begins with either an historiated or a decorated initial, depending on whether it introduces the Latin or the vernacular translation. Elsewhere I have shown that this iconic program represents a commentary with historical and political implications ("Commentary"). Although not all manuscripts are as sumptuous or redolent of meaning and courtly patronage as Morgan M332, every manuscript is in some sense unique in its response to the logic of the supplement.

The expression "manuscript matrix," then, is simply a shorthand way of referring to the historical mode of production for medieval texts, a reminder that the collective production of manuscripts involved much more than the reproduction of a verbal text. If text editing attempts to locate a text in the midst of flux, the manuscript matrix focuses on the agents of flux as also productive of meaning. The two goals are orthogonal in practice, but need not be antagonistic; rather they define different aspects of the truly "medieval" philological enterprise as Curtius conceived it.

PHILOLOGY AND LINGUISTICS

Not surprisingly, the two enterprises—text editing and the philology of the context—emerge from different historical roots of the last half-century or more. Empirical and eclectic text editing developed from efforts to define "philology" more precisely, in reaction to complaints of imprecision in the connotation of the word, by moving it in the direction of linguistics. The Dutch philologist Joseph Engels formulated these trends concisely in 1953 when he published the text of a talk: "Philologie romane—linguistique—études littéraires."

Engels cited the broad range of (frequently conflicting) definitions of "(Romance) philology" going back a century or more. Laying special emphasis on the inability of contemporary philologists like Auerbach, Tagliavini, Rohlfs, and Curtius[7] to agree on a meaning that could define a clear discipline, he located the softness of meaning less in nineteenth-century trends than in twentieth-century misunderstanding, particularly of philology's evolution. For Engels this took the form of the then prevailing wisdom that held Romance philology to have been a creation of German Romanticism at the beginning of the nineteenth century, a time which witnessed the birth of comparative philology or grammar (linguistics) and a fascination with medieval Romance literature on the part of such German Romantics as the Schlegel brothers, the Grimm brothers, and like-minded contemporaries. This thesis had been advanced by Gertrud Richert in 1913. Its attraction for the early twentieth century lay in the powerful legitimacy it conferred on the construction of Romance philology as a discipline that focused both on the origins and nature of Romance languages and on the origins and appreciation of texts, following the lead of classical philology (Engels, "Philologie" 14–16).

Engels attacked Richert's thesis, and thus the historical basis for linking two questionably compatible tendencies, by noting that there was no evidence that comparative linguistics ever called itself philology except, improperly, in England,[8] and that moreover the term "Romance philology" had not been introduced early in the century, but only towards 1863:

> Ce fait, très significatif, est une première indication de ce que, dans la première moitié du XIXe siècle, en Allemagne, l'idée d'une science philologique romane, une, nettement articulée (et qui proviendrait de la fusion de la "grammaire comparée" et de l'intérêt pour les littératures méridionales), n'était point présente aux esprits. À vrai dire, ces deux courants . . . sont restés beaucoup plus distincts qu'on ne l'admet généralement. (16)

> [This significant fact offers an initial indication that in the first half of the nineteenth century in Germany, the idea of a Romance philological science, integral, clearly articulated (and which would proceed from the fusion of comparative grammar and the interest in southern literatures), was not present in people's minds. In fact, these two currents . . . remained much more separate than is generally admitted.]

The divergence of the two supposedly merging trends could also be seen in their contrasting attitudes towards classical philology as it evolved in the eighteenth century. Classical philology developed methods for making literary texts available as well as for instructing in their appreciation. The classical philologist "saw in [the discipline] a valuable, and in fact an indispensable, means of gaining a first-hand knowledge of the literature which was his chief concern" (Jespersen, 64). At the core of classical philology, in the words of E. R. Curtius, lies a "universal concept of Antiquity, which unites philology and history," a conjugation that "has borne rich fruit" for classical scholarship (*European* 519). Since the Romance literatures needed to make their texts available and valued, classical philology offered an up-to-date (for the period) method adaptable to Romance literature.

STEPHEN G. NICHOLS

While classical philology may have served as a model for early Romance literature and language scholars, it played just the opposite role in the development of comparative grammar (linguistics). Engels points out that the putative first influence on the development of Romance philology, the comparative study of grammar, actually developed in opposition to classical philology. In 1922, in his book *Language: Its Nature, Development, and Origin*, Otto Jespersen showed how what he prefers to call comparative linguistics had emancipated the study of language from the subordination to literary study promoted by classical philology.

> The beginning of the 19th c. witnessed a growing differentiation between philology and linguistics in consequence of the new method introduced by comparative and by historical grammar; it was nothing less than a completely new way of looking at the facts of language and trying to trace their origin. *While to the philologist the Greek or Latin language, etc., was only a means to an end, to the linguist it was an end in itself.* . . . The linguist cared not for the literature as such, but studied languages for their own sake, and might even turn to languages destitute of literature because they were able to throw some light on the life of language in general or on forms in related languages. The philologist as such would not think of studying the Gothic of Wulfila, as a knowledge of that language gives access only to a translation of parts of the Bible, the ideas of which can be studied much better elsewhere; but to the linguist Gothic was extremely valuable. (64–65; my italics)[9]

In seeking language models outside the realm of literature, comparative linguistics struck at the heart of philology's initial *raison d'être*. In so doing, however, it laid the groundwork for the ultimate *querelle* philology was to pick with itself, the issue at the heart of philology's discontent: language study narrowly focused on textual study versus literary language as a manifestation of culture. Clearly Engels admired the crispness of vision traced by Jespersen when he showed the evolution of language study from comparative grammar to linguistics. He noted with approval

Jespersen's insistence on distinguishing philology—the historical study of the culture of a nation—from linguistics, which focused solely on the way language functioned: "While the philologist looked upon language as part of the culture of some nation, the linguist looked upon it as a natural object; and when in the beginning of the nineteenth century philosophers began to divide all sciences into the two sharply separated classes of mental and natural sciences (*Geistes- und Naturwissenschaften*), linguists would often reckon their science among the latter" (Jespersen 65). The appeal of Jespersen for Engels seems to have been the focus on language as the tangible element, the "hard" substance at the center of the various components of a Romance philology increasingly difficult to pin down in any way that seemed practical. Salvation, or at least logic, lay for Engels in reformulating philology to move it closer to a Jespersen-like linguistics.

Engels begins with an avowedly traditional definition of philology as encompassing two spheres, language and literature: "Philologie romane sera un terme traditionnel pour indiquer dans une seule expression *l'étude des langues et des littératures romanes*" (20). He quickly moves to delimit the definition of "littératures," however, in a new and untraditional way to encompass only the role of language in literature as linguistic communication in a restricted, formal sense. He does so in part by distinguishing between philology and literary study. Language that "begins to be the expression of an artistic thought"[10] is language as a vehicle for literary esthetics ("le beau littéraire"); "to employ the term 'philology' for this purpose would serve only to create misunderstanding and confusion."[11] In other words, Engels effectively rules the study of literature out of bounds to philology, since literary texts will simply serve as tokens or "informants" providing examples of language to be studied from a purely linguistic viewpoint. This represents a decontextualization of the linguistic token, since it is only in the context of the literary setting that a given expression can have its full meaning. "Songe" and "mensonge" in the *Roman de la rose* of Guillaume de Lorris, for instance, have very different meanings from what we find in other places. The decontextualizing gesture is a crucial one, for it invokes the empiricist

STEPHEN G. NICHOLS

rationale of common sense, e.g., stripping the problem down to basics, in this case to "communication."

Indeed, the second thrust of Engels's proposal deals directly with the definition of the study of language as communication.[12] The thrust of this section can only be termed a de-definition of philology as the study of language in a cultural context in favor of an approach consistent with linguistic methodology. Thus philology, or "Romance linguistics" as Engels prefers to call it, should not deal with matters like the range of temporal values in verbs in the past tense or those of the subjunctive mood, still less the different nuances of the indefinite pronoun *on*, since such questions belong more to the domain of literary studies. Rather Romance linguistics should more properly investigate the phonetico-morphological question of the endings *-ais, -ais, -ait* of the imperfect tense, or the linguistic functions of the subjunctive, or take part in discussions on the origin of the pronoun *on* (22). Romance linguistics will not treat texts as such in any form, whether literary or non-literary (22).

We need pursue no further Engels's distinctions between literary and linguistic study, which led him to argue for abandoning the term "philology" that originally linked them (23). We should, however, note that Engels clearly sees philology construed as linguistics as a tool for a more rigorous textual study and text editing practice. Normalised editions produced by nineteenth-century philologists not only resulted from a defective conception of linguistics, but also from "un manque de respect pour les textes" (22). Engels asserts that a linguistically oriented philology, fully attuned to the idea of language as communication, will show that language is both "parlée et écrite ('texte')" (22). In seeking to separate literary study from that of language, Engels ranges textual studies in the latter camp.

The impulse towards a more scientific definition of philology, as Jespersen noted in 1922, had already manifested itself in the mid-nineteenth century. Why then, in 1952, do we find Engels, author of studies on the *Ovide moralisé*, taking so bold a stance in favor of the scientific and empiricist view of philology? What made the timing seem appropriate, especially when the weight of such *éminences* as Curtius, Tagliavini, Croce and Auerbach espoused a contrary position?

In retrospect, Engels's talk to the twenty-first Congress of Romance Philology in Holland appears a harbinger of the times. The period coincided generally with a shift to empirical approaches in literary studies and text editing, especially in the Anglo-American sphere. Paradoxically, American New Criticism and eclectic text editing shared the same formalist postulates and textual idealism, even though each saw itself as engaged in a very different enterprise from the other. Jerome McGann has recently reflected on these matters in his book *The Textual Condition*;[13] I mention them only by way of noting the congruence of Anglo-American Old French textual studies with this larger movement. In sum, then, the quest for a more precise, practical, and "scientific" philology led to a narrowly focused and formalist conception within the field of historical linguistics. In a correlated movement, the practical "arm" of philology, text editing and textual study, evolved an editorial equivalent, eclectic or empirical approaches to text editing.

MATERIAL PHILOLOGY[14]

Thanks to this trend, our texts are excellent from a linguistic and rhetorical viewpoint. Yet these gains, it seems to me, came at the expense of certain other aspects of medieval works, particularly manuscripts as cultural artifacts. As I suggested earlier, we have given less attention to the contextual aspects of literary objects, particularly to the life of the text in its manuscript context. This was understandable in the heyday of New Criticism and structuralism, but has become less tenable now, and indeed, a number of recent studies do address the kinds of issues I am talking about.[15]

Text in/as Context. With the understanding then that we are in some sense describing a movement that is already *en cours*, rather than a departure or breakthrough, let me conclude by extending my earlier thoughts to suggest more concretely two kinds of

STEPHEN G. NICHOLS

issues, one general, the other specific, that material philology might address.

In the first place, material philology can expose the fallacy, at least so far as medieval studies are concerned, that meditation on literary context necessarily implies a turning away from the literary text. This is a charge—whatever its merits—that proponents of empirical approaches to textual studies have levelled against literary pragmatics, seen as overly concerned with usage, particularly "idealized usage." Empirical literary studies, on the contrary, are said to "focus on the actual behavior of real readers in their engagement with literary texts" (see Steen 110–14). Such dichotomies may hold for a print culture, where one possesses different states of a work moving from authorial manuscript(s), to contemporary editions corrected and overseen by the author, to texts printed at various periods after the author's death—although Jerome McGann argues the contrary, affirming that "the circumstances of publication [hence of context] *always* bear upon literary meaning" ("What" 190).

In a manuscript culture, however, where context determines text—as a recoverable historical phenomenon—distinctions of the sort Steen asserts just don't make sense. I do not mean simply that medieval literary works survive as historical artifacts only in manuscript versions. That is certainly one form of historical context, and we'll come back to it in a moment. But first let's be clear on the concept of context; for if we learned anything from Engels's article and the movement towards textuality narrowly construed that it typified, it is that context is not invariant, still less value-neutral, but rather a cultural and normative variable.

Was it not precisely the point made earlier in the discussion of text editing that the medieval context dictates the strategies of modern editors? For, as T. B. W. Reid so cogently puts it, "Of all the extant manuscripts of Old French texts, there is not one that anybody would maintain to be a completely faithful copy of the original," a fact justifying editors' "indulging in what Vinaver has called 'disguised collaboration with the author'—but it was widely felt that this was not really a very high price to pay for the labours of a good editor" ("Right" 1–4).

Across the Channel, Jacqueline Cerquiglini-Toulet sees the same historical bind as Reid. She pinpoints the dilemma of contextuality with her usual talent for apt summation:

> Le mythe du texte médiéval commence avec son édition. Sphère dont le centre est partout, la circonférence nulle part, l'activité éditrice est vécue par ses pratiquants les plus clairvoyants sous le signe de la mauvaise conscience, par ses utilisateurs les plus avertis dans le malheur. Angoisse de la non-transparence pour les uns, peur de la tromperie, chez les autres, signes de notre distance aux textes. Irréductiblement signifiant, le geste de l'éditeur est perçu par tous comme parasite, mal obligé dans ce rêve, mythique, d'une compréhension première, directe, dans cette écoute d'une voix qu'on voudrait sans interférences. Mais y a-t-il *une* voix des textes au Moyen Âge, ne faut-il pas toujours, dans la pratique, pluraliser l'origine? (337–38)

> [The myth of the medieval text begins with its edition. A sphere whose center is everywhere and whose circumference nowhere ⟨to paraphrase the medieval definition of God—S.G.N.⟩, text editing is experienced by its most clairvoyant practitioners with an uneasy conscience, and by its most experienced users with despair. The anguish of non-transparence for some, fear of mistakes for others: signs of our distance from the texts. Irreducibly signifying, the editor's act is seen by all as parasitic, an unwelcome necessity in this (mythic) dream of a primal understanding, by live coverage, eavesdropping on a voice that one longs to hear without interference. But is there *one* voice for medieval texts; must one not always, in practice, multiply the origin?]

In the textual perspective, then, "context" takes on both a negative and a positive dimension. It is negative in postulating an historical context unfavorable to the accurate transmission of texts faithfully embodying original states. This view focuses on the transmission of the verbal text: production and reception in a pre-print environment where every manuscript has the potential to offer a different "version" of a text and thus to "stray" from authorial intention. The response, as we have seen, has been to postulate a concept of *transhistorical* context as a positive counterbalance. This formula relies on the modernist notion of (scientific) progress to conceive an archeology of textual recuperation, a process of "image enhancement" done through a kind of partnership between the modern text editor and the medieval author.

In this process, the medieval context—the material historical forms of the text—constitute an interference, a distorting mirror that must be minimized where it cannot be eliminated. The process is transhistorical in the sense of privileging developments *through* or *over* time, rather than particular moments *in* time. It may be helpful to think of the transhistorical context as "punctual" rather than as a continuum, in that it postulates (for each edition) a link between a lost, originating point in the past and the scientifically produced recuperative text in the present. We would be mistaken in assuming that such willed achronicity violates medieval practice. On the contrary, it engages a sophisticated dialectic with period procedures. Multiple versions of medieval works, like the different retellings of the *Chanson de Roland* or of the *Roman de Tristan*, came about, at least in the most interesting cases, precisely because poets and jongleurs sought a version of a given work more in keeping with their own views. When a medieval jongleur states that others have told a given story before, but that his version is the true one, he invokes the same transhistorical vision as the modern text editor.

Marie de France, in the prologue to her *Lais*, gave philosophical shape to this impulse by asseverating as a matter of principle that interpretation was a collaboration through time by authors or philosophers in one period and reader-interpreters in subsequent eras.[16] The principal difference between medieval poets and jongleurs and modern text editors lies less in intent than in the direction their efforts take. Whereas the former sought to perfect or improve upon a work they took to be an imperfect original, thereby privileging present over past, the latter focus retrospectively on a past they seek to recover. In either case, the text produced in the "present" is deemed superior, but the methods used to obtain them are quite different: the one method being marked by context-*valorization*, the other by a deliberate context-

neutrality. It is the context-sensitivity of the medieval poets and jongleurs that motivates their rewritings of original versions deemed not to accord with changing tastes, for example the prosification of verse romance. On the other hand, modern text editing seeks to be context-neutral, that is, proof against the encroachment of the *historical* context on the author's original text. Each sees context as determinant, but one in a positive, the other in a negative sense.

All this means that in a pre-print culture, at least in a manuscript culture as defined by the European Middle Ages, one cannot legitimately separate text and context. No matter what tasks the medievalist sets for him- or herself, nor what methodology is espoused, one is never free from the pervasive effects of the historical context of the literary work. Moreover, all forms of production affect the texts we read. At the same time, we've seen that context varies according to focus. By way of marking the nuances entailed in the variability of context, as well as to distinguish clearly their differing foci, I would propose the terms "textual context" to refer to the transhistorical continuum on which the text editor concentrates, and "manuscript context" to designate the materiality of the manuscript culture *quâ* historical continuum. My final remarks will illustrate some examples of how material philology can help to explore the textual condition of the manuscript context.

Material Culture and the Manuscript Context. While we have seen the speciousness of the text/context dichotomy as a putative ground separating textual context from manuscript context, there is one dichotomy that text editing inevitably fosters: the split between verbal text and visual text. To predicate a transhistorical verbal text, a "sphere whose center is everywhere and whose circumference nowhere," to repeat Jacqueline Cerquiglini-Toulet's witty evocation of the medieval definition of God, inevitably bespeaks an idealized text, a text that may be thought rather than seen, *con*ceived rather than *per*ceived. Perhaps no single element so clearly distinguishes textual from manuscript context as the fundamental principle of the iconic or visual text.

STEPHEN G. NICHOLS

Visual attributes are a basic condition of material artifacts—we can see them even before we can touch them. At the same time, nothing may be quite so historically determined and context-bound as visual properties. Iconic elements include not only illuminations, decorated and historiated initials, marginal decorations, and the like, but also graphic aspects: rubrication, commentary, and the script itself of the text. All of these elements bespeak their immediate period to the point where paleography developed dating techniques based on script.[17] Medieval manuscripts therefore present a visual system much more closely tied to the taste and convention of the time of execution than to those of the poet's own period, the time of the original composition. The chronological disjunction between the initial creation of the poetic text and its rendering as a visual text in a manuscript may be very great at times, especially in the case of a popular work like the *Roman de la rose,* which continued to be reproduced well into the sixteenth century.

For example, a fifteenth-century version of the *Roman de la rose* like the Bodleian Library's Douce 195 will have a verbal text consonant with, though certainly not identical to, versions from the late thirteenth or early fourteenth centuries; in other words, the chronological disparity between versions of the poetic text will tend to be conservative. On the other hand, the material (and visible) aspects of the manuscript—illuminations, decorations, script, and rubrication—accord rather with their immediate fifteenth-century historical context. Bespeaking its aristocratic patronage—it was produced for Charles d'Orléans, Comte d'Angoulême, and his wife Louise de Savoie at the end of the fifteenth century—Douce 195 indulges in a more sumptuous display of visual art than earlier manuscripts, with illuminations tending to be more consistently "painterly," more numerous, and bolder. Each illumination resembles less a sketch or illustration than a carefully executed composition including varied perspectival backgrounds with carefully painted, detailed châteaux, landscapes complete with horizon, and "skyscapes" including cloud formations. This befits, perhaps, the status of a signature work—the illuminations are attributed to Robinet Testard or his atelier. Let me describe but two instances where the paintings differ markedly from those in earlier manuscripts and almost seem to "upstage" the poetic text.

Illuminations in fourteenth-century manuscripts portray the ekphrastic portraits of the courtly vices excluded from the *jardin de Déduit* that the lover discovers painted on the outside wall of the garden more or less as the poetic text *says* the lover sees them (i.e., as paintings), but not as the poetic text actually *describes* them. The ekphrastic portraits in the poetic text are virtuoso metamorphoses of texts into images, lively descriptions slyly suggesting that poetry possesses greater resources than art when it comes to dynamic description (Nichols, "Ekphrasis, Iconoclasm, and Desire").

Douce 195 appears to accept the challenge of the poetic text by portraying these exemplary figures (Avarice, Envy, Old Age, Hypocrisy, and so on) as free-standing, active portraits of "real" people. The fiction of portraits on a wall vanishes, or at least yields to colorful depictions of recognizable character types. In place of the wall, we see only pedestals or niches against a fully rendered natural background of hills, shrubs, trees, and clouds. The artist decontextualizes the portraits, to all intents and purposes, the better to display his own skill. That skill lives in the details of the portrait, details of dress and class, for instance, where Villainy appears as a meanly dressed, barefoot peasant woman (fol. 2), while Tristesse clearly comes from the upper class and holds a knife which she seems about to plunge deep within her (fol. 3v, left); see p. 191. Such details complement the poetic text, but they also clearly distinguish the two spheres of rival artistic activity.

Another touch of independence comes from the artist's decision to represent the castration of Saturn by Jupiter (fol. 76v) and, later, Origen's self-castration (fol. 122v) see p. 192. Both incidents are mentioned in the verbal text, but neither is so graphically described, nor have I found such explicit illustrations in earlier manuscripts. Perhaps in keeping with a more permissive atmosphere of sexual reference in fifteenth-century society, Robinet Testard depicts the male genitalia with full erections and large testicles in each case. The visual text here "raises the ante" over the poem, since the debate between Lady Reason and the Lover concerns only the propriety of *naming* generative organs by their familiar, everyday terms (such as *couilles*, "testicles") as opposed to using a euphemism. The debate is iconoclastic in the sense that the Lover, who chides Lady Reason for using "crude" language when she refers to Saturn's "couilles," really attacks the image-making quality of language.[18] Direct naming evokes the image of the thing named, according to this position. To name the shameful thing with images associated with sensuality, or susceptible of invoking sensual intention, *ipso facto* convicts one of vicious intent, as the Lover illustrates in his attack on Reason:

> "Or vaut pis," dis je, "que devant,
> Car bien vois ore apercevant
> Par vostre parleüre baude
> Que vous estes fole ribaude;
> Car, tout ait Deus les choses faites
> Que ci devant m'avez retraites,
> Les moz au meins ne fist il mie
> Qui sont tuit plein de vilenie." (ed. Langlois, vv. 6979–86)

["Well this is worse than before," I said, "for I see now clearly from your bawdy speech that you are a loose woman. God may have made the *things* you've laid before me, but at least he didn't make the *words* that are so filled with baseness."]

The Lover wants Reason to use euphemism (vv. 6932–42) that will name the thing indirectly by conjuring a substitute image (e.g., "relics," "wallet," "harness," "family jewels," v. 7143).[19] The hearer may choose or not choose to make the correct identification between the metaphor and the intended object, though, as Reason remarks (vv. 7109–15), to someone looking for nastiness, any word designating the thing would be deemed offensive.

Now the paintings in Douce 195, by clearly depicting not only the testicles with knives at their base, but also fully erect penises, interject themselves in the polemic on the side of Reason. She argues, citing the *Timaeus*, that naming a thing created by Nature does not by itself imply vicious intent (vv. 7081–7184). Language was given by God to increase understanding; words give intellectual and esthetic, not lascivious, pleasure:

> Coilles est beaus nons e si l'ains;
> Si sont, par fei, coillon e vit;
> Onc nus plus beaus guieres ne vit.
> Je fis les moz e sui certaine
> Qu'onques ne fis chose vilaine;
> E Deus, qui est sages e fis,
> Tient a bien fait quanque je fis. (vv. 7116–7121)

[Testicles is a beautiful name, and I like it; so are, if it comes to it, balls and prick; one has scarcely ever seen any more beautiful. I made the words and am certain that I never made a base thing; and God, who is wise and fine, considers well made whatever I make.]

The artist, in choosing to aggregate in one scene Reason's separate references to the sexual organs, conveys the rationale (though not Reason's intent) for their mutilation in these exempla: to disarm the male weapon. In so doing, he seeks to disarm the kind of critique literal readers like the Lover aim at visual texts, whether in the form of verbal or visual images. At the same time, the aggressively realistic portrayal of the male organs demonstrates how problematic desire can be. Just as Saturn's castrated testicles cast into the sea recycle themselves in the birth of Venus, so Douce 195's paintings, frozen in the manifestation of potency before castration, suggest the ability of the image—verbal or visual—to confirm ambiguity. These are nuances contained in the poetry, certainly, but the paintings develop them in a powerful manner, and a manner not found in earlier versions.

All of the visual details in Douce 195—style of dress, hairstyles, architecture, decoration, and so forth—bespeak an esthetics as well as an historical verisimilitude of the late fifteenth century, more than two hundred years after Guillaume de Lorris and Jean de Meun wrote their respective parts of the poetic work. The tangible experience of reading the *Rose* in such late manuscripts is to make the work contemporaneous with the manuscript, at least in "feel" and "look."

STEPHEN G. NICHOLS

I want to suggest at least two elements of the "iconic text" that convey historical understanding but that we lose when relying solely on edited texts. The first, described summarily in the previous paragraph, involves the image of the work that the manuscript matrix conveys to the reader. Second, the formal and marginal annotations and commentaries supplementing the verbal text in different manuscripts convey crucial aspects of the work as revealed by its interaction with subsequent historical moments. Image and commentary—how the work looked and how the work was thought about—have much to tell us about the way literature interacted dialectically with its audience(s) and how it adapted to historical change.

Marie de France, as we noted, understood this crucial role of readers and commentators in rethinking cultural artifacts from generation to generation. Hugh of Saint Victor argued similarly, albeit more systematically, in his *Didascalicon. We* may tend to think of medieval literature in terms of orality, reading or reciting aloud to an audience—the archetypal communal activity. But medieval literature was also, especially from the thirteenth century on, a *visual* experience. The simple appearance of an *incipit* tells us much about the importance accorded to the work by the patron who commissioned it, and thus its reception at various levels of society. In other words, the manuscript matrix may be construed as a cultural artifact that functions both as commentary and as image.

This dual role has serious implications for the theoretical and critical study of medieval works; it can only be perceived by studying them in the context of the manuscript matrix, and the historical understanding so obtained makes it difficult to imagine how one might continue to think of the edited work as sufficient unto itself, either for scholarly or pedagogical purposes. By way of a modest proposal, I would suggest that by giving equal time to both the textual context of editions and the manuscript context, we may accomplish at least two important tasks.

First, we will restore the concept and practice of philology to a fuller sense of the term—something more akin to the ideas of predecessors like Roger Bacon, Fontenelle, Gianbatista Vico, Émile

Littré, Gaston Paris, Ernest Renan, E. R. Curtius, and Erich Auerbach, for whom philology embraced both the textual and material contexts in a historicism that incorporated the full range of states of medieval artifacts, their situation in the present—including the methodologies deployed to convey and interpret them—as well as their historical context. Secondly, the practice of material philology in concert with textual criticism will more surely respond to Jacqueline Cerquiglini-Toulet's injunction, quoted above, to provide a polyphonic account of the origins of our works ("pluraliser l'origine"); that is, to extend them through time and in history.

NOTES

I would like to express my thanks to Professors Mary Speer of Rutgers University and Siegfried Wenzel of the University of Pennsylvania, and Ms. Amy Wygant of The Johns Hopkins University for reading early drafts of this paper and for their generous and thoughtful responses to it. While they should not be held accountable for the outcome, I learned much and the paper profited from their questions and comments.

　　1. Peter Dembowski, in his essay for this volume, recommends the term "textual philology" in place of "textual criticism" by way of marking the anti-theoretical nature of Old French philology. In her recent article, "Editing Old French Texts in the Eighties: Theory and Practice," Mary Speer consistently uses the terms philology/philologist (in contradistinction to theory/theorist or literary criticism/critic) in conjunction with textual study and editing in such formulations as "the traditional practice of textual criticism and its central role in Old French philology. . ." (15). Karl Uitti makes an appeal for philological text editing: "No other scholarly ambition can hold a candle to it" ("On Editing" 291). Elsewhere Uitti cites his Berkeley mentor, Edward Billings Ham, on the virtues of text editing as the surest way of acquiring research techniques necessary to do Old French scholarship—far more instructive than any "life-and-works production about some neglected later author (or, let us add, 'as any style of critical investigation that happens to be at the time in vogue')" ("Preface," *Poetics* 7).

　　2. Foulet and Speer are careful to deal only with the practical aspects of text editing in their manual, making no claims at all regarding the centrality of text editing to philology. In a private communication to me (15 August 1992), Mary Speer notes: "Indeed, we tried our best to limit our

discussion to practical concerns, rather than to engage in theoretical debate over the purpose of philology."

3. Alfred Foulet, "On Grid-Editing Chrétien de Troyes" and "On Editing Chrétien's Lancelot."

4. Speer puts these problems succinctly: "Although the *NRCF* [i.e., Noomen and Van den Boogaard] is a heroic editorial undertaking destined to remain useful for several generations, it has limitations: it may not always offer the most appropriate fabliau texts for general readers or those unwilling to scrutinize its notes; as a specific statement about textuality, it hardly lends itself to direct imitation by editors of other texts; and in any event, its size and expense preclude imitation" ("Editing Old" 28).

5. I would like to make clear at the outset of this study that the medieval manuscript as a class comprehends an enormously diverse range of instantiations. Partly because they are interesting, and also because they represent a significant patronage level, I will be talking primarily about illuminated manuscripts, a group that actually represents a relatively limited range of extant codices. Unadorned manuscripts like the Bodleian's Ms. Digby 23 (the so-called Oxford version of the *Chanson de Roland*) or Ms. 927 of the Bibliothèque municipale of Tours, containing the unique copy of the *Mystère d'Adam*, are "plain" manuscripts lacking the full panoply of iconic attributes found in more sumptuous codices. Nonetheless, even such minimalist manuscripts illustrate the properties I associate with the iconic text. Although less complex, they are produced in the same way as more elaborate manuscripts; they may have fewer "bells and whistles" for us to analyze and from which we may work out their history, but they necessarily have iconic elements such as initials, rubrication, script, *mise-en-page*.

6. Uitti points to Chrétien's "predilection" for such poetic constructions as chiasmus, *annominatio*, and rich rhyme, and to "Guiot's bias against the sort of literary adornment that Chrétien clearly relished" ("On Editing" 291).

7. Auerbach, *Introduction aux études de philologie romane*; Tagliavini, *Le origini delle lingue neolatine*; Rohlfs, *Romanische Philologie*; Curtius, "Über die altfranzösische Epik," 246; see also Curtius, "Gustav Gröber und die romanische Philologie."

8. Engels follows Otto Jespersen here. In Jespersen's colorful formulation: "[Philology] is often in English used in a sense unknown to other languages and really objectionable, namely as a synonym of (comparative) study of languages. . ." (64).

9. Jespersen is cited in part by Engels, 16–17. Jespersen's study went through numerous printings; the last edition was brought out by W. W. Norton in 1964, twenty-one years after Jespersen's death.

10. The expression comes from Tagliavini's *Origini:* "La filologia, in senso più stretto, prende la lingua come ogetto di studio solo là dove essa comincia ad essere attestata letteriamente o comunque ad essere l'espressione di un pensiero artistico. . ." (36; "Philology, in the strictest sense of the word, takes language as its object of study only when language begins to be attested as literature or, at least, when it begins to be the expression of artistic thought").

11. Engels's entire paragraph excluding artistic language from the proper sphere of philology reads: "Pourtant, 'la langue qui commence à être l'expression d'une pensée artistique,' c'est là, à notre avis, précisément la définition de l'objet des *études littéraires:* la langue en tant que véhicule du beau littéraire. Employer ici le terme 'philologie' ne servirait qu'à créer des malentendus et des confusions. Je dis *études littéraires,* au pluriel, pour rendre possibles toutes les classifications et divisions ultérieures" ("Philologie" 20; "However, 'language which begins to be the expression of an artistic thought' is, in my opinion, precisely the definition of the object of literary studies: language as a vehicle of literary beauty. To employ the term 'philology' for this purpose would serve only to create misunderstanding and confusion. I say 'literary studies,' in the plural, to anticipate all later classifications and divisions").

12. "La linguistique sera donc l'étude de la langue *comme moyen de communication*" (ibid. 21).

13. I am thinking, in particular, of McGann's first three essays: "Introduction: Texts and Textualities"; chapter 1, "Theory, Literary Pragmatics and the Editorial Horizon"; chapter 2, "What is Critical Editing?"

14. I want to differentiate my position in the following section from what Jerome McGann calls "bibliographic criticism," a notion developed in a number of his writings. See most recently *The Textual Condition,* especially chapter 6, "Pound's *Cantos:* A Poem Including Bibliography." McGann says, in part, "I want to explore *how* meanings operate at the work's most primary material levels. In carrying out this particular exercise, we shall trace an exemplary textual scene where the material forms and events of writing and printing call attention to the parts they play in the signifying system of the work" (130). McGann's concept of bibliographic criticism aims at making more complete critical editions. Indeed, his example in the Pound chapter features the difference in printed versions of

the *Cantos* between ones overseen by Pound himself and the New Directions version lacking Pound's input. Although McGann's is a project of historicizing critical editions, and I am concerned with historicizing the study of medieval literature by replacing it in the visual context of the manuscript, the fundamental difference between print technology and manuscript reproduction separates our positions. Print technology is copy technology. Manuscript propagation may be viewed as a means of copying pre-existing texts, and that is the way text editing and textual studies have regarded manuscripts. This is a reductive view—based on the empirical or functional observation that since manuscripts were to provide copies of works for reading, they must have been *copies*. A reproduction may indeed be a copy, but a copy with a difference—a difference born of the intervention of an author, someone who sees and reports (reproduces) what is seen, transposing it into his own dialect, and so forth. It is this difference that makes the manuscript a space of representation, a space of supplementation, and not simply a copy. By the late Middle Ages supplementary practices had become pronounced, if not dominant, in many manuscripts of secular works. This phenomenon is as important to our understanding of the Middle Ages, and the role of art in its culture, as is the quest for an ideal text of Chrétien de Troyes's *romans*. These are the issues material philology seeks to explore.

139

15. For example, the following: Michael Camille, *Image on the Edge: The Margins of Medieval Art* and *The Gothic Idol: Ideology and Image-Making in Medieval Art*; Georges Didi-Huberman, *Devant l'image: Question posée aux fins d'une histoire de l'art*; A. N. Doane and Carol Braun Pasternack, eds., *Vox Intexta: Orality and Textuality in the Middle Ages*; Wlad Godzich and Jeffrey Kittay, *The Emergence of Prose: An Essay in Prosaics*; Sylvia Huot, *From Song to Book: The Poetics of Writing in Old French Lyric and Lyrical Narrative Poetry*; Laura Kendrick, *The Game of Love: Troubadour Wordplay*; Samuel N. Rosenberg and Hans Tischler, *The Monophonic Songs in the Roman de Fauvel*; Linda Seidel, *Stories of an Icon: Jan van Eyck's Arnolfini Wedding Portrait Re-Viewed*; Gabrielle Spiegel, *Romancing the Past: The Rise of Vernacular Prose Historiography in Thirteenth-Century France*; Margaret Switten, *The Cansos of Raimon de Miraval: A Study of Poems and Melodies*; Siegfried Wenzel, *Macaronic Sermons in the Age of Chaucer: Social Discourse and Private Reform*. Some of my own essays in this area include "Commentary and/as Image," "Ekphrasis, Iconoclasm, and Desire," "Marie de France's Common Places," and "On the Sociology of Manuscript Illumination."

16. "Custume fu as ancïens, / Ceo testimoine Precïens, / Es livres ke jadis feseient, / Assez oscurement diseient / Pur ceus ki a venir esteient / Et ki aprendre les deveient, / K'i peüssent gloser la lettre / E de lur sen le surplus mettre. / Li philesophe le saveient, / Par eus meïsmes entendeient, / Cum plus trespassereit li tens, / Plus serreient sutil de sens / Et plus se savreient garder / De ceo k'i ert a trespasser" (Rychner, ed., *Lais*, "Prologue" vv. 9–22; "It was the ancients' custom / so Priscian says, / to speak cryptically / in the books they made in those days, / so that those who were to come / and who would learn them, /might gloss the letter, / and supplement it from their own understanding. / Poets knew / and understood themselves, / That the more time would pass, / the more subtle they would be in understanding / and the more they would retain / from that which was there to surpass").

17. "In addition to providing instruction in the correct decipherment of old handwriting, the traditional task of palaeography was to provide the means of dating manuscripts. . . . The breakthrough to the recognition of what script could tell us about history was achieved by Léopold Delisle and by Ludwig Traube, who linked it closely with Latin philology and the study of text transmission" (Bischoff 1–2).

18. Reason's speech rhymes "coilles" and "andoilles" (sausages made from hog's intestines) in a vivid passage linking the castration of Saturn with the birth of Venus, goddess of desire: "Joustice, qui jadis regnot, / Ou tens que Saturnus regne ot, / Cui Jupiter copa les coilles, / Ses fiz, con se fussent andoilles, / (Mout ot ci dur fill e amer), / Puis les gita dedenz la mer, / Don Venus la deesse issi, / Car li livres le dit issi" (Langlois, ed., vv. 5535–42); "Justice which used to reign / in the days when Saturn ruled / whose balls Jupiter, his son, / lopped off, like sausages, / (you might say a hard and bitter son) / Then he threw them in the sea / Whence the Goddess Venus arose, / for that's how the books tell it").

19. Of course there is considerable irony in the Lover's position since, not being a philologist, he does not realize that "coilles" is philologically just such a euphemism as he chides Reason for not using. Old French *coille* comes from Vulgar Latin *colea, Latin *coleus, "leather sack or wallet." By the same token, Old French *vit*, "prick," which the Lover also reproaches Reason for naming, is also philologically a euphemism derived from Latin *vectis*, "lever, crowbar." Jean de Meun could have had Reason use a latinate term such as *genitaires* (the term used by Douce 195, fol. 122v, in rubricating Origen's self-castration) or *genitailles*. Indeed the Latin book that Reason cites in her original mention of *coilles* uses the

euphemism *naturalia* for testicles: "Juppiter patri naturalia resecavit et in mare projecit, et ex iis nata est Venus, dea libidinis" (Langlois, ed., 2:344, n. to vv. 5537–42, citing Mai, vol. 3, § 102). The fact that Jean insists on the vernacular and popular terms suggests the complex layers of the intellectual and linguistic agenda played out in the debate.

NEW DIRECTIONS

BEYOND THE BORDERS OF NATION AND DISCIPLINE

Joan M. Ferrante

I am honored to be included in this gathering of distinguished French medievalists, though I do not feel I belong. I console myself with the thought that I have been invited as a comparatist, that I can make comments from an odd angle looking in, while others make them from the center looking out. I shall offer an informal presentation in the spirit of a round-table discussion; not a master plan for the decade to come, but a list of suggestions for future work.

Nothing of what I have to suggest is radically different from what has been or is being done; it is mainly a plea for more of the same or for somewhat different emphases, since by and large I admire what my colleagues here have done and think it has considerably advanced medieval studies in general. I would like to see (and not only in French) more opening out to international, interdisciplinary, and "intersexual" studies. I would like to see the emphasis in the study of medieval literature continue to shift, and shift much further, from close investigations of individual texts to placing those texts in a much larger picture, in relation to the literature of other languages, to the cultural, historical, political, economic context of the work and its audience or audiences. This is not to say that we should ever give up close reading of texts, but that we should step back and look at them from various distances and angles—and in some cases that means we have to help build the scaffolds from which we look—before, or at least while, we do it. (I would suggest a moratorium on close reading while we work on the context, if I thought I could respect it myself.)

As a first step, I would like to see a technical development that would benefit us in every area. Such a project may be in the works, but if it is I am not aware of it. This would be to put on disk, and to make available to libraries and to individuals by modem, all the still unpublished medieval works—the critical editions or studies on decaying paper or in small out-of-date editions or in dissertation form, in short anything that would have too small a market to be published commercially, but that could be of use to scholars.

Despite the astonishingly large number of chansons de geste that have been published, there are still some that are only mentioned, as far as I can make out, such as *Renier*. Most of the prose romances summarized by Löseth are still unpublished, as are the *Histoire ancienne jusqu'à César* and the *Échecs amoureux*. We do not have all the continuations of Perceval, nor all the volumes of *Le roman de Perceforest*. Even someone drawing as much scholarly attention as Christine de Pisan (see p. 193) is not yet completely available: the *Lettre d'Othéa* and the *Cité des dames* have been translated, but edited only in dissertations; *Le livre des fais d'armes et de chevallerie* is available only in a dissertation while the *Livre des trois vertus* has been translated but not edited.[i] There is no collection of the "chansons de nonne"; some of the lesser known and later Provençal poets have not been fully edited or published, and many poems that have been are in old and not easily accessible journals; a complete edition of the poems of the trobairitz only came out in 1991.[2] If as interesting a work as the *Roman de Silence* was not published in a book until 1972 (ed. Thorpe), one wonders what else might be out there. Do we have all the drama, all the saints' lives, all the chronicles, the books of manners, the medical treatises? Do we not need to expand our knowledge of popular culture in the Middle Ages considerably?

In the best of all possible worlds, should we not have editions like Pickens's of Jaufré Rudel that give us all the variant readings in context? Stephen Nichols warned recently of the dangers of reading a lyric innocent of that context ("Introduction" 3). How different would our understanding of *Partonopeu de Blois* be if we could read it in all its variations? Is it asking too much to think we might someday have texts available in the larger context of their entire manuscripts, the particular version with the other works in exactly the form in which they accompany it in one manuscript or another—something Sylvia Huot has whetted our appetite for—or even, given the infinitely expanding possibilities of technology, that we might in the future be able to see the text in its visual context, a reproduction of the manuscript's verbal format and illuminations in our own libraries?

We have as models both the Dartmouth Dante Project that is making available on disk Dante commentaries from the fourteenth century on, and the Brown Women Writers Project that will give us greater access to women's writings in English from 1330 to 1830. They are evidence that determined scholars working together can at least begin such massive projects.[3]

Meanwhile, as one step in enlarging the picture, I would like to see more work across national and language borders: aesthetic and cultural rather than source studies of Provençal and Arabic lyrics (there is much to be done here by way of literary analysis and historic investigation, including the role of Arabic slave-women as singers and composers of lyrics), comparative studies of Provençal and German lyric, of German and Italian/Sicilian lyric. A literary study of the Sicilian court of Frederick II might be particularly fruitful; it included Arabs, Jews, Italians, and Germans, and many poets. Frederick was a patron of Walter von der Vogelweide, as well as of Giacomo da Lentini and Pier della Vigna, and he himself composed poetry in Italian, while his father, Henry VI, had composed in German, and his father-in-law, Jean de Brienne, in French (Contini 1:46). Is there not also something to be learned from a comparison of the texts recorded and the variations in those texts in French and Italian manuscripts of the troubadours?

I would like to see studies made of different versions of the same story such as the *Roman d'Eneas* and Heinrich von Veldecke's *Eneide,* Chrétien de Troyes's *Érec* or his *Yvain* and Hartmann von Aue's, or Chrétien's *Conte del graal* and Wolfram von Eschenbach's *Parzival,* not to say the many Tristans, studies that would seek to show not influence or sources, but a contemporary response to the works. We can, for instance, see the problems Chrétien posed for at least part of his audience in the attempts Hartmann makes to explain or explain away certain details: Enite's father, in Hartmann's *Erec*, is understandably dubious about Erec's proposal of marriage because they are so poor; Enite is able to see and hear better than Erec on the road because his armor inhibits his vision and hearing; when Erec is angry at Enite's speaking, he punishes her by making her take care of the horses, and she has a difficult time managing eight of them until she ties the bridles together. There must have been many literal-minded hearers who worried about the same things. Does the German tendency to name even the most minor characters say something about German culture, or does it suggest that at least some in Chrétien's audience were confused by the number of nameless actors in his stories?

We have, I think, come a long way from the searches for Celtic sources in Chrétien, or even from the sophisticated stylistic study of Thomas and Gottfried by Dijksterhuis which resulted in this chauvinistic conclusion: "These differences between Thomas and Gottfried are not without implications beyond the two poets. For they are not simply a difference between two independent individuals, they belong to their people and their time. In the people, there is the Romance-Germanic difference; the German always with the drive towards movement, opening out, the Romanic towards peace and self-enclosure."[4] We are more likely, if we look at works in other languages at all, to treat both works with equal respect, not to use the comparison to put one of them down. But some traces of that chauvinism remain in attention to critical works. A critic I much admire, in a very interesting article on *Silence*, makes a point about Dante and cites Pézard and Vance as the sources.[5] While I respect the work of both, I found myself distressed at the certainly unintended implication that French Dante criticism is all that matters, particularly since the same point had been made by Dorothy Sayers, though only a year earlier than Pézard, and she credits it to the sixteenth-century commentary of Gelli.[6] Perhaps my reaction to this slight was exaggerated by my suspicion that her remarks were ignored because they were made in the notes to her translation—serious scholars do not read translations—just as Robert Hanning and I feel our remarks about Marie de France have often been ignored because they were made in the notes to a translation.

What I am really concerned with, however, is the need to expand our vision beyond national boundaries, to include in our studies of particular works the response to them in the courts or cities of other nations as another way of getting at possible meanings for their contemporaries. Even more important, of course, is the attempt to establish a historical and cultural context for those works at home. What sorts of courts were they being written for? What other poets or scholars were connected with them? What relations did they have with other courts, and so forth? One can profitably study the "text's social logic" from a historian's point of view, as Gabrielle Spiegel does with the Pseudo-Turpin chronicles, to understand the influence of social and political changes on the evolution of prose historiography. Or one can look at the allusions to political and social phenomena in particular works or poets, Chrétien's romances, the *Nibelungenlied*, the *Divine Comedy*, to help in understanding or explaining the poets' meanings or the meanings that might have occurred to their audiences.

In the case of Chrétien, such allusions reveal an increasing cynicism through his work. In *Érec*, the socio-political allusions are slight: perhaps in the court Arthur holds at Nantes for Érec and Énide's coronation there is a reflection of the court Henry II held at Nantes to have his barons do homage to himself and his son, the Young King. If so, this is presumably an admiring allusion to the harmony between kings and vassals, with its promise of international peace, a "centripetal" movement, to borrow Vance's word. This mood does not last. In *Cligés*, though the first part offers a happy solution to the problems of Alexandre and Sordamor within the Arthurian setting, the second introduces troubles immediately after Cligés's birth when his uncle usurps his lands, and gets progressively worse through the broken promises and betrayals of the various marriage arrangements. Fourrier has documented the contemporary events, the succession to the Byzantine throne of the younger brother Manuel Comnenus, rather than the elder Isaac, the complicated series of marriage negotiations, some successful some not, between Byzantium, the German empire, and the English and French monarchies, all of which must have been exciting subjects of gossip for Chrétien's audience. But Fourrier did not discuss the implications for Chrétien of this second part, so filled with intrigues, deceptions, and hypocrisy (not least in the love of the hero and heroine), following and replacing the harmony achieved in the first part. Never mind that this is a Tristan parody (which replaces the Tristan adultery with a scarcely more palatable false marriage); we are left at the end with a rather bitter taste from the actions of all the characters. Though Alis is wrong to have stolen Cligés's inheritance, and Fenice's father is wrong to renege on the promised marriage because he gets a better offer—making the marriage of Fenice and Alis wrong from every point of view—Fenice is nonetheless not right to claim greater purity than Isot because she does not sleep with her husband while, ignoring her position as empress, she does run off with her lover. Clearly, the ideals represented by the Arthurian court have been destroyed by the political realities of the world.

These unpleasant realities begin to invade the Arthurian world in Chrétien's remaining romances, making their message more and more cynical. In *Yvain*, the historic references are less specific. We are shown social injustice in a series of emblematic episodes, in which women must be defended from various kinds of violence and oppression and exploitation, the most striking of which is that of the silk-workers in the Pesme Aventure. The hero, who seems to be moving towards an enhanced sense of social responsibility through his adventures as the Knight of the Lion, is distressed by the plight of the three hundred maidens, but does not offer to do anything for them. They do not fit into the normal chivalric context and he would presumably leave them there, despite his sympathy, if he were not forced to fight the two demons who hold them, and thus coincidentally release the workers. Since Chrétien shows us the young girl reading a romance to her father who is reclining on silk ("se gisoit sor un drap de soie," ed. Reid, vv. 5363–4) in the garden of the same establishment, oblivious to the factory and the plight of its workers, one is forced to make a connection. She is presumably reading escape literature, the kind that has "no redeeming social purpose," as it were, not the kind Chrétien writes with its serious messages of social re- 151 sponsibility, but Chrétien's hero, though sympathetic to the workers when their situation is forced on his consciousness, is no more moved than the family in the garden to help them. The hero's developing sense of social responsibility seems to include only noble women in distress, but even at this level he is not able to follow through. He must return at the end of the story to the duty he had assumed in his reckless youth of defending Laudine's fountain, a duty that involves him in continuous and pointless vi- olence and that does not even enable him to prevent the periodic destruction of the land. Has Chrétien become disillusioned with the world around him and the power of his poetry to move people to proper action?

It certainly seems so in *Lancelot,* where we probably again have a specific historic event at the core, the imprisonment of a queen suggesting the continuing captivity of Eleanor of Aquitaine (1174–89), the mother of Chrétien's patron, Marie de Champagne. Since Marie was the daughter of Eleanor and Louis VII, it does not seem farfetched to connect, or to wonder if Chrétien's audience connected, Guenievre's husband Arthur with Louis, and her arro- gant, lustful, treacherous captor and would-be husband, Melea- gant, with Eleanor's second husband, Henry II. At the beginning of the story, Chrétien treats the queen with great sympathy, show- ing her to be at the mercy of Arthur's dubious attachment to his seneschal Kes; she sacrifices herself to the needs of the king and the self-delusions and self-importance of his hatchet-man—I can think of no better explanation for Arthur's attachment to Kes. But when Guenievre the political victim, who inspired extraordinary courage and devotion in Lancelot, becomes Guenievre the tyrant in love, Chrétien's attitude changes (D. Kelly, *Sens* 54ff.). Now she becomes a destructive force, luring her devoted knight into ac- tions that lead inevitably to his being immured in a tower, "par traïson" Chrétien says when he alludes to the event in *Yvain* (ed. Reid, v. 4744). But is the "traïson" Meleagant's treachery or Lancelot's betrayal of his king or both? And is Lancelot perhaps a figure for Richard Lionheart, inspired to chivalric and poetic feats by the traditions of his mother's Provençal heritage, but also to rebellion against his father by his mother's political intrigues? In any case, it seems clear that the lessons of contemporary politics have so far disillusioned Chrétien that he can no longer pretend that the literary model works any better.

Richard Lionheart may be in the background of the *Nibelungenlied* as well, as one of the examples of contemporary dirty politics, because of his capture on the way home from crusade by Leopold of Austria and the large ransom paid for him to the German emperor, Henry VI; in both parts of the poem, it is dangerous, indeed fatal, to heroes to travel to or through supposedly friendly lands. But far more important to the story are the power struggles between key nobles and the emperor: Frederick Barbarossa, lacking the centralized power of the English and French monarchies, had been forced to make concessions to his princes to keep their support, concessions which only increased their strength, perhaps reflected in Gunther's position as the king of the Burgundians, forced to rely on the strength of Siegfried against his enemies in battle and unable to control the political intrigues of his strongest vassal, Hagen. (There may be a good deal of Henry VI, far less effective a ruler than his father, in Gunther as well.) Might the audience have seen in Siegfried a reflection of Henry the Lion, Duke of Bavaria and a rival candidate for the crown, who was eventually forced into exile, his lands given to Frederick's loyal supporter, Otto (Hagen)?[7]

In the poem, Hagen is at the center of a power struggle. Ostensibly in the service of his king, he uses and then eliminates the most powerful figure on the scene and his possible rival, Siegfried, then seizes/steals Siegfried's treasure from his widow, Kriemhild; she takes Siegfried's place as Hagen's opponent and finally destroys both Hagen and the king, though at great cost to her new land. The place of women in the power struggle is the most puzzling element of the poem. Although the rivalry between Brunhild and Kriemhild is the cause of the death of Siegfried and ultimately of the destruction of the Burgundian nation, and although Kriemhild is described as a devil when she obsessively pursues her revenge, the poet betrays some sympathy for the two women in his treatment of their feudal status. He shows both of them early on being deprived of their feudal and legal rights, as if to suggest that their later destructive actions are a result of those wrongs.

When Brunhild, who has been a powerful and respected ruler in her own right, is tricked into marrying the unworthy Gunther, she leaves her land in the care of an uncle until her husband can assume control of it (a detail that is not followed up—presumably he is never strong enough to assert his right there). Meanwhile, however, her husband's men dispense her treasure lavishly, saying she will have enough wealth from her husband. This sounds generous, but in fact it leaves her without the means to build a power base in her new land. Deprived of any official role, she broods about the feudal status of her sister- and brother-in-law, and is drawn into the disastrous rivalry with Kriemhild.

Kriemhild, too, has been deprived of her feudal rights; at her marriage, she demanded her share of her family lands and a third of their knights. Her brothers do not deny her claim, but her husband refuses the land. After Siegfried's death, she makes several unsuccessful attempts to take legal action. When his wounds bleed in the presence of Hagen, she makes a public accusation, but nothing is done. (Had a man made such a well-founded accusation, it is hard to imagine how he could have been so easily ignored.) When she claims and takes possession of Siegfried's treasure at her family's greedy suggestion but then begins to spend it in order to buy the loyalty that will help her avenge her husband, Hagen seizes the treasure and refuses to return it. When she accepts Etzel's offer of marriage, it is because it gives her a much more powerful base of operations, from which she will finally get revenge on Hagen. That revenge comes, however, only after Hagen has publicly offended her by flouting his possession of Siegfried's sword, as if gloating over the unavenged murder of her husband. To a man, in epic, this would be justification for murder (compare

Beowulf, ed. Klaeber, vv. 2041–62). Kriemhild does indeed murder Hagen and bring about the destruction of the whole dynasty he has served, but her action horrifies her husband's men, and she is quickly executed.

I am curious, but have not yet been able to determine why two of the figures involved in the great power struggles of the poem are women. Is the poet making a critical comment on those vassals who oppose imperial authority by portraying them as women? If so why does he suggest that they have been wronged in the first place? Or is he alluding to actual women, like Beatrice the heir to Burgundy, whom Frederick married presumably in order to extend his control in the South and consolidate his power? What role, if any, did she play in imperial politics? Is he alluding to Constance, heiress of Sicily, who married Frederick's son, Henry VI, turning his attention to the South and the Middle East, while the imperial structure his father had built collapsed? It is not easy to find the kind of information about these or other women it would take to answer such questions—yet another sort of gap that needs to be filled.

The role of contemporary history in the *Divine Comedy* would not be overlooked by even a casual reader of Dante, but the extent of its importance to the structure and meaning of the poem is not always apparent even to Dantisti. I will give only a few examples, because I have written on this elsewhere (*Political Vision*), and also because I seem to be moving far from the subject of the conference—though my point is partly that these things are also our subject. That Dante was deeply involved in the Church-state debate raging in France and Italy and Germany, we know from his letters and the *Monarchia*, but it is not so obvious to us as it was to contemporaries that the *Comedy* is part of this debate, not only in the passages that explicitly mention the Donation of Constantine and papal assumptions of secular power, but throughout the poem through use of imagery intimately associated with that debate. The two swords of Peter in Luke 22:38 are taken by papalists to stand for spiritual and temporal power, both ultimately in the pope's hands though one is usually delegated, whereas Dante has the angels who represent the Church in Purgatory—a Church that is pure spirit—carry only one sword. Similarly, the sun and the moon are used by papalists to represent respectively the papacy as the source of light and power on earth, and secular monarchy, taking its light and power from the Church; Dante, in contrast, has Marco Lombardo speak of two suns, one eclipsing the other, in Purgatory. In Paradise, where he cannot deny the order of the planets, he places failed religious in the moon and great teachers (most of them religious or clergy) in the sun, but the secular rulers who serve justice are in the sphere of Jupiter above both the moon and the sun. Dante also subverts the papalist argument that Christendom is one body, and a body, if it is not to be a monster, can have only one head—as Christendom must have the pope. In the drama of Church history at the top of Purgatory, Dante presents the Church as a chariot, not a body but an inanimate object, which nonetheless, when it takes on secular wealth and power in the eagle's feathers, becomes a monster of seven heads and ten horns, indeed the monster of the Apocalypse, far more powerful as a poetic image than discursive arguments could be.

Law and legal practice are another important part of the contemporary scene for medieval literature (see Bloch, *Medieval French Literature and Law*). The world of secular wealth, trade, and banking is yet another. Chrétien de Troyes was composing in the commercially active area of Northern France, Dante in the then financial center of the western world, Northern Italy. For both, as for many other writers, commercial thought and language are part of their art, a point that has been made for *Yvain* by Eugene Vance in "Chrétien's *Yvain* and the Ideologies of Change and Exchange," where he argues for the need to recognize the presence and influence of economic interests in late-twelfth-century culture and in Chrétien's poems in particular. Judith Kellogg, in "Economic and Social Tensions Reflected in the Romance of Chrétien de Troyes," looks at the effects of the changing economic climate on the aristocracy, as seen in *Érec et Énide* and in *Yvain*. These studies are necessary and fruitful corrections to our limited literary perspective. We already know, from their own lips, how important financial reward is to poets and minstrels. We need to know much more about the economic underpinnings of their courts and towns, not to say countries.

In Dante's case, we know that the banking cities of North Italy, like Florence and Lucca, were power-brokers throughout Europe, that financiers were as important in Dante's world as politicians and churchmen, that Dante had close connections with this world, but we have not paid enough attention to the reflections of these facts in Dante's poem.[8] Dante could not have failed to include financiers among his intended audience, if he wanted to reach the sources of power, and indeed we know from the letters of merchants in the Datini archives that they were enthusiastic readers of the *Comedy*.

    It is not surprising, then, to find that the poem is full of commercial language, which is not always obvious in translation, but which would certainly have been noted by his audience. Not only are sins condemned in such language, as one might expect: he says of those who foment division in Church and state that "they acquire their load by dividing, for which here they pay their fee" ("si paga il fio / a quei che, scomettendo, acquistan carco," ed. Singleton, *Inf.* 27.135–36); a simoniac comments that "on earth he put wealth, here he puts himself in a purse" ("su l'avere e qui me misi in borsa," *Inf.* 19.72); the weights borne by the hypocrites "make their scales creak" ("li pesi / fan così cigolar le lor bilance," *Inf.* 23.101–2). But in their penance as well, souls in Purgatory "pay their debt" to God ("il debito si paghi," *Purg.* 10.108), "pay their fee for pride" ("di tal superbia qui si paga il fio," *Purg.* 11.88), "pay such coin in satisfaction" ("cotal moneta rende / a sodisfar," *Purg.* 11.125–26). The sharing of love is contrasted to the distribution of wealth in economic terms that imply the difference between spiritual and corporal usury: earthly goods are lessened by partnership, while heaven's are increased by the number of possessors (*Purg.* 15.5off.). Even Dante's religious faith is a coin he has in his purse whose "alloy and weight have been examined . . . so shining and round that there is no doubt of its minting" ("assai bene è trascorsa / d'esta moneta già la lega e'l peso . . . sì lucida e sì tonda / che nel suo conio nulla mi s'inforsa," *Par.*

24.83–87), and the knowledge he gathers on his journey is cargo he is loading on his ship (*Purg.* 26.73–75). Dante is a merchant loading the ship of his mind, "la navicella del mio ingegno," with wares, doctrine both political and religious, he hopes to sell his audience.[9] That Dante's concern with commerce is not purely metaphorical is clear from his attention to specific economic sins: he condemns "grave usura," not simple lending—unlike the Church, Dante does not place usury within fraud, but only in its shadow, though he condemns other kinds of illicit profit in the circle of fraud, particularly commercial fraud (theft), as betrayal of one's fellows. Like Aquinas, he recognizes trade and finance as essential components of his society which must be controlled.

Since money and language are the basic means of social exchange, Dante treats the abuses of both similarly: gibberish first appears in the circle of avarice, blasphemy and usury are in the same section of violence against God, and lying and counterfeiting are in the lowest section of fraud, because falsifying coins is as dangerous to social stability as falsifying words. Numismatics is another, if minor, area that bears some attention. Contemporary coins (see p. 193) suggest added meaning in at least two passages in the *Comedy:* the coins of Boniface VIII, Dante's arch-villain, and of no other contemporary pope, use the form "Pape" (others use "Papa" or various abbreviations). Might Dante's audience not have connected the monster's greeting in *Inferno* 7, "Pape Satan aleppe," with Boniface, giving an added fillip to the reading "Pope Satan"? Luccan coins had the image of the *Santo Volto* on them, which gives another twist to the devil's comment to the upended barrator (*Inf.* 21.48), "Qui non ha loco il Santo Volto," literally "There is no place for the *Santo Volto* here," or in other words, "You can't bribe your way out of here." Given the wide diffusion of minting and the great variety of coins thereby produced, an investigation of northern coins might produce something interesting as well.

A far more obvious area of visual investigation is art and architecture—the world outside the text and the world of the text, what the literary audience might see or be likely to call to mind. Anthony Cassell has shown us how much church sculpture can add to our sense of Dante's meaning, by his elegant juxtapositions of Christ rising from the tomb with Farinata rising from his tomb, so that we see Farinata also as a perverted Christ. The sense of Satan, frozen in the ice, as a perverted figure of God is enhanced by the images of Christ half submerged at his baptism. And a particularly telling comment is made on Pier della Vigna's actions when we connect his soul to be hung on the tree of his body not only with Christ, the body hung on a tree, but also with the body of Judas hanging from a tree. Jeffrey Schnapp has also made exciting connections between Dante's heaven of Mars and the mosaics of Sant' Apollinare in Ravenna, christianizing the Anchises-Aeneas echoes and adding a political dimension, Ravenna's independence from Rome and dependence on the Christian emperor, as the setting for the saint's life.

Much is yet to be learned from the images that surrounded poet and audience in their daily lives, where we still have access to them, and much from the images that surround the text. We can assume that the illuminations in a manuscript had some significance for the meaning of a text from the care that certain authors took with them. Christine de Pisan may have wanted to be sure her presentation copies were impressive, but she presumably had some interest in preventing the images from distorting the meaning. Certainly Hildegard of Bingen would have been concerned that the images of her visions were as true to their divine origins as her descriptions. Although we do not have many illustrations that can be connected with the composers of the text, we can still look to them for help with understanding later readings—though not without the help of art historians to warn about clichés and conventions. Alone, we and they are limited; working together we can get much further. We should also be paying more attention to the musical context of the text, the relation of sound and meaning, the possible parodies derived not only from words but from using old music for a new poem; without the music we cannot have even a vague sense of audience reception. Here again, of course, a modern sense of music, however sophisticated, is not sufficient; we need musicologists to tell us what were the expected effects of different modes, what were the acceptable and unacceptable intervals. We should also ask why some poems were set to music and

JOAN M. FERRANTE

others were not and how far back that practice goes (in each vernacular). Perhaps many of these questions cannot be answered, but if we don't have them in mind we will never know.

Finally, I would like to point to a large area of investigation in which it is crucial to have questions in mind in order to notice the answers as they present themselves, that is, the place of women in the literary history of the Middle Ages. I am sure that if we look, we will be able to learn much more about their roles as authors, as patrons, as audience, and as performers. There are sufficient hints of women performing as minstrels, *joglaritz*, to suggest a real presence: not only the court ladies who compose and sing lais, like Isot in the *Tristans* of both Thomas and Gottfried, and heroines who disguise themselves as minstrels, Nicolette and Silence, but a "spilwîp" who carries messages in Wolfram's *Parzival* (ed. Leitzmann, 7.363.1), and the dangerous "joculatrix" in the anonymous cleric's warning: "Item, sicut auceps possit in laqueo vel rethe aviculam unam doctam quae volitando alas quasi libera extendat et cantet: sic Dyabolus aliquam joculatricem quae sciat cantiones ad choreas adducit, ut alias secum trahat" ("Similarly, as the hunter of birds can [place] in his snare or net a tamed bird which, flying, may extend its wings and sing as if it were free, so the devil draws some female joglar who knows songs to dances so that she may draw others with her").[10] Duggan cites this passage as part of a series of attacks on joglars, which is quite important, but I suggest that we must also look for passages which are specific to women.

The presence of women as patrons has been documented to some extent, but only as individual details within the larger picture of patronage.[11] We should look more closely at the role women actually played in the development of medieval literature, at the kinds of works women sponsored, not just translations into the vernacular—assumed to be needed because women could not understand Latin, though there is good evidence that laywomen were better able to understand Latin than laymen before the thirteenth century—but Latin works. The *Patrologia latina* has many references to religious works requested by or dedicated to women from Jerome and Augustine to Fulgentius, Alcuin, and Abelard.

Historical works are also addressed to women: Ethelweard's chronicle for Matilda, a granddaughter of Otto I; indeed the life of Otto was written by a woman, Hrotsvit, at the request of a woman, Gerberga, but presented to the Ottonian court; Adela, daughter of William the Conqueror, urged Hugues of Fleury to write his chronicle; one Latin life of Edward the Confessor was written for and dedicated to Edward's queen; another, in Anglo-Norman, was written by a nun of Barking; there are histories written for women in French from Wace's *Brut* and Gaimar's *Estoire des Engles/Anglais* to Froissart and Joinville. There is at least one chanson de geste, *Enfances Ogier le Danois*, dedicated to Marie de Brabant, and there are the various romances: Benoît de Sainte-Maure most probably dedicated the *Roman de Troie* to Eleanor, "riche dame de riche rei" (ed. Constans, v. 13468). Gautier d'Arras began *Eracle* for one of Eleanor's daughters, Marie de Champagne (for whom Chrétien de Troyes composed *Lancelot*, however grudgingly), and for the husband of another daughter, Aelis de Blois, for whom *Partonopeu de Blois* may also have been written (Keller, "Literary" 197). We do not know what role, if any, a third daughter, Matilda, wife of Henry of Saxony, played in the literary life of her court, for which Eilhart may have written his *Tristrant*. Perhaps we cannot find out, but unless we look we will never know.

No doubt there are still women patrons to be identified, and then there are other questions to be asked, such as those raised by June McCash in "Marie de Champagne's 'Cuer d'ome et cors de fame.'" She looks into the nature of Marie de Champagne's literary influence by comparing the works known to have been written for her, Evrat's *Genesis*, the translation and gloss of "Eructavit cor meum," and the *Lancelot*, as well as one that may have come from her court, Andreas Capellanus's *De arte honeste amandi*. There is much to be learned from such studies.

There is also much to be learned from asking questions of the text about the presence of women in the audience, the female audience inscribed in the text. From Cercamon on, we have references to women in the audience: "These troubadours, between truth and falsehood, confound lovers and wives and husbands" ("Ist trobador, entre ver e mentir, / afollon drutz e molhers et espos," ed. Wolf and Rosenstein, 8.19–20); many poets address at least one stanza in a poem to their lady. The troubadour *Vidas* and *Razos* tell us that women are particularly interested in the honor they can derive from being the subjects of poems, and encourage poets in order to enhance their reputations, to the envy of other women (ed. Boutière and Schutz, XI.F.4, XVIII.B.3, XXXIII.B.3–11). In a particularly interesting reference, Bernart de Ventadorn takes comfort that his lady is literate, that "she knows and understands letters and it pleases me that I write the words and, if she pleases, she reads them for my good" ("sap letras et enten / et agrada·m qu'eu escria / los motz, e s'a leis plazia, / legis los al meu sauvamen," ed. Appel, 17.53–56).

The notion of a literate female audience brings up other issues. We know there were trobairitz (the body of even their extant texts may be larger than we have thought, as various people argue in Paden's *The Voice of the Trobairitz*); we have examples of women engaging in love debates with men in the many *pastorelas* and the dialogues of Andreas Capellanus, where the women consistently debunk the male rhetoric of love. In these cases, we have men writing in a woman's voice, but Andreas tells us that noble women are quick to censure and ridicule men: "nobilis enim mulier sive nobilior promptissimo reperitur et audax hominis nobilioris facta vel sermones arguere multumque laetatur, si suis ipsum pulchre possit dictis illudere" ("for a noblewoman or a woman of the higher nobility is found to be very ready and bold in censuring the deeds or words of a man of the higher nobility, and she is very glad if she has a good opportunity to say something to ridicule him").[12] Is it not likely, then, that women engaged in playful or even serious debates with men at court, and is it not at least possible that they also engaged in poetic debates to a much greater extent than the few *tensos* that have been attributed to them suggest? When Marcabru and Peire d'Alvernhe send birds as messengers to their ladies, might they not be asking for an answering poem from them? In Italian there are answering poems supposedly between men and women by Cielo d'Alcamo, Guittone d'Arezzo, and the Amico di Dante, as well as by the one woman we know of who wrote in Italian in this period, the Compiuta Donzella. The exchange is always attributed to one poet, but can we be sure that two were not involved? Think of the answering poems of Guido Cavalcanti and Dante, cited in the *Vita nuova,* playing on the same rhyme schemes and words—if we did not know Guido as a poet in his own right could we be sure Dante had not written both? I do not know that we can ever determine male and female authorship of particular poems, but if we at least consider both possibilities, we may see things we have not seen before.

There is no need to suggest that more work be done on the women writers we already know. That will, certainly, take care of itself. And perhaps it will lead to investigations into yet un-published material that may turn up other women writers. I have been studying letters written to or by women through the Middle Ages and have been pleasantly surprised at the extent of correspondence involving women and at the range of subject matter. Surely there are other unexplored areas. In this, as in all the other topics of investigation, we have only to be open to the possibilities.

NOTES

1. Loukopoulos, "Classical Mythology in the Works of Christine de Pisan, with an Edition of *L'Epistre Othea* from the Manuscript Harley 4431"; Chance, trans., *Letter of Othea to Hector;* Curnow, "The *Livre de la cité des dames* of Christine de Pisan: A Critical Edition"; Richards, trans., *The Book of the City of Ladies;* Laennec, "Christine *antygrafe:* Authorship and Self in the Prose Works of Christine de Pizan with an edition of B.N. Ms. 603 *'Le livre des fais d'armes et de chevallerie' ";* Lawson, trans., *The Treasure of the City of Ladies.*

2. The Rieger edition had not appeared when the conference was held.

3. I have recently learned from Robert Hollander, who got the Dartmouth project started, that Princeton is considering establishing a center for machine-readable texts that would include, though not be limited to, medieval works. Any move in this direction is welcome.

4. "Dieser Unterschied zwischen Thomas und Gottfried ist nicht ohne weiteres der zwischen zwei Dichtern. Denn sie sind nicht auf sich selbst stehende Individualitäten, sie gehören ihrem Volk und ihrer Zeit an. In dem Volk ist es der Unterschied romanisch-germanisch; der Germane hat vor allem den Trieb zur Bewegung, zur Offenheit, der Romane zur Ruhe und Geschlossenheit" (Dijksterhuis 44).

JOAN M. FERRANTE

5. "That is why, as A. Pézard and E. Vance have shown, Dante associates blasphemy, sodomy and usury. . ." (Bloch, "Silence" 92).

6. Pézard's *Dante sous la pluie de feu* was published in 1950; Sayers's translation of *Hell*, in which the comment appears, was first published in 1949 (see endnotes to canto 17).

7. Haymes gives political and social background, but specifically refrains from making such connections.

8. One notable exception is Garrani; I have also discussed these issues in chapter six of *The Political Vision*.

9. The implied metaphor of the artist as merchant occurs in the Tristan poems too, particularly in Eilhart and Gottfried von Strassburg. Both merchant and artist sell themselves and their wares to a receptive audience, both are messengers between cultures.

10. Paris, Bibliothèque nationale lat. 16515, cited by Duggan 731, who cites Faral as his source.

11. See particularly Holzknecht and Legge, from whom many of the details about specific works in this paragraph are drawn. (Also, for more local studies, see Benton and Lejeune.—W. D. P.)

12. Trojel, ed., beginning of dialogue 8. The translation is from Parry, 107. For a fuller discussion of women as debunkers of the male rhetoric of love, see Ferrante, "Male Fantasy and Female Reality in Courtly Literature."

OLD FRENCH LITERATURE AND THE NEW MEDIEVALISM

R. Howard Bloch

Word's out. There's something exciting going on in medieval studies. And maybe just a little bit in the Renaissance too. While those who study classical French literature have witnessed the virtual disappearance not of a field but of *the* battlefield upon which the modern critical wars—what was known in the mid-sixties as "La Nouvelle Critique"—erupted, and while modernists are currently so mired in the question of who did what to whom during World War II that they have lost a sense of intellectual urgency, the study of medieval literature and culture has never been more alive or at a more interestingly innovative stage.

The institutional signs of a New Medievalism are everywhere: in the appointment of medievalists at major university centers, many of which remained without specialists in Old French after the deaths or retirements of the dominating philological figures in the forties, fifties, and sixties; in renewed interest among graduate students, many of whom are even returning to earlier questions having to do with the material conditions of the medieval text; in a number of recent scholarly gatherings pitched to new understandings of the Middle Ages or to plotting the future of medieval studies, including this very one; in the book and monograph series enumerated by William Paden (see p. 23 in this volume); in the founding of scholarly journals like *Assays, Exemplaria, Médiévales, Envoi;* in special issues of established reviews like *Yale*

French Studies (ed. Brownlee and Nichols), *Romanic Review* (ed. Nichols), *Esprit créateur* (ed. Uitti), *Littérature* (ed. Poirion); and—*mirabile dictu*—in the recent appearance of an issue of *Speculum* devoted to the so-called "New Philology" (ed. Nichols). Then too, a renaissance of interest in the Middle Ages can be seen in the symptomatic self-consciousness that has begun to creep into the discipline. By this I mean a certain belated thinking about just what it is we do when we study medieval culture, what such a gesture might mean in the late twentieth century, and especially in a world in which the old nationalistic boundaries that separated countries at the time our discipline was founded, and indeed account for the founding articulations of the field, may now be disappearing.

The question occurs naturally: Where do we go from here?

I have no answer to such a question. I shall, however, outline a number of trends which are already underway and which will, I think, continue into the next decade. In my opinion, these are the areas in which Old French studies are both most interesting and most powerfully promising of new answers not only to essential disciplinary questions, but to the possibility of moving beyond what has historically been a somewhat self-contained disciplinary preserve.

As I have said, we are currently witness to a phenomenon of increased self-consciousness on the part of medievalists, a trend which is not in and of itself a goal, but, I think, a necessary step in the understanding of the historical determinants of the field and thus of its future. An important consequence of the recent increase of interest in the Middle Ages is that questions which have in the past simply been taken for granted as being the immutable and natural defining issues of the field have begun to seem increasingly opaque. Indeed, those who write about the millennium between the fall of Rome and the discovery of the New World have come more and more to see that their assumptions regarding this period are as historically determined by the framing perceptions of the last century as they are by the artifacts of the medievalist's study. The necessary historicization or relativization of the past entailed by such a perception might be nothing more than a liberating pretext for change, or simply for imagining other possibilities than those already in place.

In this the field of medieval studies is not alone but part of a larger movement: almost every discipline within the social sciences and the humanities is currently wallowing in the question of its origins. Historians since Hayden White's work in the seventies have become more aware of the rhetorical underpinnings of the historical enterprise, just as anthropologists since the publication of Lévi-Strauss's *Tristes tropiques* have discovered the literary and even biographical elements that comprise the anthropological voyage, otherwise known as fieldwork. So too, medievalists have begun to write the external history of the discipline from a perspective, or I should say perspectives, that would have been unthinkable twenty years ago. Here one can identify several stages, which are, in reality, more logical than chronological.

The first stage can be seen in the attempt to write the history of medieval studies from within the perspective of the discipline itself, that is, from a point of view implying a minimum distance of the historian from his or her object of study. The Iordan-Orr history of romance philology, of course, springs immediately to mind. This is a work whose highly narrative structure, based upon intellectual genealogies, who did their thesis with whom, merely repeats the movement of the philologist's desire for origins, which, as I have maintained elsewhere, also mirrors medieval thinkers' own obsession with etymologies and genealogies. Janette Dakyns's book on medievalism in nineteenth-century France, which includes the assimilation of medieval material in both primary literary works and in criticism, and which seeks to define not a single but a multiplicity of Middle Ages according to the political motivations of particular classes and regimes, represents an important step, I think, beyond the old history. So, too, the first chapter of Lee Patterson's *Negotiating the Past* represents a more sophisticated version of Dakyns's undertaking within the realm of Middle English studies.

A second stage implies, indeed is defined by, a recognition of and insistence upon a certain identity between the medieval period and our own. Here one thinks of a series of articles and books that have appeared, or lectures that have been delivered, over the last fifteen years—Eugene Vance's "The Modernity of the Middle Ages in the Future: Remarks on a Recent Book" (1973), Peter Haidu's "Making it (New) in the Middle Ages: Towards a Problematics of Alterity" (1974), Hans Robert Jauss's *Alterität und Modernität der mittelalterlichen Literatur* (1977), Paul Zumthor's lectures on the modernity of the Middle Ages given at the Pompidou Center in January 1979 (*Speaking of the Middle Ages*, 1986), Alexandre Leupin's "The Middle Ages, The Other" (1983), and the first chapter of my own *Etymologies and Genealogies: A Literary Anthropology of the French Middle Ages*, which also appeared that same year. Such a disparate group of writings is united by a certain enthusiastic sense of wonder at the discovery of how familiar the Middle Ages seem within the context of the contemporary discourses of cultural criticism, and thus a sense of relief that those who study medieval texts are not as irrelevant to the present as many of our own teachers had hoped we would be. The astonishment of a whole generation of medievalists at a certain moment was occasioned by the healing of a certain wounded narcissism among baby-boomers no longer content merely to hide behind the foil of philological expertise, which for decades in the academy had served not as a tool to make medieval literature accessible, but as a *cordon sanitaire* to prevent the reading of such works, and thus to inhibit dialogue between medievalists and specialists in other fields. The discovery that the period we study not only had something to say to modernists but also might serve to unsettle or historicize what has come to be known as "theory" spells relief.

Finally, for some time now a number of medieval historians, art historians, philologists, and specialists of almost every national literature have felt the need for some more sustained external history of the various disciplines of medieval studies, which, in fact, is already under way. Brian Stock has written a brilliant article on Erich Auerbach; Hans Aarslef, one on Joseph Bédier; Hans Ulrich Gumbrecht, a ground-breaking essay on Friedrich Diez, Gaston Paris, and the development of romance philology in both Germany and France. Just last year Bernard Cerquiglini published a monograph-length synthesis of the relation between medieval textual practice and medievalism: *Éloge de la variante: Histoire critique de la philologie*. This phase of the "New Medievalism" would thus serve to place in historical context the cultural appropriations of the study of the Middle Ages as it has been practiced since the middle of the eighteenth century. And this seems to point to what I see as a subject worthy of still further study.

One could imagine, for example, a history of medievalisms aimed at exploring the ways in which medieval studies have been determined by the specific ideological or local, nationalistic or religious, political or personal interests (including class, race, and gender) of those who have shaped the field. Such a history might include consideration of questions normally excluded from the canon of traditional or of high medieval studies, topics like connoisseurship, professionalization, and popularization; the relation of philology to other disciplines and to semiology and linguistics; the role of collections, journals, bibliographies, textual series, and of authoritative manuals like Gröber's *Grundriss* as well as that edited by Jauss and Köhler. It might include the effects of presuppositions about paleography upon editions and hence upon the interpretation of medieval texts; important figures, schools, and movements; defining questions and debates (that would not simply rehash the terms but would contextualize the stakes and motivations) and even the scholarly quarrel as a form of communication conceived to be productive of knowledge; the logical, philosophical, epistemological, and even moral presuppositions implicit to the notion of knowledge about the Middle Ages; the effects of anecdote, rumor, personality, and historical events; the role of academic, nationalistic, religious, and professional associations and institutions (including the university, the Société Arthurienne, the Société Rencesvals, or the Medieval Academy); the place of secular theology in medieval studies; the role of congresses and seminars; the politics of specialization, of edition, and of reviewing; the relation of medieval studies to other disciplines within the liberal arts curriculum. Then too, one might seek to evaluate the current rationale for the study of the Middle Ages as well as to assess the potential effects of the study of medieval concepts, theories, and texts upon contemporary criticism, upon the canon, and upon such modern disciplines as psychoanalysis and semiotics—the work of Jacques Lacan and Umberto Eco, for example. In what ways can the study of the Middle Ages teach us to historicize the field of critical theory?

Which is another way of asking, to what extent do our own strategies and desires determine the questions we pose and the answers we give? One cannot escape the obligation to clarify our own agendas so that we do not, under the illusion that we might escape our own blindnesses, merely refill the Augean stables once they have been cleaned. This, again, is a current trend which medieval studies shares with other disciplines both within the humanities and the social sciences, and which entails some recognition of the specificity of the inquiring subject in what has been since the Renaissance an enterprise assuming the supposed disinterestedness of knowledge, the objectivity of philological science.

Here one can, I think, identify a landmark in Paul Zumthor's *Speaking of the Middle Ages*, which not only speaks eloquently to the question of what it means to study the medieval past in the twentieth century, but does so in the first person singular. "Along the way, I will not apologize for speaking in the first person," writes Zumthor.

> This is not a stylistic device, but an intellectual necessity. . . . It is not a question of speaking about oneself, still less of retreating into a den of memories. It is a matter of choosing . . . the most directly accessible reference point. Others are free to illustrate a half century of scholarly or social achievement by tracing the biography of a mentor or colleague. But why take that course when what counts in the end is neither he nor I? What counts is the possibility of identifying in an emblematic way the social function fulfilled by that individual (that is, by his work) as part of a given project, a given task, a given field of thought or research to which events (for want of a natural inclination) attached him for a fairly long time. In this way, the project, the task, or the field may be considered through the mediation of a person, that is, otherwise than in the library. (3–4)

Zumthor's personalized voice is justified by what he rightly points to as a crisis of method in the social sciences, and especially in the field of medieval studies, coupled nonetheless to "the weight of mental habits" inherited from the nineteenth century: a sort of inability to tear ourselves away from "an unexamined positivism" which forms the basis of the prejudice called "objectivity," shared by Zumthor's mentors, and eliciting ironically something on the order of confession:

> Edmond Faral, with his dry, distinguished manner and his aseptic language, who was good enough to encourage my early efforts although they were unfaithful to his teachings; Karl Voretzsch, proud of the imperial title of "Geheimrat" which made up for his small size, who was said to have boasted, in August 1914, that he would soon enter conquered Arles at the head of the Provençal regiment; Walter von Wartburg, who knew everything but who had only a few, rather narrow ideas, and who left to his memory alone the task of structuring knowledge; Robert Bossuat, who in 1935 gave me a 2 out of 20 on my Old French examination. That is not my motive for writing these lines! But none of these details are "objectively" insignificant. (17)

Zumthor's long essay is significant in its acknowledgement of the role of personal memory combined with cultural critique in an "objective" history of medieval studies.

When I refer to *Speaking of the Middle Ages* as a landmark in the history of the discipline I do not mean to imply that it caused the sudden irruption of a personalized subject in the otherwise objective discourse of medievalism. Certainly both American and Continental feminism are responsible more generally for such a trend, which also informs recent Lacanian readings of medieval texts, beginning with Grail literature but including the courtly lyric and romance as well, as receptive referents seeking the desire of the modern reader. If you doubt what I say, take, for example, the report by Baschet and others in *Médiévales* for 1984 describing the answers to a poll of medievalists in Europe and America concerning their motivations for choosing the Middle Ages. The answers ran the gamut from ponderous confessions of having seen the Holy Grail while visiting Europe's cathedrals with pious parents to some Californian smart aleck who replied "C'est ça qui me plaît et que j'aime" (15). Or consider the special issue of *Speculum* (ed. Nichols), where you can find an almost obligatory identification of the personal voice on the part of authors who had no prior knowledge of each other's contributions. Thus Siegfried Wenzel begins:

> As the following remarks are to reflect my own scholarly commitment and experience, I should begin by saying that they come from a medievalist who in his work is always conscious of dealing with the works of a past civilization. They also come from a historian of literature, who in contrast to political or economic historians makes written documents the subject of his study, and who in contrast to linguists looks at them as works of verbal art. And finally, they come from a professor of English who works closely with colleagues whose ultimate aim. . . . (11)

Suzanne Fleischman introduces her article on philology and linguistics via the story of her "initial encounter with the Oxford *Roland*" (19). My entry on the "New Philology and Old French" contains an inevitably witty first footnote identifying my own subjective relation to the subject, a footnote that might also have served in the present context.

The introduction of the subject into the heretofore supposedly objective field of medieval studies is the symptom of a warming of the discipline, which has since the late 1800s considered itself sufficiently detached and coldly Other to prevent the identification of the scholar with the others he or she studies, the kind of identification which, for example, makes literary and cultural work on the Renaissance and subsequent periods seem so transparent and familiar. And this brings me to what I see as the second feature of a future that is already under way.

The time has come when the medievalist can no longer hide behind the barrier of philology, the safety net of specialization, but is obliged for the first time since the nineteenth century to enter the mainstream of the university. This implies that the medievalist must not only know his or her speciality, but must know more generally the disciplines of the Sciences of Man—history, linguistics, philosophy, anthropology, psychoanalysis—with respect to which he or she can no longer feign neutrality or disinterest, can no longer say, "It's not my century." On the contrary, given the seeming aimlessness of many modernists, the present moment offers a golden opportunity to renew the conviction that many of the pressing issues of modernism have a long and complex history in the Middle Ages. The best work in medieval studies is already and will in the future be truly interdisciplinary—interdisciplinary not in the sense that deans dream of, or in the sense merely of the tendency to contrast and compare more than one national literature. On the contrary, the isolation of national literatures from each other or from the study of Latin culture will, in my opinion, no longer be viable in the Europe of the 1990s. Nor, if I had to bet on it, would I wager that the narrow specialities that have served historically to isolate the study of Old French from its broader culture will survive within the university of the twenty-first century. Which is less a grim prospect than an opportunity. Indeed, there has never been a moment more ripe for the teaching of the works of philosophers, historians, and poets who themselves imagined the possibility of what Dante termed the *imperium*, the known world unified under one rule. The medievalist should, I think, exploit the development of the European community to press upon the university curriculum the universalising aspects of medieval culture. But in order to do so, he or she will no longer be able to pretend to be beyond, or below, or outside of that which for better or worse has become the metalanguage of cross-cultural study— that is, literary theory.

This is not an assertion alien to the spirit of the Middle Ages, for Old French literature always contains a certain imbrication of theory and practice. If one looks carefully, there is almost no work that does not contain a sophisticated indication of how it should be read and of how literary works signify more generally. Conversely, as the manuals of Poetic Art, the *artes poeticae* of the thirteenth century (Matthieu de Vendôme, Geoffroi de Vinsauf) make clear, it is just as difficult to imagine a medieval theory without the examples that are its practice. Moreover, if I had to indicate a specific direction in which medieval theory might make the greatest impact not only on our understanding of medieval literature, but on modern thought as well, it would be in the return to the master theoreticians of the Middle Ages, the Church Fathers, a return which, already under way, signals one of the essential directions of contemporary medieval studies. Here lies my third point.

Recent interest in late Roman and early Christian culture has produced significant changes in our understanding both of the substance and the relevance of Patristic thought. Indeed, the writings of the Church Fathers, once dismissed under the twin paralogisms of theology and scholasticism, have come increasingly to be seen as essential to our own esthetic and intellectual sense. This is not a view which emanates from the current worldwide wallowing in religious fundamentalism, nor from the tendency to push the origins of modernism toward an ever more distant past, nor even from the impulse toward analogy on the part of those anxious to root contemporary theory in some more subsuming context. The return of the Patristic writers, inspired perhaps by reconsideration of ancient civilization and philosophy by the makers of our own critical temper (Vernant, Vidal-Naquet, Detienne on classical Greece, Derrida on Plato, Foucault on the Hellenic period, Lacan on Augustine), stems from a recognition of the numerous and important similarities between a culture for which speculation about representation (verbal signs in particular) was essential to speculation about the wider universe and our own attempt to rethink the relation of linguistics, isolated since the Renaissance in the solitude of science, to the erotic, to the social, to ontology, and even to metaphysics.

The history of the early Church has indeed begun to become detached, strictly speaking, from the limits of religious doctrine and from narrow intellectual history to become the focus of an anthropology of the formative Christian period. I refer not only to comparative religious studies and reconsiderations of major figures in the light of psychoanalysis, political theory, and even semiotics, but also to a certain turning upon the writings of the Church Fathers and the institutions mobilized by their writings of questions normally reserved by the Sciences of Man for non-Western cultures. A good deal of work has been done in the course of the past decades on heresy and reform, sainthood, friendship, poverty, and asceticism alongside the monumental reformulations of the meaning and impact of Gnosticism and the Stoics. More important, a wave of fresh scholarly activity has revitalized the ways we have traditionally understood religious ideals and movements by placing them within the broader perspective of social, political, legal, and economic institutions while at the same time enriching our knowledge of the everyday life of the Mediterranean world—habits of eating, fasting, excreting, and even starvation; modes of make-up, adornment, and dress; medical and sexual practice. In particular, the intense scrutiny accorded Roman and early medieval family structure, not the least of which has come from anthropologists, has tended toward a radical revision of our notion of the relation of kinship to Patristic writings on sexuality and gender.

This brings me to a fourth and final area in which the medieval past corresponds so powerfully with the modern temper as to render its study compelling and urgent—that of gender. There can be little doubt that the study of gender has come to constitute, at least in America and at least for the time being, an independent discipline. Nor can the myriad of books that appear each year on the question of women in the Middle Ages—historical studies, literary studies, studies in the history of religion—leave any doubt that this is one of the most vital aspects of present-day medievalism. With a zeal that must surely resemble that of the nineteenth-century scholars' discovery and publication of unknown manuscripts, the most committed scholars of our discipline are writing the hidden history of the medieval period, the history of private life, but also the history of literature written by women, and, more difficult, the history of women's experience. Such intense interest in the question of gender signals, of course, a shift in the composition of the scholarly community. The medievalist of the future will not only adjust to changes in the canon, to the recognition of female writers who have historically been neglected, but he or she will take into account the determining effect of women scholars upon the redefinition of what was until relatively recently an almost exclusively male preserve.

Here too lies a bridge between medieval studies and the larger university community, indeed another area in which the medievalist might not only speak to those in other disciplines, but might take the lead. The conception of gender as we know it in the West came into being in the first centuries of the Christian era and has survived more or less intact from that time to the present era. To be both precise and quick, it was among the Church Fathers that the flesh became gendered feminine, that the feminine became estheticized, and that esthetics became theologized.[1] You can find all of these elements in preexisting and surrounding tradition; in fact, you can find any two, but you cannot find this triple nexus which is characteristic of gender in the West. And any contemporary discussion which does not take into account this fundamental shift in the cultural expression of the difference between the sexes risks, I maintain, merely projecting our own views of gender upon the past and thus, by essentializing, risks being caught in the movement of the very thing that such discussions seek to undo. What I am suggesting is, then, not so much the dismissal of Patristic views of sexuality as stultifying or archaic, not so much simply the positive identification of sources in previous tradition, but an understanding of just how deeply determining the Patristic "invention" of sexuality as we know it really was. Such a move, already under way, includes studies of the male and female body, homosexuality, transvestism, androgyny, prostitution, impotence and frigidity, conception, contraception and fertility, abortion, eroticism, intercourse (position specific), orgasm, menstruation, and, in particular, the ideal (and the practice) of sexual renunciation. So great, in fact, is the abundance of work on the theme of virginity that it alone practically constitutes an independent field.[2] And here too, many of the most significant contributions to the current reinterpretation of the Patristic period come from women writing from a feminist perspective: studies of feminine piety and of the role of women in the primitive Church, of female patronesses, friends, missionaries, prophets, and heroic martyrs, explanations of the appeal of early Christianity, despite

175

the condemnation of the feminine among the Fathers, to women anxious to escape the patriarchy of the ancient world.[3]

Here, then, is less a program for the future than the identification of four current trends in medieval studies which seem to me promising for the coming decade: (1) medievalists are becoming increasingly aware of the premises which inform their discipline, and thus are (2) beginning to enter the mainstream of the university in ways that have not been possible since the late nineteenth century, and in ways that, given the universalism of medieval culture, are particularly appropriate to the coming Europeanism of the nineties. (3) The engagement with other disciplines within the university, which implies something on the order of a common language, or theory, is enabled by study of the Patristic texts, as well as medieval philosophers, who themselves tended to think through all issues in what would today be theoretical terms. (4) Finally, I conclude with the suggestion that the founding articulation of gender in the beginning centuries of our era represents one of the strong bridges between the modern temper and the study of the medieval past.

NOTES

1. For fuller discussion see Bloch, *Medieval Misogyny and the Invention of Western Romantic Love.*—W. D. P.

2. See, for example: Brown, *The Body and Society: Men, Women, and Sexual Renunciation in Early Christianity;* Bugge, *Virginitas: An Essay in the History of a Medieval Ideal;* Castelli, "Virginity and Its Meaning for Women's Sexuality in Early Christianity"; Clark, "Ascetic Renunciation and Feminine Advancement: A Paradox of Late Ancient Christianity"; Crouzel, *Virginité et mariage selon Origène;* McNamara, "Sexual Equality and the Cult of Virginity in Early Christian Thought"; Pagels, *Adam, Eve, and the Serpent;* Rousselle, *Porneia: De la maîtrise du corps à la privation sensorielle, IIe–IVe siècles de l'ère chrétienne;* Ruether, "Misogynism and Virginal Feminism in the Fathers of the Church"; Schulenberg, "The Heroics of Virginity: Brides of Christ and Sacrificial Mutilation"; Sissa, *Le corps virginal.*

3. See, for example: Børresen, *Subordination and Equivalence: The Nature and Role of Women in Augustine and Thomas Aquinas;* Brock and Harvey, *Holy Women of the Syrian Orient;* Bynum, *Jesus as Mother:*

Studies in the Spirituality of the High Middle Ages; Cameron and Kuhrt, eds., *Images of Women in Antiquity*; Clark, *Jerome, Chrysostom, and Friends*; Daly, *The Church and the Second Sex*; Fiorenza, *In Memory of Her: A Feminist Theological Reconstruction of Christian Origins*; Hayter, *The New Eve in Christ*; Ruether and McLaughlin, eds., *Women of Spirit: Female Leadership in the Jewish and Christian Traditions*; Parvey, "The Theology and Leadership of Women in the New Testament"; Ruether, "Mothers of the Church: Ascetic Women in the Late Patristic Age"; Trible, "Depatriarchalizing in Biblical Interpretation"; Warner, *Alone of All her Sex*; Yarbrough, "Christianization in the Fourth Century: The Example of Roman Women."

A NEOPHILOLOGICAL ALBUM

1. Gaston Paris (1839–1903). Paris studied in Germany with Friedrich Diez; lectured on the *Song of Roland* as a national monument during the German siege of Paris, 1870; succeeded his father, Paulin Paris, in the Collège de France, 1872; founded the journal *Romania*, with Paul Meyer, in the same year; and was elected to the Académie des inscriptions, 1876. Frontispiece from the *Bibliographie des travaux de Gaston Paris*, ed. Joseph Bédier and Mario Roques (Paris: Bouillon, 1904).

2. Joseph Bédier (1864–1938). Raised on Reunion Island in the Indian Ocean, where his family had been established for two centuries, Bédier was born in Paris and educated at the École normale. He succeeded Gaston Paris at the Collège de France in 1903 and assumed a chair at the Académie française in 1921. Frontispiece from Ferdinand Lot, *Joseph Bédier 1864–1938* (Paris: Droz, 1939).

3. Marcelino Menéndez Pelayo (1856–1912), professor of Spanish literature, University of Madrid, member of the Royal Spanish Academy, and director of the National Library, Madrid. The *Edición nacional de las obras completas de Menéndez Pelayo* runs to sixty-two volumes. Frontispiece from his *Historia de las ideas estéticas en España*, ed. Enrique Sánchez Reyes, *Edición nacional*, I (Santander: S.A. de Artes Gráficas, 1940).

4. Ramón Menéndez Pidal (1869–1968) as a young man. Menéndez Pidal was
the dominant Hispanic philologist of his nearly centenarian time and editor of
the *Poema del Cid* among many other texts. At the time of his death a news-
paper published a cartoon showing "the Cid, seated on a cloud and smiling
broadly at the small bespectacled figure who is coming toward him; the cap-
tion has the Cid say in welcome, '¡Hombre, ahora vamos a hablar de nuestras
cosas!' " [Man, now we'll talk about our business!] (Colin Smith, *Ramón Menéndez Pidal 1869–1968, A Lecture . . .* [London, n.p., 1970], 1). Photograph
from the family album, reproduced here from the necrology by Yakov Malkiel,
" 'Era omme esencial . . . ,' " *Romance Philology* 23 (1970): 371–411, opposite
page 372.

5. Federico García Lorca (1898–1936) at Columbia University, New York, October 1929. The poet sent this photograph to his family with a letter explaining that it shows him seated before a prodigious porphyry globe, part of the university clock. From the Fundación García Lorca, Madrid.

6. Edward Billings Ham (1902–1965), for many years professor of French at the University of Michigan and then at California State College, Hayward, was a prolific editor of Old French texts. Frontispiece from *Romance Studies in Memory of Edward Billings Ham*, ed. Urban Tigner Holmes, California State College Publications, 2 (Hayward, Calif.: California State College, 1967).

7 (above). Alfred Foulet (1900–1987), professor of French, Princeton University, and author (with Mary Blakely Speer) of *On Editing Old French Texts*, Edward C. Armstrong Monographs on Medieval Literature, 1 (Lawrence: Regents Press of Kansas, 1979). From the dedication by Yakov Malkiel and Karl D. Uitti of the "Lucien Foulet Memorial—Alfred Foulet Testimonial," a special issue of *Romance Philology* 22.4 (1969): 369–72.

8 (opposite). Neck amphora by the Alkimachos Painter (5th century B.C.). Theseus seizes Procrustes before his (Procrustean) bed, preparing to slay him. The legendary robber was said to stretch his smaller victims out to the size of his bed, or to chop the larger ones down to fit; in the traditional depiction Theseus killed him with his own hammer. His name, originally a surname, means "the Stretcher," from the verb meaning "to beat or hammer out, to stretch out," a technical term for the activity of the smith. In Racine's *Phèdre*, Procrustes figures among the "brigands punis" whom Hippolyte credits to his father's account (I, i, 79–80). Reproduced from John Boardman, *Athenian Red Figure Vases: The Classical Period, A Handbook* (London: Thames and Hudson, 1989), fig. 44.

Buona pulcella fur eulalia. Bel auret corps bellezour anima
Voldrent la ueintre li do inimi. Voldrent la faire diaule seruir
Elle nont eskoltet les mals conselliers. Quelle do raneiet chi maent sus en ciel
Ne por or ned argent ne paramenz. por manatce regiel ne preiement
Niule cose non la pouret omq pleier. La polle sempre n amast lo do menestier
E poro fut presentede maximiien. chi rex eret a cels dis soure pagiens
Il li enortet dont lei nonq chielt. qued elle fuiet lo nom xpiien
Ellent adunet lo suon element. Melz sostendreiet les empedementz
Quelle p desse sa uirginitet. Poros furet morte a grand honestet
Enz enl fou la getterent com arde tost. Elle colpes non auret por o nos coill
Pro zo nos uoldret concreidre li rex pagiens. Ad une spede li roueret tolir lo chief
La domnizelle celle kose non contredist. Volt lo seule lazsier si ruouet krist
In figure de colomb uolat a ciel. Tuit oram que por nos degnet preier
Qued auuisset de nos xps mercit. Post la mort et a lui nos laist uenir
Par souue clementia

RITH MUS TEYTONICUS DE PIE MEMORIE HLUDUICO REGE
FILIO HLUDUICI AEQ REGIS.

Einan kuning uueiz ih. Heizsit her hluduig.
Ther gerno gode thionot. Ih uueiz her imos lonot
Kind uuarth her faterlos. Thes uuarth imo sar buoz
Holoda inan truhtin. Magaezogo uuarth her sin
Gab her imo dugidi. fronisc githigini
Stual hier in urankon. So brache heriz langa
Tho az gideilder thanne Sar mit kurilmanne

9. Valenciennes, Bibliothèque municipale, MS 150, folio 141v, containing the oldest poem preserved in the French language, the ninth-century "Sequence of Saint Eulalia."

9a (opposite). The page begins with the words "Buona pulcella," the beginning of the sequence; the eighth line down appears to begin "Ellent adunet" (verse 15), but see figure 9b. Reproduced from *Les plus anciens monuments de la langue française: album*, ed. Gaston Paris, SATF (Paris: Firmin-Didot, 1875).

9b (above). The word "aduret," misread as "adunet" until publication of an article by Henry Dexter Learned, "The *Eulalia* MS. at Line 15 Reads *aduret*, not *adunet*," *Speculum* 16 (1941): 334–35. Learned explains that "an accidental smear extends downward from the horizontal stroke of the *r*, giving it at first sight the appearance of an *n*," but that the correct reading is evident in daylight through a magnifying glass. Thus the saint is called upon to *adore* a pagan god, not to *unite* one (!). Reproduced from *Speculum* 16 (1941), opposite p. 335.

10. Manuscripts of the *Roman de la rose.*

10a (above). New York, Pierpont Morgan Library, MS M. 332, folio 1. Jean de Meun presents his translation of Boethius to Philippe IV. Courtesy of the Pierpont Morgan Library, New York.

10b (top). Oxford, Bodleian, Douce 195, fol. 2. Villainy appears as a
barefoot peasant woman, meanly dressed. Courtesy of the Bodleian
Library, Oxford.

10c (bottom). Oxford, Bodleian, Douce 195, fol. 3v, left. Tristesse
threatens to plunge a knife into her breast. Courtesy of the Bodleian
Library, Oxford.

10d (above). Oxford, Bodleian, Douce 195, fol. 76v. Jupiter castrates Saturn. Courtesy of the Bodleian Library, Oxford.

10e (bottom). Oxford, Bodleian, Douce 195, fol. 122v. Origen, the Christian philosopher (died c. 254 A.D.), castrates himself. Courtesy of the Bodleian Library, Oxford.

11. London, British Library, MS Harley 4431 (French, early fifteenth century), fol. 4. Christine de Pizan in her study. The picture illustrates the opening passage of her *Book of the City of Ladies:* "According to the habit I have, and which organizes the pattern of my life, that is, in frequenting the study of letters, one day, when I was sitting in my cell surrounded by volumes on diverse subjects . . . , I raised my face from my book, thinking . . . to look for some amusement in the words of the poets." Courtesy of the British Library, London.

193

12. Two Italian coins suggestive of meanings in the *Divine Comedy.*

12a (left). Coin minted in Lucca, 1209–18. The obverse is inscribed SVVLT' DE LUCA, that is, Sanctus Vultus de Lucca, "the Holy Face of Lucca." In *Inferno,* when a devil says there is no place for the Santo Volto here (21.48), he may be referring to the coin, saying "You can't bribe your way out of this," or "You can't buy favors here." Cf. Joan M. Ferrante, *The Political Vision of the Divine Comedy* (Princeton: Princeton University Press, 1984), p. 346. Photograph courtesy of the American Numismatic Society, New York.

12b (right). Coin minted by Pope Boniface VIII, who reigned from 1294 to 1303. The inscription on the obverse, difficult to make out in this exemplar, reads DOMINI • BO • PAPE, "Of Lord Boniface, Pope." The form PAPE, usually PP, PAPA, PA, or PAP on the coins of other popes, suggests a possible allusion in *Inferno* when Pluto cries out, "Papè Satàn, Papè Satàn aleppe" (7.1). Perhaps the cry means "Pope Satan . . . ," with reference to Boniface as he is named on coins such as this one. Cf. Ferrante, *The Political Vision of the Divine Comedy,* p. 338. Reproduced from Francesco Muntoni, *Le monete dei Papi e degli Stati pontefici* (Rome: P & P Santamaria, 1972), 1:24, no. 1.

13. The AT&T Building, New York (1978), designed by Philip Johnson, shows playful qualities characteristic of postmodern architecture and, perhaps, postmodern philology. Photograph copyright by Brian Rose, New York City.

14. The Opéra de la Bastille, Paris (1990), designed by Carlos Ott. The first production, on March 17, 1990, was Berlioz's *Les Troyens*. The production may be considered as a version of the *translatio studii* topos since it depicted the flight of Aeneas from Troy to Italy; was played on the Place de la Bastille, the site of the fall of the *ancien régime* and the triumph of the Revolution; and inaugurated a new impulse in diffusion of nineteenth-century French culture to a global audience at the end of the twentieth century. Courtesy of the Service de presse, Opéra de la Bastille. Photograph Moatti / Kleinefenn.

❦ CONTRIBUTORS

R. Howard Bloch, Professor of French, University of California, Berkeley

Peter F. Dembowski, Distinguished Service Professor of French, University of Chicago

Joan M. Ferrante, Professor of English and Comparative Literature, Columbia University

Hans Ulrich Gumbrecht, Professor of Comparative Literature, Stanford University

Stephen G. Nichols, James M. Beall Professor of French, The Johns Hopkins University

William D. Paden, Professor of French, Northwestern University

Rupert T. Pickens, Professor of French, University of Kentucky

❦ WORKS CITED

Aarsleff, Hans. "Scholarship and Ideology: Joseph Bédier's Critique of Romantic Medievalism." *Historical Studies and Literary Criticism.* Ed. Jerome J. McGann. Madison: University of Wisconsin Press, 1985. 93–113.

Amalric, Jacques. "Les inquiétudes de M. Mitterrand." *Le monde: Sélection hebdomadaire, édition internationale* 23–29 Nov. 1989: 2.

Appel, Carl, ed. *Bernart von Ventadorn: Seine Lieder.* Halle: Niemeyer, 1915.

Armstrong, Edward C., and others, eds. *The Medieval French Roman d'Alexandre.* Elliott Monographs in the Romance Languages and Literatures, 36–42. 7 vols. Princeton: Princeton University Press, 1937–76.

Assmann, Aleida, and Jan Assmann, eds. *Kanon und Zensur: Archaeologie der literarischen Kommunikation, II.* Munich: Fink, 1987.

Auerbach, Erich. *Introduction aux études de philologie romane.* Frankfurt: V. Klostermann, 1949.

Baist, Gottfried, ed. *Crestien's von Troyes Contes del Graal (Percevaus li galois), Abdruck der Handschrift Paris, français 794.* Freiburg, 1909; rev. 1912.

Baschet, Jérome, Christine Lapostolle, Michel Pastoureau, Yvonne Régis-Cazal. "Profession médiéviste." *Médiévales* 7 (1984): 7–64.

Baum, Richard. *Recherches sur les oeuvres attribuées à Marie de France.* Annales Universitatis Saraviensis, Reihe: Philosophische Fakultät, 9. Heidelberg: Winter, 1968.

Bédier, Joseph. "De l'édition princeps de la *Chanson de Roland* aux éditions les plus récentes: Nouvelles remarques sur l'art d'établir les anciens textes." *Romania* 63 (1937): 433–69; 64 (1938): 145–244, 489–521.

————. *De Nicolau Museto (gallice Colin Muset), francogallico carminum scriptore, thesim Facultati litterarum Parisiensi proponebat Joseph Bédier.* Paris: Bouillon, 1893.

————. *Les fabliaux: Études de littérature populaire et d'histoire littéraire du moyen âge.* Paris: Bouillon, 1893.

————, ed. "Le lai de l'ombre." By Jean Renart. *Index lectionum quae in Universitate Friburgensi per menses aestivos anni MDCCCXC . . . habebuntur.* Fribourg, 1890. [1]–[59].

————, ed. *Le lai de l'ombre par Jean Renart.* SATF, 109. Paris: Firmin-Didot, 1913.

————. "La tradition manuscrite du *Lai de l'ombre:* Réflexions sur l'art d'éditer les anciens textes." *Romania* 54 (1928): 161–96, 321–56. Published as a pamphlet 1929; rpt. Paris: Champion, 1970.

Benton, J. F. "The Court of Champagne as a Literary Center." *Speculum* 36 (1961): 551–91.

Berg, Irwin A., and L. A. Pennington. *An Introduction to Clinical Psychology.* 3rd ed. New York: Ronald Press, 1966.

Bergman, Ingmar, dir. *The Seventh Seal [Det Sjunde Inseglet].* Svensk Filmindustri, 1956.

Binder, David, and Barbara Crossette. "As Ethnic Wars Multiply, U.S. Strives for a Policy; In Baring Old Hatreds, the Cold War's End Imperils the Peace." *New York Times*, 7 February 1993: Y1+.

Bischoff, Bernhard. *Latin Palaeography: Antiquity and the Middle Ages.* Trans. Dáibhí ó Cróinín and David Ganz. Cambridge, UK: Cambridge University Press, 1990.

Bloch, R. Howard. *Etymologies and Genealogies: A Literary Anthropology of the French Middle Ages.* Chicago: University of Chicago Press, 1983.

————. "The Lay and the Law: Sexual / Textual Transgression in *La chastelaine de Vergi,* the *Lai d'Ignaure,* and the *Lais* of Marie de France." *Stanford French Review* 14.1–2 (Spring-Fall 1990): 181–210.

————. *Medieval French Literature and Law.* Berkeley: University of California Press, 1977.

————. *Medieval Misogyny and the Invention of Western Romantic Love.* Chicago: University of Chicago Press, 1991.

————. "The Medieval Text—'Guigemar'—as a Provocation to the Discipline of Medieval Studies." *The Legitimacy of the Middle Ages.* Ed. Stephen Nichols. 63–73. Rpt. in *The New Medievalism.* Ed. Brownlee, Brownlee, and Nichols. 99–112.

————. "New Philology and Old French." *The New Philology*. Ed. Nichols. 38–58.

————. "Silence and Holes: The *Roman de Silence* and the Art of the Trouvère." *Yale French Studies* 70 (1986): 81–99.

Børresen, Kari Elisabeth. *Subordination and Equivalence: The Nature and Role of Women in Augustine and Thomas Aquinas.* Washington: University Press of America, 1981.

Boutière, Jean, and A. H. Schutz, eds. *Biographies des troubadours.* Rev. Jean Boutière and I.-M. Cluzel. Paris: Nizet, 1964.

Brakelmann, Julius. "Die Pastourelle in der nord- und süd-französischen Poesie: Ein Beitrag zur franz. Litteraturg. des M.A. nebst einem Anhange ungedruckter Pastourellen." *Jahrbuch für romanische und englische Literatur* 9 (1868): 155–89, 307–37.

Brochier, Jacques-Elie. "Deux mille ans d'histoire du climat dans le Midi de la France: Étude sédimentologique." *Annales: Économies, sociétés, civilisations* 38 (1983): 425–38.

Brock, Sebastian P., and Susan Ashbrook Harvey. *Holy Women of the Syrian Orient.* Berkeley: University of California Press, 1987.

Brown, Peter. *The Body and Society: Men, Women, and Sexual Renunciation in Early Christianity.* New York: Columbia University Press, 1988.

Brownlee, Kevin. "Discourse as *Proueces* in *Aucassin et Nicolette.*" *Yale French Studies* 70 (1986): 167–82.

————, Marina Scordilis Brownlee, and Stephen G. Nichols, eds. *Boundary and Transgression in Medieval Culture.* Special issue of *Stanford French Review* 14.1–2 (1990): 1–274.

————, and Stephen G. Nichols, eds. *Images of Power: Medieval History / Discourse / Literature.* Special issue of *Yale French Studies* 70 (1986): 1–253.

Brownlee, Marina S., Kevin Brownlee, and Stephen G. Nichols, eds. *The New Medievalism.* Baltimore, MD: The Johns Hopkins University Press, 1991.

Brunetière, Ferdinand. "Les fabliaux du moyen âge et l'origine des contes." *Revue des deux mondes* 119 (1893): 189–213.

Bugge, John. *Virginitas: An Essay in the History of a Medieval Ideal.* The Hague: Martinus Nijhoff, 1975.

Burgess, Glyn S. *The Lais of Marie de France: Text and Context.* Athens: University of Georgia Press, 1987.

Burke, James F. *Structures from the Trivium in the Cantar de mio Cid.*

University of Toronto Romance Series, 66. Toronto: University of Toronto Press, 1991.

Busby, Keith, ed. *Chrétien de Troyes: Le roman de Perceval ou le Conte du graal*. Tübingen: Niemeyer, 1993.

Bynum, Caroline Walker. *Jesus as Mother: Studies in the Spirituality of the High Middle Ages*. Berkeley: University of California Press, 1982.

Cameron, Averil, and Amélie Kuhrt, eds. *Images of Women in Antiquity*. Detroit: Wayne State University Press, 1983.

Camille, Michael. *The Gothic Idol: Ideology and Image-Making in Medieval Art*. New York: Cambridge University Press, 1989.

———. *Image on the Edge: The Margins of Medieval Art*. Cambridge, MA: Harvard University Press, 1992.

Carroll, Carleton W., ed. *Chrétien de Troyes: Erec and Enide*. New York: Garland, 1987.

Cassell, Anthony K. *Dante's Fearful Art of Justice*. Toronto: University of Toronto Press, 1984.

Castelli, Elizabeth. "Virginity and Its Meaning for Women's Sexuality in Early Christianity." *Journal of Feminist Studies in Religion* 2 (1986): 61–88.

Cerquiglini, Bernard. *Éloge de la variante: Histoire critique de la philologie*. Des Travaux. Paris: Seuil, 1989.

———, Jacqueline Cerquiglini, Christiane Marchello-Nizia, and Michèle Perret-Minard. "L'objet 'ancien français' et les conditions propres à sa description linguistique." *Méthodes en grammaire française*. Ed. Jean-Claude Chevalier and Maurice Gross. Initiation à la Linguistique, B 6. Paris: Klincksieck, 1976. 185–200.

Cerquiglini-Toulet, Jacqueline. "Le *Voir dit* mis à nu par ses éditeurs, même: Étude de la réception d'un texte à travers ses éditions." *Mittelalter-Rezeption: Zur Rezeptionsgeschichte der romanischen Literaturen des Mittelalters in der Neuzeit*. Ed. Reinhold R. Grimm. Begleitreihe zum GRLMA, 2. Heidelberg: Carl Winter, 1991. 337–80.

Chance, Jane, trans. *Letter of Othea to Hector*. Focus Library of Medieval Women. Newburyport, MA: Focus Information Group, 1990.

Clark, Elizabeth A. "Ascetic Renunciation and Feminine Advancement: A Paradox of Late Ancient Christianity." *Anglican Theological Review* 63 (1981): 240–57.

———. *Jerome, Chrysostom, and Friends: Essays and Translations*. Studies in Women and Religion, 2. New York: E. Mellen Press, 1979.

Constans, Léopold, ed. *Le roman de Troie par Benoît de Sainte-Maure*. 6 vols. SATF. Paris: Firmin Didot, 1904–12.

Contini, Gianfranco, ed. *Poeti del Duecento*. 2 vols. Milan: Ricciardi, 1960.

Coover, Robert. "The End of Books." *New York Times Book Review*, 21 June 1992: 1+.

Cornilliat, François, Ullrich Langer, and Douglas Kelly, eds. *What is Literature? France 1100–1600*. Edward C. Armstrong Monographs on Medieval Literature, 7. Lexington, KY: French Forum, 1993.

Crist, Larry S., ed. *Saladin: Suite et fin du deuxième cycle de la croisade*. Textes Littéraires Français, 185. Geneva: Droz, 1972.

——, and Robert F. Cook, eds. *Baudoin de Sebourc: Chanson d'aventures du XIVe siècle*. SATF, forthcoming.

Crouzel, Henri. *Virginité et mariage selon Origène*. Paris: Desclée de Brouwer, 1963.

Culler, Jonathan, ed. *On Puns: The Foundation of Letters*. Oxford: Blackwell, 1988.

Curnow, Maureen Cheney Lois, ed. "The *Livre de la cité des dames* of Christine de Pisan: A Critical Edition." Diss. Vanderbilt University, 1975. *Dissertation Abstracts International* 36.7A (1976): 4536.

Curtius, Ernst Robert. *European Literature and the Latin Middle Ages*. Trans. Willard R. Trask. Bollingen Series, 36. New York: Pantheon Books, 1953.

——. "Gustav Gröber und die romanische Philologie" (1952). *Gesammelte Aufsätze zur romanischen Philologie*. Bern: Francke Verlag, 1960. 428–55.

——. "Über die altfranzösische Epik." *Zeitschrift für romanische Philologie* 64 (1944): 233–320.

Dagenais, John. *The Larger Gloss: The Ethics of Reading the Libro de buen amor*. Princeton: Princeton University Press, forthcoming.

Dakyns, Janine R. *The Middle Ages in French Literature 1851–1900*. London: Oxford University Press, 1973.

Daly, Mary. *The Church and the Second Sex*. Boston: Beacon Press, 1985.

Danto, Arthur C. "The End of Art." *The Death of Art*. Ed. Berel Lang. Art and Philosophy, 2. New York: Haven, 1984. 5–35.

Delany, Sheila. "Anatomy of the Resisting Reader: Some Implications of Resistance to Sexual Wordplay in Medieval Literature." *Exemplaria* 4 (1992): 7–34.

Dembowski, Peter F. "De nouveau: *Érec et Énide*, Chrétien et Guiot." "*Et c'est la fin pour quoi sommes ensemble*": *Hommage à Jean Dufournet, professeur à la Sorbonne nouvelle; Littérature, histoire et langue du Moyen Age*. Ed. Jean-Claude Aubailly and others. Paris: Champion, 1993. 409–17.

————. "The 'French' Tradition of Textual Philology and Its Relevance to the Editing of Medieval Texts." *Modern Philology* 90 (1993): 512–32.

————. "Intertextualité et critique des textes." *Littérature* 41 (1981): 17–29.

————, ed. *Jourdain de Blaye (Jordains de Blaivies): Chanson de geste*. Chicago: University of Chicago Press, 1969. 2d ed. CFMA, 112. Paris: Champion, 1991.

————, ed. *La vie de sainte Marie l'Égyptienne*. Publications Romanes et Françaises, 144. Geneva: Droz, 1977.

Di Salvatore, Brian. "Vehement Fire." *New Yorker* 27 Apr. 1987: 42 + ; 4 May 1987: 38 + .

Didi-Huberman, Georges. *Devant l'image: Question posée aux fins d'une histoire de l'art*. Paris: Minuit, 1990.

Dijksterhuis, Aaltje. *Thomas und Gottfried: Ihre Konstruktiven Sprachformen*. Groningen-Batavia: Noordhoff, 1935.

Doane, A. N., and Carol Braun Pasternack, eds. *Vox Intexta: Orality and Textuality in the Middle Ages*. Madison: University of Wisconsin Press, 1991.

Douglas, Wallace. "Accidental Institution: On the Origin of Modern Language Study." *Criticism in the University*. Ed. Gerald Graff and Reginald Gibbons. TriQuarterly Series on Criticism and Culture, 1. Evanston: Northwestern University Press, 1985. 35–61.

Duby, G., A. Joris, J. Dufournet, C. Bourel de la Roncière. "*Le Moyen âge a un siècle*." *Moyen âge* 94 (1988): 159–82.

Dufour, Jean-Paul, and Franck Nouchi. "Un entretien avec M. Hubert Curien." *Le monde* 26 July 1989: 16.

Duggan, Joseph. "Social Functions of the Medieval Epic in the Romance Literatures." *Oral Tradition* 1 (1986): 728–66.

Eagleton, Terry. "The End of English." *Textual Practice* 1.1 (1987): 1–9.

Eisenstein, Sergei, dir. *Ivan the Terrible [Ivan Groznyi]*. Mosfilm Studios; Part 1, 1944; Part 2, 1946 (released 1958).

Engels, Joseph. *Études sur l'Ovide moralisé*. Groningen–Batavia: J. B. Wolters, 1945.

————. "Philologie romane—linguistique—études littéraires." *Neophilologus* 37 (1953): 14–24.

Étiemble, René. *Parlez-vous franglais?* Paris: Gallimard, 1964.

Faral, Edmond, ed. *La conquête de Constantinople*. By Geoffroi de Villehardouin. Classiques de l'Histoire de France au Moyen Âge, 18–19. 2 vols. Paris: Belles Lettres, 1938–39.

Ferguson, Priscilla Parkhurst. "Preface to the Paperback Edition: *Literary France* Revisited." *Literary France: The Making of a Culture*. By Priscilla Parkhurst Clark. Berkeley: University of California Press, 1987. Paperback 1991. xv–xvii.

Ferrante, Joan M. "Male Fantasy and Female Reality in Courtly Literature." *Women's Studies* 11 (1984): 67–97.

———. *The Political Vision of the Divine Comedy*. Princeton: Princeton University, 1984.

Fineman, Joel. "'The *Pas de Calais*': Freud, the Transference and the Sense of Woman's Humor." *On Puns: The Foundation of Letters*. Ed. Culler. 100–14.

Fiorenza, Elisabeth Schüssler. *In Memory of Her: A Feminist Theological Reconstruction of Christian Origins*. New York: Crossroad, 1983.

Fleischman, Suzanne. "Philology, Linguistics, and the Discourse of the Medieval Text." *The New Philology*. Ed. Nichols. 19–37.

———. *Tense and Narrativity: From Medieval Performance to Modern Fiction*. Austin: University of Texas Press, 1990.

Flutre, L.-F. "Nouveaux fragments du manuscrit dit d'Annonay des oeuvres de Chrétien de Troyes." *Romania* 75 (1954): 1–21.

Foerster, Wendelin, ed. *Erec und Enide*. By Chrétien de Troyes. Romanische Bibliothek, 8. Halle: Niemeyer, 1890.

Foucault, Michel. *Les mots et les choses: Une archéologie des sciences humaines*. Paris: Gallimard, 1966.

Foulet, Alfred. "On Editing Chrétien's Lancelot." *The Romances of Chrétien de Troyes*. Ed. D. Kelly. 287–304.

———. "On Grid-Editing Chrétien de Troyes." *Poetics of Textual Criticism*. Ed. Uitti. 15–23.

———, and Mary Blakely Speer. *On Editing Old French Texts*. Edward C. Armstrong Monographs on Medieval Literature, 1. Lawrence: Regents Press of Kansas, 1979.

———, and Karl D. Uitti, eds. *Le chevalier de la charrette (Lancelot)*. By Chrétien de Troyes. Classiques Garnier. Paris: Bordas, 1989.

Fourquet, Jean. "Fautes communes ou innovations communes?" *Romania* 70 (1948): 85–95.

———. "Linguistique et philologie." *Actes du Colloque des 29 et 30 avril 1977: "Linguistique et philologie" (applications aux textes médiévaux)*. Ed. Danielle Buschinger. Paris: Champion, 1977. 7–14.

———. "Le paradoxe de Bédier." *Mélanges 1945*. Publications de la Faculté des Lettres de l'Université de Strasbourg, 105. Paris: Belles Lettres, 1946. 2:1–16.

Fourrier, Anthime. *Le courant réaliste dans le roman courtois en France au moyen-âge.* Paris: Nizet, 1960.

Freeman, Michelle A. *The Poetics of Translatio Studii and Conjointure: Chrétien de Troyes's Cligés.* French Forum Monographs, 12. Lexington, KY: French Forum, 1979.

Fukuyama, Francis. "The End of History?" *The National Interest* 16 (Summer 1989): 3–18.

———. *The End of History and the Last Man.* New York: Free Press, 1992.

Gadamer, Hans-Georg. *Wahrheit und Methode: Grundzüge einer philosophischen Hermeneutik.* 2nd ed. Tübingen: Mohr, 1965.

García Lorca, Federico. "El cante jondo (primitivo canto andaluz)." *Obras completas.* Ed. Arturo del Hoyo, Jorge Guillén, Vicente Aleixandre. 16th ed. Madrid: Aguilar, 1971. 39–56.

———. "La imagen poética de don Luis de Góngora." *Obras completas.* Ed. Arturo del Hoyo, Jorge Guillén, Vicente Aleixandre. 16th ed. Madrid: Aguilar, 1971. 62–85.

Garrani, Giuseppe. *Il pensiero di Dante in tema di economia, monetaria e creditizia.* Palermo: Cassa di Risparmio, 1965.

Gilson, Etienne. *Les idées et les lettres.* Paris: Vrin, 1932.

Godzich, Wlad, and Jeffrey Kittay. *The Emergence of Prose: An Essay in Prosaics.* Minneapolis: University of Minnesota Press, 1987.

Gravdal, Kathryn. "Camouflaging Rape: The Rhetoric of Sexual Violence in the Medieval Pastourelle." *Romanic Review* 76 (1985): 361–73.

Greenblatt, Stephen. "Psychoanalysis and Renaissance Culture." *Literary Theory / Renaissance Texts.* Ed. Parker and Quint. 21–24.

Grimes, Joseph E. "Outlines and Overlays." *Language* 48 (1972): 513–24.

Gröber, Gustav, ed. *Grundriss der romanischen Philologie.* 2 vols. in 4 parts. Strassburg: Trübner, 1897–1906.

Guiette, Robert. "D'une poésie formelle en France au moyen âge." *Revue des sciences humaines,* N.S., 54 (1949): 61–68. Expanded in: Guiette, Robert. *Questions de littérature.* Romanica Gandensia, 8. Ghent: Romanica Gandensia, 1960. 9–32. Published separately: Guiette, Robert. *D'une poésie formelle en France au moyen âge.* Paris: Nizet, 1972.

Gumbrecht, Hans Ulrich. "A la sombra del reino hermeneutico." *Filología* 24 (1989): 165–80.

———. "L'auteur comme masque: Contribution à l'archéologie de l'imprimé." *Masques et déguisements dans la littérature médiévale.* Ed. Marie-Louise Ollier. Montréal: Presses de l'Université de Montréal, 1988. 185–92.

————. "Beginn von 'Literatur': Abschied vom Koerper?" *Der Ursprung von Literatur: Medien, Rollen, Kommunikationssituationen zwischen 1450 und 1650.* Ed. Gisela Smolka-Koerdt, Peter-Michael Spangenberg, Dagmar Tillmann-Bartylla. Munich: Fink, 1988. 15–50.

————. "The Body Versus the Printing Press: Media in the Early Modern Period, Mentalities in the Reign of Castile, and Another History of Literary Forms." *Poetics* 14 (1985): 209–27.

————. "Bulky Baggage from the Past: The Study of Literature in Germany." *Comparative Criticism* 11 (1989): 97–109.

————. *Eine Geschichte der spanischen Literatur.* Frankfurt: Suhrkamp, 1990. English translation forthcoming from Stanford University Press, 1993.

————. "Inszeniertes Leben: Alltag und Kunst in der spanischen Provinz um die Jahrhundertwende." *In memoriam Erich Köhler.* Special issue of *Romanistische Zeitschrift für Literaturgeschichte* (1984): 141–62.

————. "Klassik in Spanien." *Literarische Klassik.* Ed. Hans-Joachim Simm. Frankfurt: Suhrkamp, 1988. 155–81.

————. "Lebende Vergangenheit: Zur Typologie der 'Arbeit am Text' in der spanischen Kultur." *Das fremde Wort: Studien zur Interdependenz von Texten, Festschrift für Karl Maurer zum 60. Geburtstag.* Eds. Ilse Nolting-Hauff and Joachim Schulze. Amsterdam: Gruner, 1988. 148–176.

————. "Das Nicht-Hermeneutische: Die Theorie weiss von der Unmöglichkeit des Verstehens." *Frankfurter Allgemeine Zeitung,* 19 February 1992. N3.

————. "(N)On (Literary) Interpretation." *Poetics* 18 (1989): 375–87.

————. "'Un souffle d'Allemagne ayant passé': Friedrich Diez, Gaston Paris, and the Genesis of National Philologies." *Romance Philology* 40 (1986): 1–37.

————. "'Las versiones que agradan a mi imaginación,' oder: Von Menéndez Pidal zur postmodernen Editionspraxis." *Quevedo-Textüberlieferung / Textkritik / Textkommentar.* Ed. Ilse Nolting-Hauff. Amsterdam: Gruner, forthcoming.

————. "Warum gerade Góngora? Poetologie und historisches Bewusstsein in Spanien zwischen Jahrhundertwende und Buergerkrieg." *Lyrik und Malerei der Avantgarde.* Ed. Rainer Warning and Winfried Wehle. Munich: Fink, 1982. 145–92.

————, and K. Ludwig Pfeiffer, eds. *Materialität der Kommunikation.*

207

Frankfurt: Suhrkamp, 1988. Trans. as *Materialities of Communication*. Stanford: Stanford University Press, forthcoming 1993.

———, eds. *Paradoxien, Dissonanzen, Zusammenbrüche: Situationen offener Epistemologie*. Frankfurt: Suhrkamp, 1991.

———, and Juan José Sánchez. "Menéndez Pelayo, ¿per omnia saecula saeculorum?" *Arbor* nos. 467–68 (1984): 215–31.

Habermas, Jürgen. "Modernity's Consciousness of Time and Its Need for Self-Reassurance." *The Philosophical Discourse of Modernity: Twelve Lectures*. Trans. Frederick Lawrence. Cambridge, MA: MIT Press, 1987. Lecture 1.

Haidu, Peter. "Making it (New) in the Middle Ages: Towards a Problematics of Alterity." *Diacritics* (Summer 1974): 1–11.

Haidu, Peter, Alexandre Leupin, and Eugene Vance. "Medievalism: Testing Ground for Historicism(s)? Round Table Discussion." *Paroles gelées: UCLA French Studies* 9 (1991): 1–32.

Ham, Edward Billings, ed. *Five Versions of the Venjance Alixandre*. Paris: Presses Universitaires de France, 1935.

———, ed. *Girart de Roussillon: Poème bourguignon du XIVe siècle*. New Haven: Yale University Press, 1939.

———, ed. *Renart le bestorné*. Ann Arbor: University of Michigan Press, 1947.

———. "Textual Criticism and Common Sense." *Romance Philology* 12 (1959): 198–215.

———. *Textual Criticism and Jehan Le Venelais*. Ann Arbor: University of Michigan Press, 1946.

———, ed. *La venjance Alixandre*. Paris: Presses Universitaires de France, 1931.

Hanning, Robert, and Joan Ferrante, trans. *The Lais of Marie de France*. New York: Dutton, 1978.

Hardison, O. B., Jr. *Disappearing Through the Skylight: Culture and Technology in the Twentieth Century*. New York: Viking Penguin, 1989.

Hawking, Stephen W. *A Brief History of Time: From the Big Bang to Black Holes*. Toronto: Bantam, 1988.

Haymes, Edward R. *The Nibelungenlied: History and Interpretation*. Urbana: University of Illinois Press, 1986.

Hayter, Mary. *The New Eve in Christ: The Use and Abuse of the Bible in the Debate about Women in the Church*. London: SPCK, 1987.

Heinemann, Edward A. "Textual Criticism or Literary Criticism? Echo (Or Is It Redundancy?) and the Shifting Text of the Old French Epic."

Text: Transactions of the Society for Textual Scholarship 4 (1988): 121–33.

Hempel, Wido, ed. Portraits of scholarly journals in Romance languages and literatures. *Romanische Forschungen* 100.1–3 (1988): ii–vii, 1–342.

Henahan, Donal. "'Troyen' Grandly Inaugurates the Bastille." *New York Times* 19 Mar. 1990: B1–B4.

Hilka, Alfons, ed. *Das altfranzösische Rolandslied*. Sammlung Romanischer Übungstexte, 3–4. Halle: Niemeyer, 1926.

——, ed. *Der Percevalroman (Li contes del graal)*. Christian von Troyes: Sämtliche Erhaltene Werke, ed. Wendelin Foerster, 5. Halle: Max Niemeyer, 1932. Rpt. Amsterdam: Rodopi, 1966.

Hofmann, Conrad, ed. *Amis et Amiles und Jourdains de Blaivies: Zwei altfranzösische Heldengedichte des kerlingischen Sagenkreises*. Erlangen: T. Blaesing, 1852. 2d ed. 1882.

Holmes, Urban T., Jr., ed. *Adenet le Roi's Berte aus grans piés*. University of North Carolina Studies in Romance Languages and Literatures, 6. Chapel Hill: University of North Carolina Press, 1946.

——. Review of Ham, *Textual Criticism and Jehan le Venelais*. *Speculum* 22 (1947): 468–70.

Holzknecht, Karl Julius. *Literary Patronage in the Middle Ages*. Philadelphia: University of Pennsylvania, 1923. Rpt. New York, Octagon: 1966.

Hult, David F. "Lancelot's Two Steps: A Problem in Textual Criticism." *Speculum* 61 (1986): 836–58.

——. "Reading It Right: The Ideology of Text Editing." *The Legitimacy of the Middle Ages*. Ed. Nichols. 74–88.

——. "Steps Forward and Steps Backward: More on Chrétien's *Lancelot*." *Speculum* 64 (1989): 307–16.

Hunt, Tony. "Chrestien de Troyes: The Textual Problem." *French Studies* 33 (1979): 257–71.

Huot, Sylvia. *From Song to Book: The Poetics of Writing in Old French Lyric and Lyrical Narrative Poetry*. Ithaca: Cornell University Press, 1987.

Iordan, Iorgu, and John Orr. *An Introduction to Romance Linguistics, Its Schools and Scholars*. Rev. Rebecca Posner. 2d ed. Berkeley: University of California Press, 1970.

Iseley, Nancy V., ed. *La chançun de Willame*. University of North Carolina Studies in Romance Languages and Literatures, 13. Chapel Hill: University of North Carolina Press, 1952. Rev. ed. University of North Carolina Studies in Romance Languages and Literatures, 35. 1961.

Jauss, Hans Robert. *Alterität und Modernität der mittelalterlichen Literatur: Gesammelte Aufsätze 1956–1976.* Munich: Fink, 1977.

Jauss, Hans Robert, and Erich Köhler, eds. *Grundriss der romanischen Literaturen des Mittelalters.* 13 vols. projected. Heidelberg: Winter, 1968– .

Jeanroy, Alfred. *De nostratibus medii aevi poetis qui primum lyrica Aquitaniae carmina imitati sint.* Paris: Hachette, 1889.

———. *La poésie lyrique des troubadours.* 2 vols. Toulouse: Privat, 1934.

Jenkins, T. Atkinson, J. M. Manly, Mildred K. Pope, Jean G. Wright, eds. *La seinte resureccion from the Paris and Canterbury MSS.* Anglo-Norman Text Society, 4. Oxford: Blackwell, 1943.

Jespersen, Otto. *Language: Its Nature, Development and Origin.* London: G. Allen & Unwin, 1922. New York: Norton, 1964.

Johnson, E. N. "American Mediaevalists and Today." *Speculum* 28 (1953): 844–54.

Katzner, Kenneth. *The Languages of the World.* Rev. ed. London: Routledge and Kegan Paul, 1986.

Kay, Sarah. *Subjectivity in Troubadour Poetry.* Cambridge, UK: Cambridge University Press, 1990.

Keller, Hans-Erich. "Literary Patronage in the Time of Philip Augustus." *The Spirit of the Court: Selected Proceedings of the Fourth Congress of the International Courtly Literature Society (Toronto, 1983).* Ed. Glyn S. Burgess and Robert A. Taylor. Cambridge, UK: Brewer, 1985. 196–207.

———, ed. *La vie de sainte Marguerite.* By Wace. Beihefte zur Zeitschrift für Romanische Philologie, 229. Tübingen: Niemeyer, 1990.

Kellogg, Judith L. "Economic and Social Tensions Reflected in the Romance of Chrétien de Troyes." *Romance Philology* 39 (1985): 1–21.

Kelly, Amy. *Eleanor of Aquitaine and the Four Kings.* Cambridge, MA: Harvard University Press, 1950.

Kelly, Douglas, ed. *The Romances of Chrétien de Troyes: A Symposium.* Edward C. Armstrong Monographs on Medieval Literature, 3. Lexington, KY: French Forum, 1985.

———. *Sens and Conjointure in the "Chevalier de la charrette."* The Hague: Mouton, 1966.

Kendrick, Laura. *The Game of Love: Troubadour Wordplay.* Berkeley: University of California Press, 1988.

Kermode, Frank. *The Sense of an Ending: Studies in the Theory of Fiction.* Oxford: Oxford University Press, 1967.

Kibler, William. *Introduction to Old French*. New York: The Modern Language Association of America, 1984.

Klaeber, Fr., ed. *Beowulf and The Fight at Finnsburg*. 3rd ed. Boston: Heath, 1950.

Kleinhenz, Christopher, ed. *Medieval Manuscripts and Textual Criticism*. Chapel Hill: University of North Carolina Dept. of Romance Languages, 1976.

Köhler, Erich. "Observations historiques et socioligiques sur la poésie des troubadours." *Cahiers de civilisation médiévale* 7 (1964): 27–51.

Laennec, Christine Moneera. "*Christine antygrafe*: Authorship and Self in the Prose Works of Christine de Pizan with an edition of B.N. Ms. 603 '*Le livre des fais d'armes et de chevallerie*.' " Diss. Yale University, 1988. *Dissertation Abstracts International* 50.11A (1990): 3581.

Langlois, Ernest, ed. *Le roman de la rose par Guillaume de Lorris et Jean de Meun*. 5 vols. Paris: Firmin-Didot, 1914–24.

Lawson, Sarah, trans. *The Treasure of the City of Ladies*. By Christine de Pisan. Harmondsworth: Penguin, 1985.

Le Goff, Jacques. "For an Extended Middle Ages." *The Medieval Imagination*. Trans. Arthur Goldhammer. Chicago: University of Chicago Press, 1988. 18–23.

Learned, Henry Dexter. "The *Eulalia* MS. at Line 15 Reads *aduret*, not *adunet*." *Speculum* 16 (1941): 334–35.

Lecoy, Félix, ed. *Le conte du graal (Perceval)*. Les Romans de Chrétien de Troyes Édités d'Après la Copie de Guiot (Bibl. nat. fr. 794), 5. 2 vols. CFMA, 100, 103. Paris: Champion, 1973–75.

Legge, Mary Dominica. *Anglo-Norman Literature and its Background*. Oxford: Clarendon Press, 1963.

Leitzmann, Albert, ed. *Wolfram von Eschenbach: Parzival*. 3 vols. Altdeutsche Textbibliothek, 12–14. Tübingen: Niemeyer, 1961–65.

Lejeune, Rita. "Rôle littéraire d'Aliénor d'Aquitaine et de sa famille." *Cultura neolatina* 14 (1954): 5–57. Rpt. in Lejeune, Rita. *Littérature et société occitane au moyen âge*. Liège: Marche Romane, 1979. 403–48.

———. "Rôle littéraire de la famille d'Aliénor d'Aquitaine." *Cahiers de civilisation médiévale* 3 (1960): 319–37. Rpt. in Lejeune, Rita. *Littérature et société occitane au moyen âge*. Liège: Marche Romane, 1979. 449–72.

Lemaire, Anika. *Jacques Lacan*. London: Routledge and Kegan Paul, 1977.

Lepage, Yvan G., ed. *Les rédactions en vers du Couronnement de Louis*. Textes Littéraires Français, 261. Geneva: Droz, 1978.

Lerner, Robert E. "Literacy and Learning." *One Thousand Years: Western Europe in the Middle Ages.* Ed. Richard L. DeMolen. Boston: Houghton Mifflin, 1974. 165–233.

Leupin, Alexandre. "The Middle Ages, the Other." *Diacritics* (Fall 1983): 22–31.

———. "*Raoul de Cambrai:* La bâtardise de l'écriture." *The Legitimacy of the Middle Ages.* Ed. Nichols. 89–104.

Löseth, Eilert. *Le roman en prose de Tristan, le roman de Palamède, et la compilation de Rusticien de Pise; Analyse critique d'après les manuscrits de Paris.* Paris: Bouillon, 1890.

Loukopoulos, Halina Didycky. "Classical Mythology in the Works of Christine de Pisan, with an Edition of *L'Epistre Othea* from the Manuscript Harley 4431." Diss. Wayne State University, 1977. *Dissertation Abstracts International* 38.11A (1978): 6706.

Lukacs, John. *The End of the Twentieth Century and the End of the Modern Age.* New York: Ticknor & Fields, 1993.

Lucas, Harry H. "L'édition des textes lyriques: schéma d'ensemble ou schéma individuel?" *Actes du Xe Congrès international de linguistique et de philologie romanes, Strasbourg 23–28 avril 1962.* Ed. Georges Straka. Paris: Klincksieck, 1965. 2: 697–703.

Lyotard, Jean François. *The Postmodern Condition: A Report on Knowledge.* Trans. Geoff Bennington and Brian Massumi. Theory and History of Literature, 10. Minneapolis: University of Minnesota Press, 1984. Trans. of *La condition postmoderne: Rapport sur le savoir.* Paris: Minuit, 1979.

McCann, James. "Dissertations in Progress." *French Review* 65 (1991): 99–113.

McCash, June Hall. "Marie de Champagne's 'Cuer d'ome et cors de fame': Aspects of Feminism and Misogyny in the Twelfth Century." *The Spirit of the Court: Selected Proceedings of the Fourth Congress of the International Courtly Literature Society (Toronto, 1983).* Ed. Glyn S. Burgess and Robert A. Taylor. Cambridge, UK: Brewer, 1985. 234–45.

McCrum, Robert, William Cran, Robert MacNeil. *The Story of English.* New York: Viking Penguin, 1986.

McGann, Jerome J. *A Critique of Modern Textual Criticism.* Chicago: University of Chicago Press, 1983.

———. *The Textual Condition.* Princeton: Princeton University Press, 1991.

———. "What Difference Do the Circumstances of Publication Make to

212

the Interpretation of a Literary Work?" *Literary Pragmatics*. Ed. Roger D. Sell. London and New York: Routledge, 1991. 190–207.

McKibben, Bill. *The End of Nature*. New York: Random House, 1989.

McNamara, Jo Ann. "Sexual Equality and the Cult of Virginity in Early Christian Thought." *Feminist Studies* 3 (1976): 145–58.

Mai, Angelo, ed. *Classicorum auctorum e Vaticanis codicibus editorum tomus I [–X]*. 10 vols. Rome: Typis Vaticanis, 1828–38.

Masson, Jeffrey Moussaieff. *Against Therapy: Emotional Tyranny and the Myth of Psychological Healing*. New York: Atheneum, 1988.

Maurer, Christopher, ed. "Federico García Lorca escribe a su familia desde Nueva York y La Habana (1929–1930)." *Poesía: Revista ilustrada de información poética* 23/24 (1985): 5–151.

Meier, C. A. *Soul and Body: Essays on the Theories of C. G. Jung*. Santa Monica: Lapis Press, 1986.

Méla, Charles, ed. *Chrétien de Troyes: Le conte du graal, ou Le roman de Perceval*. Lettres Gothiques. Paris: Livre de Poche, 1990.

Meltzer, Françoise. "Eat Your *Dasein*: Lacan's Self-Consuming Puns." *On Puns: The Foundation of Letters*. Ed. Culler. 156–63.

Ménard, Philippe. "La composition d'*Aucassin et Nicolette*." *Mélanges de philologie et de littératures romanes offerts à Jeanne Wathelet-Willem*. Ed. Jacques de Caluwé. Liège: Cahiers de l'ARULg, 1978. 413–32.

———. *Manuel d'ancien français: 3. Syntaxe*. 2d ed. Bordeaux: SOBODI, 1972.

Menéndez Pidal, Ramón, ed. *Flor nueva de romances viejos*. 6th ed. Madrid: Austral, 1984.

———. *El romancero español: conferencias dadas en la Columbia University de New York los días 5 y 7 de abril 1909*. New York: The Hispanic Society of America, 1910.

———. *La epopeya castellana a través de la literatura española*. Buenos Aires: Espasa-Calpe Argentina, 1954.

Menocal, María Rosa. *Shards of Love: Exile and the Origins of the Lyric*. Durham, NC: Duke University Press, forthcoming.

Micha, Alexandre, ed. *Cligés*. Les Romans de Chrétien de Troyes, 2. CFMA, 84. Paris: Champion, 1957. Rpt. 1970.

———. *La tradition manuscrite des romans de Chrétien de Troyes*. Publications Romanes et Françaises, 90. Paris 1939. Rpt. Geneva: Droz, 1966.

Minnelli, Vincent, dir. *An American in Paris*. With Gene Kelly, Leslie Caron. Metro-Goldwyn-Mayer, 1951.

Minnis, A. J. *Medieval Theory of Authorship*. 2nd ed. Philadelphia: University of Pennsylvania Press, 1988.

Mortier, Raoul, gen. ed. *Les textes de la Chanson de Roland*. 10 vols. Paris: Geste Francor, 1940–44.

Nelson, Lowry, Jr. "Comparing Literatures in the Wake of Modernism." *Sewanee Review* 90 (Fall 1982): 555–67.

Nichols, Stephen G. "Commentary and/as Image." *Commentary as Cultural Artifact*. Ed. Lee Patterson and Stephen G. Nichols. Special issue of *South Atlantic Quarterly* 91 (1992): 965–92.

———. "Ekphrasis, Iconoclasm, and Desire." *Rethinking the Romance of the Rose: Text, Image, Reception*. Ed. Kevin Brownlee and Sylvia Huot. Philadelphia: University of Pennsylvania Press, 1992. 133–66.

———. "Introduction: Philology in a Manuscript Culture." *The New Philology*. Ed. Nichols. 1–10.

———, ed. *The Legitimacy of the Middle Ages*. Special issue of *Romanic Review* 79.1 (1988): 1–248.

———. "Marie de France's Commonplaces." *Contexts: Style and Values in Medieval Art and Literature*. Ed. Daniel Poirion and Nancy Freeman Regalado. Special issue of *Yale French Studies*. New Haven: Yale University Press, 1991. 134–48.

———, ed. *The New Philology*. Special issue of *Speculum* 65.1 (1990): 1–108.

———. "On the Sociology of Manuscript Illumination." *Annotation and Its Texts*. Ed. Stephen Barney. Oxford: Oxford University Press, 1991. 43–73.

Nichols, Stephen G., and John A. Galm, with A. Bartlett Giamatti, Roger J. Porter, Seth L. Wolitz, Claudette M. Charbonneau, eds. *The Songs of Bernart de Ventadorn*. University of North Carolina Studies in Romance Languages and Literatures, 39. Chapel Hill: University of North Carolina Press, 1962.

Noomen, Willem, and Nico van den Boogaard, eds. *Nouveau recueil complet des fabliaux (NRCF)*. 5 vols. to date. Assen: Van Gorcum, 1983– .

Owens, Joseph. "*Mediaeval Studies* Fifty Years After." *Mediaeval Studies* 50 (1988): xi–xvi.

———. *Towards a Philosophy of Medieval Studies*. Toronto: Pontifical Institute of Mediaeval Studies, 1986.

Paden, William D. "Alfred Jeanroy (1859–1953)." *Dictionary of Medieval Scholarship*. Ed. Helen Damico and Joseph B. Zavadil. New York: Garland, forthcoming.

————. "Rape in the Pastourelle." *Romanic Review* 80 (1989): 331–49.

————. Review of L. Kendrick, *The Game of Love: Troubadour Wordplay. Studies in the Age of Chaucer* 11 (1989): 256–63.

————. "Tenebrism in the *Song of Roland*." *Modern Philology* 86 (1989): 339–56.

————, ed. *The Voice of the Trobairitz: Perspectives on the Women Troubadours*. Philadelphia: University of Pennsylvania Press, 1989.

Paden, William D., and Patricia Harris Stäblein, eds. "'De Tradicione Guenonis': An Edition with Translation." *Traditio* 44 (1988): 201–51.

Pagels, Elaine. *Adam, Eve, and the Serpent*. New York: Random House, 1988.

Panofsky, Erwin. "Die Perspektive als 'Symbolische Form.' " *Vorträge der Bibliothek Warburg* (1924–25): 258–330.

Paris, Gaston. "*La chanson de Roland* et la nationalité française." Collège de France. Paris, 8 Dec. 1870. Published in *La poésie du moyen âge: Leçons et lectures*. Paris: Hachette, 1886; 2d ed. 1887. 87–118.

————. "La poésie du moyen âge." *La poésie du moyen âge: leçons et lectures*. 2d ed. Paris: Hachette, 1887. 1–39.

————. Review of Foerster, ed. *Érec und Enide. Romania* 20 (1891): 148–66.

————, ed. *La vie de saint Alexis: poème du XIe siècle et renouvellements des XIIe, XIIIe et XIVe siècles*. Bibliothèque de l'Ecole Pratique des Hautes Études, Sciences philologiques et historiques, 7. Paris: A. Franck, 1872. Preface reprinted in *Romania* 1 (1872): 111–13.

————, ed. *La vie de saint Alexis, poème du XIe siècle*. Paris: F. Vieweg, 1885.

————, ed. *La vie de saint Alexis, poème du XIe siècle*. 1903; rpt. CFMA, 4. Paris: Champion, 1911.

Parker, Patricia, and David Quint, eds. *Literary Theory / Renaissance Texts*. Baltimore: The Johns Hopkins University Press, 1986.

Parry, John J., trans. *The Art of Courtly Love, by Andreas Capellanus*. New York: Columbia University Press, 1941. Rpt. New York: Ungar, 1959.

Parvey, Constance F. "The Theology and Leadership of Women in the New Testament." *Religion and Sexism*. Ed. Ruether. 117–49.

Patterson, Lee. *Negotiating the Past: The Historical Understanding of Medieval Literature*. Madison: University of Wisconsin Press, 1987.

————. "On the Margin: Postmodernism, Ironic History, and Medieval Studies." *The New Philology*. Ed. Nichols. 87–108.

Pauphilet, Albert. *Le manuscrit d'Annonay*. Paris: Droz, 1934.

215

————. "Nouveaux fragments manuscrits de Chrétien de Troyes." *Romania* 63 (1937): 310–23.

Pennington, Kenneth. "The Tyranny of the Printed Text." Conference at the Medieval Institute, University of Notre Dame: "Editio Princeps: Editing and Interpretation." South Bend, Indiana, 2 March 1991.

Perspectives médiévales. Paris: Société de Langue et de Littérature Médiévales d'Oc et d'Oïl. No. 1 (June 1975)– .

Pézard, André. *Dante sous la pluie de feu (Enfer, chant XV)*. Paris: Vrin, 1950.

Pickens, Rupert T., ed. *Chrétien de Troyes, The Story of The Grail (Li contes del graal), or Perceval*. Trans. William W. Kibler. Garland Library of Medieval Literature, A: 62. New York and London: Garland, 1990.

————. "Jaufré Rudel et la poétique de la mouvance." *Cahiers de civilisation médiévale* 20 (1977): 323–37.

————, ed. *The Songs of Jaufré Rudel*. Studies and Texts, 41. Toronto: Pontifical Institute of Mediaeval Studies, 1978.

————. "Towards an Edition of Chrétien's *Li contes del graal:* Hilka vv. 1869–2024." *L'esprit créateur* 27.1 (Spring 1987): 53–66.

Pinkus, Karen. "The Hungry Eye: Anamorphosis and Anorexia." *Stanford Humanities Review* 2 (1990): 7–30.

Poirion, Daniel, ed. *Intertextualités médiévales*. Special issue of *Littérature* 41 (1981): 1–128.

Pope, M. K. *From Latin to Modern French with Especial Consideration of Anglo-Norman*. Publications of the University of Manchester, 229. Manchester: Manchester University Press, 1934. Rpt. 1961.

Potvin, Charles, ed. *Perceval le Gallois ou le Conte du graal*. Société des Bibliophiles Belges, 21. 6 vols. Mons: Dequesne-Masquillier, 1866–71.

Pound, Ezra. *Make It New: Essays*. London: Faber and Faber, [1934].

Régnier, Claude, ed. *Les rédactions en vers de la Prise d'Orange*. Paris: Klincksieck, 1966.

————. Review of Foulet and Speer, *On Editing*. *Romania* 103 (1982): 133–34.

Reid, T. B. W. "Chrétien de Troyes and the Scribe Guiot." *Medium Aevum* 45 (1976): 1–19.

————, ed. *Chrestien de Troyes: Yvain (Le chevalier au lion)*. French Classics. Manchester: Manchester University Press, 1942.

————. "The Right to Emend." *Medieval French Textual Studies in Memory of T. B. W. Reid*. Ed. Ian Short. London: Anglo-Norman Text Society, 1984. 1–32.

Richards, Earl Jeffrey, trans. *The Book of the City of Ladies*. By Christine de Pizan. New York: Persea, 1982.

———. *Modernism, Medievalism and Humanism: A Research Bibliography on the Reception of the Works of Ernst Robert Curtius*. Beihefte zur Zeitschrift für Romanische Philologie, 196. Tübingen: Niemeyer, 1983.

Richert, Gertrud. *Die Anfänge der romanischen Philologie und die deutsche Romantik*. Inaugural-Dissertation Berlin. Halle: Karras, 1913. Beiträge zur Geschichte der Romanischen Sprachen und Literaturen, 10. Halle: Niemeyer, 1914.

Riding, Alan. "À Bas Anglais! From Now On, It's the Law!" *New York Times*, 11 July 1992: Y3.

Rieger, Angelica, ed. *Trobairitz: Der Beitrag der Frau in der altokzitanischen höfischen Lyrik. Edition des Gesamtkorpus*. Beihefte zur Zeitschrift für Romanische Philologie, 233. Tübingen: Niemeyer, 1991.

Roach, William, ed. *Chrétien de Troyes: Le roman de Perceval ou le Conte du graal*. Textes Littéraires Français, 71. Geneva: Droz, 1956. 2d ed. 1959.

———, ed. *The Continuations of the Old French Perceval of Chrétien de Troyes*. 5 vols. Philadelphia: University of Pennsylvania Press, 1949–50; American Philosophical Society, 1953–83.

———, ed. *The Didot Perceval: According to the Manuscripts of Modena and Paris*. Philadelphia: University of Pennsylvania Press, 1941.

———, ed. *Le roman de Perceval ou le Conte del graal*. By Chrétien de Troyes. Geneva: Droz, 1956.

Rohlfs, Gerhard. *Romanische Philologie*. 2 vols. Heidelberg: C. Winter, 1950–52.

Roques, Mario, ed. *Le chevalier au lion (Yvain)*. By Chrétien de Troyes. CFMA, 89. Paris: Champion, 1968.

———, ed. *Le chevalier de la charrette*. By Chrétien de Troyes. CFMA, 86. Paris: Champion, 1958.

———, ed. *Erec et Enide*. Les Romans de Chrétien de Troyes, 1. CFMA, 80. Paris: Champion, 1955. Rpt. 1970.

———. "Établissement de règles pratiques pour l'édition des anciens textes français et provençaux." *Compte rendu de la séance tenue à Paris les 18 et 19 octobre 1925*. SATF. Paris: Champion, 1926. 3–9. Rpt. *Romania* 52 (1926): 243–49, and *Bibliothèque de l'École des chartes* 87 (1926): 453–59.

———. "Le manuscrit fr. 794 de la Bibliothèque nationale et le scribe Guiot." *Romania* 73 (1952): 177–99.

————. Review of Fourquet, "Paradoxe." *Romania* 69 (1946): 117–18.

Rose, Mary Beth, ed. *Women in the Middle Ages and the Renaissance: Literary and Historical Perspectives.* Syracuse NY: Syracuse University Press, 1986.

Rosenberg, Samuel N., and Hans Tischler, eds.. *The Monophonic Songs in the Roman de Fauvel.* Lincoln: University of Nebraska Press, 1991.

Rousselle, Aline. *Porneia: De la maîtrise du corps à la privation sensorielle, IIe–IVe siècles de l'ère chrétienne.* Paris: Presses Universitaires de France, 1983.

Ruether, Rosemary Radford. "Misogynism and Virginal Feminism in the Fathers of the Church." *Religion and Sexism.* Ed. Ruether. 150–83.

————. "Mothers of the Church: Ascetic Women in the Late Patristic Age." *Women of Spirit.* Ed. Ruether and McLaughlin. 71–98.

————, ed. *Religion and Sexism: Images of Woman in the Jewish and Christian Traditions.* New York: Simon & Schuster, 1974.

Ruether, Rosemary, and Eleanor McLaughlin, eds. *Women of Spirit: Female Leadership in the Jewish and Christian Traditions.* New York: Simon & Schuster, 1979.

Rychner, Jean, ed. *Les lais de Marie de France.* CFMA, 93. Paris: Champion, 1966.

————, ed. *Marie de France: Le lai de Lanval.* Textes Littéraires Français, 77. Geneva: Droz, 1958.

Sayers, Dorothy L., trans. *The Comedy of Dante Alighieri the Florentine: Cantica I, Hell (L'Inferno).* Harmondsworth: Penguin, 1949.

Schnapp, Jeffrey T. *The Transfiguration of History at the Center of Dante's Paradise.* Princeton: Princeton University Press, 1986.

Schulenberg, Jane Tibbetts. "The Heroics of Virginity: Brides of Christ and Sacrificial Mutilation." Rose, ed. *Women in the Middle Ages and the Renaissance.* 29–72.

Segre, Cesare, ed. *La chanson de Roland: Édition critique.* Rev. and trans. Madeleine Tyssens. Textes Littéraires Français, 368. 2 vols. Geneva: Droz, 1989. First ed.: *La chanson de Roland: Edizione critica.* Documenti di Filologia, 16. Milano: Ricciardi, 1971.

Seidel, Linda. *Stories of an Icon: Jan van Eyck's Arnolfini Wedding Portrait Re-Viewed.* Cambridge, UK: Cambridge University Press, forthcoming 1993.

Seminario Menéndez Pidal, ed. *Romancero tradicional de las lenguas hispánicas: Español-Portugués-Catalán-Sefardí.* Vol. 1. Madrid: Gredos, 1957.

Singleton, Charles S., ed. *The Divine Comedy*. 3 vols. Bollingen Series, 80. Princeton: Princeton University Press, 1970–75.

Sissa, Giulia. *Le corps virginal: La virginité féminine en Grèce ancienne*. Paris: J. Vrin, 1987.

Smith, Nathaniel B. "*Aucassin et Nicolette* as Stylistic Comedy." *Kentucky Romance Quarterly* 26 (1979): 479–90.

Snyder, Joel. "Picturing Vision." *The Language of Images*. Ed. W. J. T. Mitchell. Chicago: University of Chicago Press, 1980. 219–46.

Speer, Mary B. "Editing Old French Texts in the Eighties: Theory and Practice." *Romance Philology* 45 (1991): 7–43.

———. "Editing the Formulaic Romance Style: The Poetics of Repetition in the *Roman des sept sages*." *L'esprit créateur* 27.1 (1987): 34–52.

———, ed. *Le roman des sept sages de Rome: A Critical Edition of the Two Verse Redactions of a Twelfth-Century Romance*. Edward C. Armstrong Monographs on Medieval Literature, 4. Lexington, KY: French Forum, 1989.

———. "Textual Criticism Redivivus." *L'esprit créateur* 23.1 (Spring 1983): 38–48.

———. "Wrestling with Change: Old French Textual Criticism and *Mouvance*." *Olifant* 7 (1980): 311–26.

Spiegel, Gabrielle M. "History, Historicism, and the Social Logic in the Text in the Middle Ages." *The New Philology*. Ed. Nichols. 59–86.

———. *Romancing the Past: The Rise of Vernacular Prose Historiography in Thirteenth-Century France*. Berkeley: University of California Press, forthcoming 1993.

Steen, Gerard. "Understanding Metaphor in Literature: Towards an Empirical Study." *Literary Pragmatics*. Ed. Roger D. Sell. London and New York: Routledge, 1991. 110–26.

Stock, Brian. "Literary Discourse and the Social Historian." *New Literary History* 8 (1977): 183–94.

Stuip, René E. V., ed. *La chastelaine de Vergi*. Publications de l'Institut d'Études Françaises et Occitanes de l'Université d'Utrecht, 5. The Hague: Mouton, 1970.

Svidercoschi, G. G. "Unità dall'Atlantico agli Urali: Il progetto del Papa per l'Europa." *La nazione* (Umbria) 22 Aug. 1989: 2.

Switten, Margaret, ed. *The Cansos of Raimon de Miraval: A Study of Poems and Melodies*. Cambridge, MA: Medieval Academy of America, 1985.

Tagliavini, Carlo. *Le origini delle lingue neolatine*. 2d rev. ed. Bologna: R. Patron, 1952.

Thiry, Claude. Review of Foulet and Speer, *On Editing*. *Le moyen âge* 89 (1983): 281–83.

Thorpe, Lewis, ed. *Le roman de Silence: A Thirteenth-Century Arthurian Verse-Romance*. By Heldris de Cornuaille. Cambridge, UK: Heffer, 1972.

Toulmin, Stephen. *Cosmopolis: The Hidden Agenda of Modernity*. New York: Free Press, 1990.

Trible, Phyllis. "Depatriarchalizing in Biblical Interpretation." *Journal of the American Academy of Religion* 41 (1973): 30–48.

Trojel, E., ed. *Andreae Capellani regii Francorum: De amore libri tres*. Copenhagen: Libraria Gadiana, 1892. Rpt. Munich: Eidos, 1964.

Uitti, Karl D. "À propos de philologie." *Littérature* 41 (1981) 30–46.

——. "Introduction." *Trends in Romance Linguistics and Philology*. Ed. Rebecca Posner and John N. Green. 3: *Language and Philology in Romance*. The Hague: Mouton, 1982. 3–44.

——. "Philology: Factualness and History." *Literary Style: A Symposium*. Ed. Seymour Chatman. London: Oxford University Press, 1971. 111–32.

——. "The Poetico-Literary Dimensions and the Editing of Medieval Texts." *What is Literature? France 1100–1600*. Ed. Cornilliat, Langer, and Kelly. 143–79.

——, ed. *The Poetics of Textual Criticism: The Old French Example*. Special issue of *L'esprit créateur* 27.1 (1987): 1–128.

——. "Preface." *Poetics of Textual Criticism*. Ed. Uitti. 5–14.

Uitti, Karl D., and Alfred Foulet. "On Editing Chrétien de Troyes: Lancelot's Two Steps and Their Context." *Speculum* 63 (1988): 271–92.

Vance, Eugene. "*Aucassin et Nicolette* as a Medieval Comedy of Signification and Exchange." *The Nature of Medieval Narrative*. Ed. Minnette Grunmann-Gaudet and Robin F. Jones. French Forum Monographs, 22. Lexington KY: French Forum, 1980. 57–76.

——. "Chrétien's *Yvain* and the Ideologies of Change and Exchange." *Yale French Studies* 70 (1986): 42–62.

——. *From Topic to Tale: Logic and Narrativity in the Middle Ages*. Theory and History of Literature, 47. Minneapolis: University of Minnesota Press, 1987.

——. "The Modernity of the Middle Ages in the Future: Remarks on a Recent Book." *Romanic Review* 64 (1973): 140–51.

Vàrvaro, Alberto. Review of Cerquiglini, *Éloge*. *Medioevo romanzo* 14 (1989): 474–77.

Wahlund, Carl, and Hugo von Feilitzen, eds. *Les enfances Vivien: Chanson de geste*. Upsala: Librairie de l'Université, 1895.

Warner, Marina. *Alone of All Her Sex: The Myth and the Cult of the Virgin Mary*. New York: Knopf, 1976.

Warnke, Karl, ed. *Die Fabeln der Marie de France*. Halle: Niemeyer, 1898. Rpt. Geneva: Slatkine, 1974.

Watson, James D. *The Double Helix: A Personal Account of the Discovery of the Structure of DNA*. Ed. Gunther S. Stent. New York: Norton, 1980.

Weightman, John. "On Not Understanding Michel Foucault." *American Scholar* 58 (1989): 383–406.

Wenger, Luke. "Editor's Note." *The New Philology*. Ed. Nichols. [vii].

Wenzel, Siegfried. *Macaronic Sermons in the Age of Chaucer: Social Dicourse and Private Reform*. Ann Arbor: University of Michigan Press, forthcoming 1993.

———. "Reflections on (New) Philology." *The New Philology*. Ed. Nichols. 11–18.

White, Hayden. *Metahistory: The Historical Imagination in Nineteenth–Century Europe*. Baltimore: Johns Hopkins University Press, 1973.

Whitehead, Frederick, and Cedric E. Pickford. "The Introduction to the *Lai de l'ombre*: Sixty Years Later." *Romania* 94 (1973):145–56. Rpt. "The Introduction to the *Lai de l'ombre*: Half a Century Later." *Medieval Manuscripts*. Ed. Kleinhenz. 103–16.

Williamson, Harold F., and Payson S. Wild. *Northwestern University: A History, 1850–1975*. Evanston, IL: Northwestern University, 1976.

Wimsatt, James I., and William W. Kibler, eds. *Guillaume de Machaut: Le jugement du roy de Behaigne and Remede de Fortune*. The Chaucer Library. Athens: University of Georgia Press, 1988.

Winters, Margaret, ed. *The Romance of Hunbaut: An Arthurian Poem of the Thirteenth Century*. Davis Medieval Texts and Studies, 4. Leiden: Brill, 1984.

Woledge, Brian. "The Problem of Editing *Yvain*." *Medieval French Textual Studies in Memory of T. B. W. Reid*. Ed. Ian Short. London: Anglo-Norman Text Society, 1984. 254–67.

———. "Un scribe champenois devant un texte normand: Guiot copiste de Wace." *Mélanges de langue et de littérature du moyen âge et de la Renaissance offerts à Jean Frappier*. Publications Romanes et Françaises, 112. Geneva: Droz, 1970. 2:1139–54.

Wolf, George, and Roy Rosenstein, eds. *The Poetry of Cercamon and Jau-*

fre Rudel. Garland Library of Medieval Literature, 5A. New York: Garland, 1983.

Woodward, Kenneth L., with Pia Hinckle. "New Vita for an Old Lingua." *Newsweek*, 11 November 1991: 66.

222   Yarbrough, Anne. "Christianization in the Fourth Century: The Example of Roman Women." *Church History* 45 (1976): 149–165.

Zumthor, Paul. "Du nouveau sur la poésie des troubadours et trouvères." *Romanic Review* 66 (1975): 85–92.

————. *Essai de poétique médiévale*. Collection Poétique. Paris: Seuil, 1972.

————. "Intertextualité et mouvance." *Littérature* 41 (1981): 8–16.

————. *Introduction à la poésie orale*. Collection Poétique. Paris: Seuil, 1983.

————. *Langue et techniques poétiques à l'époque romane (XIe-XIIIe siècles)*. Bibliothèque Française et Romane, C: 4. Paris: Klincksieck, 1963.

————. *La lettre et la voix: De la "littérature" médiévale*. Collection Poétique. Paris: Seuil, 1987.

————. *La poésie et la voix dans la civilisation médiévale*. Collège de France, Essais et Conférences. Paris: Presses Universitaires de France, 1984.

————. *Speaking of the Middle Ages*. Trans. Sarah White. Lincoln: University of Nebraska Press, 1986.

————. "The Text and the Voice." *New Literary History* 16 (1984): 67–92.

₹ INDEX

Palaye's transcriptions, 60; in a single manuscript, 100; vs. text, 19; in text editing, 94, 116; in *Vie de saint Alexis,* 58; in *Vie de sainte Marie l'Égyptienne,* 98–99; in Villehardouin, *La conquête de Constantinople,* 60; Zumthor on, 61

Multi-text editions: B. Cerquiglini on, 69; Hult on, 85n33

Music: and literary text, 158–59

Narrative: analysis of, 83n28

Nationalism: philology and, viii, x, 53, 87, 165. *See also* Nation-state

Nation-state: in Great Renaissance, 18, 20. *See also* Nationalism

New Criticism, American: philology and, viii, 54, 126

New Medievalism. *See* Medievalism, New; Philology, New

Nibelungenlied: historical allusions, 152; women in, 152–54

Nichols, Stephen G.: on crisis in philology, 22, 53, 55; and New Philology, 13, 88–90; on return to manuscripts, 19; as text editor, 108n6

Noomen, Willem, and Nico van den Boogaard: synoptic edition of fabliaux, 117

Northwestern University: German doctorate program at, 21; humanism and, 16; postmodernism, listings of in library of, 27n5

Numismatics: and Dante, 157; Italian coins, photographs of, 196

Ott, Carlos, Opéra de la Bastille (Paris): photograph of, 195; and translatio studii, 12

Overlay: in analysis of narrative, 83n28

Owens, Joseph: philosophy of medieval studies, 4

Paleography: on script as means of dating, 131

Paris, Gaston: on *Chanson de Roland* and nation-state, 20; and Lachmannian textual criticism, 56, 73–74; and nationalism, viii; portrait of, 180; as Procrustes, 56, 91; on simplicity of Middle Ages, 18; against univocal meaning, 109n10; *Vie de saint Alexis,* editions of, 73–74

Paris, Paulin (father of Gaston Paris), 56

Paris, University of: and Latin language, 10

Paris School: and Fleischman, 64, 65

Pastourelle: and Great Renaissance, 18; history of criticism on, 7–8

Patristic studies: and gender, 175; and medieval studies, 173–74

Patterson, Lee: on crisis in medieval studies, 22; on history of Middle English studies, 166; and New Philology, 9

Perspective, in painting: Great Renaissance and, 17

Pesme Aventure (in Chrétien de Troyes, *Yvain*): theme of social responsibility, 150–51

Philippe de Thaün, *Cumpot:* mouvance in, 58

Philology: and communication, 125; history of, viii, 55; essentialism in, 32–34, 36; and European Community, viii; and linguistics, 121–26; and literature, 37, 124–25; and modernism in Spain, 32–49; modernity of, 54; origin of, in Germany, 121; origin of, in Vico, 15. *See also* Nationalism; New Criticism, American; Positivism

Philology, classical: and linguistics, 123; and medieval study, 18, 23–24, 26, 122

Philology, material. *See* Manuscript study

Philology, New: anticipated in Spain, 36; B. Cerquiglini as source of, 55–64; crisis of, 53–55; and fundamentalism, 34–35, 45; and

229

Robinet Testard (illuminator): facsimiles, 190–92; *Roman de la rose* miniatures attributed to, 131, 132

Robinson, Peter: on computer in text editing, 85n35

Romance, audience response to: call for comparative studies, 147

Romancero tradicional: and Menéndez Pidal, 39–40, 42

Romances, prose, unpublished. *See* Unpublished texts: call for computer publication of

Roman de la rose, 131–34; facsimiles of, 190–92

Romanticism: German, and creation of philology, 121; Modernism and, 12–16; in Spain, 41

Roques, Mario: Bédier's principles applied by, 102; on emending homophonic rhymes, 103; rules of, for text editing, 97

Sainte-Palaye, Jean Baptiste de La Curne de: mouvance in troubadour transcriptions of, 60

Schiller, Friedrich von: on sentimentality, 41

Schlegel, August Wilhelm and Friedrich von: origin of philology and, 121

Sculpture, ecclesiastical: and Dante, 157–58

Segre, Cesare: respect for tradition, 110n15

Self-consciousness: in medieval studies, 165–66

Sequence of Saint Eulalia: facsimile, 189; paleography and, 109n11

Serments de Strasbourg: Bloch on, 92–93

Song of Roland. See Chanson de Roland

Special issues of journals: as sign of prosperity, 164–65

Speer, Mary Blakely: respect of, for tradition, 97, 115; on text editing, 62–63, 115, 136n1

Spiegel, Gabrielle: on Pseudo-Turpin chronicles, 149

Spitzer, Leo: on authoritative text, 19

Structuralism: in literary study, 47

Subjectivity and objectivity: oscillation of, in Spanish classics, 36–37

Subjectivity in medieval studies: feminism and, 170; Lacan and, 170; in New Philology, 15–16, 171; in text editing, 97–98; in Zumthor, 169–70

Supplementation: defined, 118, 120; in manuscript matrix, 119–20, 139n14

Symbolist poetry, French: and Spanish modernism, 37

Syntax: beyond the sentence, 19

Text. *See* Author's original text; Cerquiglini, Bernard; Manuscript study; Spitzer, Leo; Text editing; Unconscious

Text editing
—practice of: and computer, 69–72, 85n35; and emendation, 127; empirical approaches to, 115; Ham as editor, 80n6; history of, 114; and hypertext, 30n32; Isely as editor, 80n6; lacuna, detecting, 104–7; Menéndez Pidal as editor, 36; mouvance in, 61–62, 94, 116; Pickens as editor, 146; practical concerns of, 136n2; pragmatic experience, examples, 98–108; recent projects concerning, in North America, 95; and restoration of missing couplets, 103–4; rhymes, correcting homophonic, 100–101, 103; and Roques's rules, 97; synoptic editions, 99, 117; text in many manuscripts, 102–7; text in one manuscript, 100–101; versification and, 103
—principles of: Bédier, 74–78; Bédier's principles applied by Roques, 102; best manuscript, 99,

Virginity: and medieval studies, 175
Visual text: in chronology, 131; elements of, 131; in manuscript study, 130–35, 147, 158; in *Roman de la rose* manuscript, 131–34

Wace, *Brut:* transcribed by Guiot, 80n9
Walter von der Vogelweide, at court of Frederick II: call for study, 147
Wenger, Luke: on state of medieval studies, 88
Wenzel, Siegfried: on New Philology, 108n3; on philological inquiry, 72–73
William of Conches: commentary of, on Boethius, *De consolatione,* 120
Woledge, Brian: on author's original text, 116
Women
—medieval: as authors of poetic debates, 161–62; female literacy, 159, 161; in implicit audience of troubadours, 160–61; in literary history, 159–62; in *Nibelungen-*

lied, 152–54; as patrons, 159–60; as performers of lyric poetry, 159; trobairitz, 161; vitality of studies on, 174
—twentieth century: impact of, on medieval studies, 174–75
Word associations: and dialects, 66–68; in New Philology, 13–15, 65–69; *lai,* 13–14, 65–68; *traire,* 14, 68
World War I: and journals in medieval studies, 23; and pastourelle, study of, 7
World War II: and Cold War, end of, 6; and journals in medieval studies, 24; and Latin language, 27n10; and New Philology, 9; and pastourelle, study of, 7

Yale University: and humanism, 16

Zumthor, Paul: Fleischman on, 64; on mouvance, 61; and New Philology, 15, 92; and subjectivity in medieval studies, 169–70